HISTORICAL
ATLAS
OF THE
RENAISSANCE

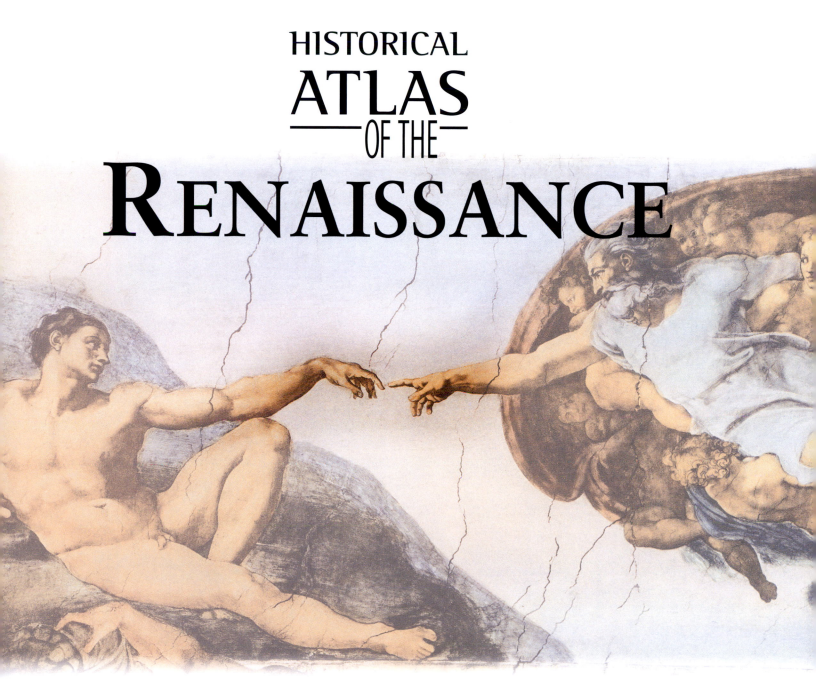

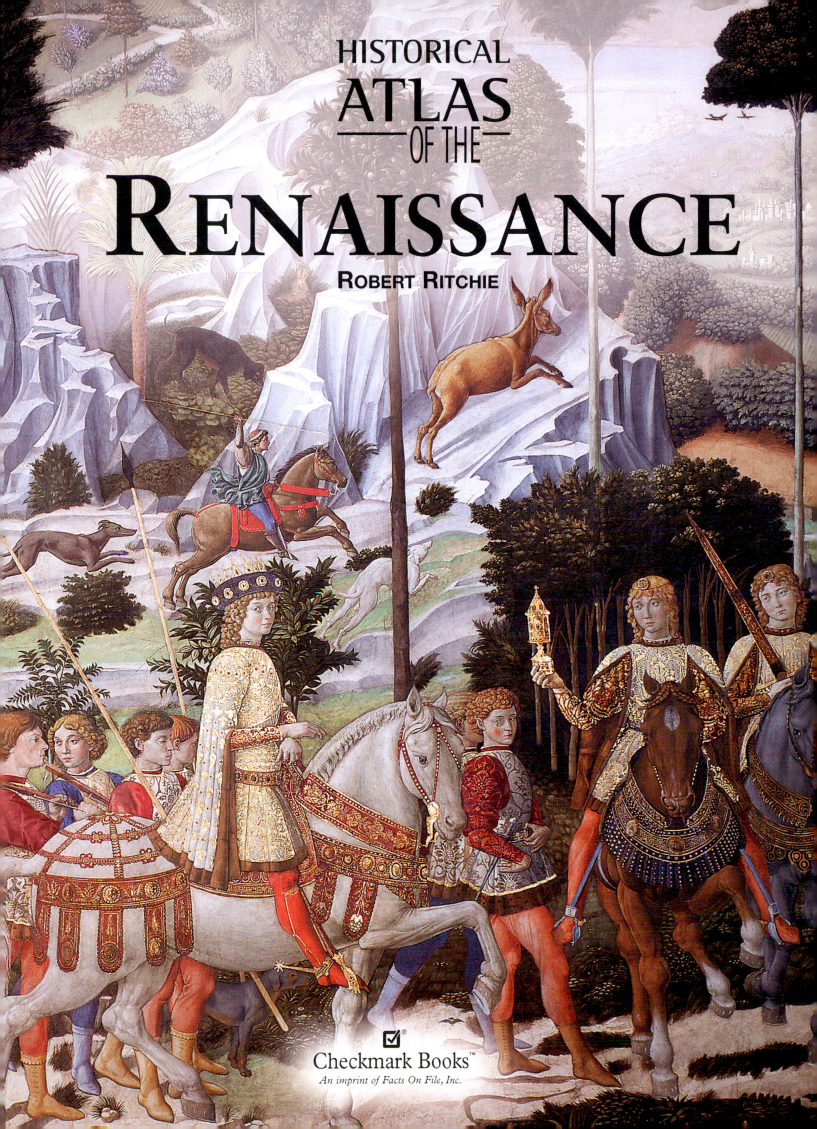

HISTORICAL
ATLAS
OF THE
RENAISSANCE

Robert Ritchie

Checkmark Books™

An imprint of Facts On File, Inc.

HISTORICAL ATLAS OF THE RENAISSANCE

Copyright © 2004 by Thalamus Publishing

Checkmark Books
An imprint of Facts On File, Inc.
132 West 31st Street
New York, NY 10001

For Library of Congress Cataloging-in-Publication data, please contact
Checkmark Books. Control Number 12803030.
    ISBN 0-8160-5731-1

Checkmark Books are available at special discounts when purchased in bulk quantities for businesses, associations, institutions or sales promotions. Please call our Special Sales Department in New York at:
(212) 967-8800 or (800) 322-8755.

You can find Facts On File on the World Wide Web at:
http://www.factsonfile.com

For Thalamus Publishing
Project editor: Warren Lapworth
Maps and design: Roger Kean

Printed and bound in Singapore

10 9 8 7 6 5 4 3 2 1
This book is printed on acid-free paper

PICTURE CREDITS

CORBIS/Alinari Archives: 15; CORBIS/Alinari Archives: 16, 28, 37 (top), 39 (top), 39 (bottom), 50, 54 (top), 57. 130 (left), 143, 145 (bottom); CORBIS/Paul Almasy: 157 (bottom); CORBIS/James L. Amos: 178, 183; CORBIS/Archivo Iconografico, S.A.: 12, 14, 17 (top). 23, 26, 32, 44, 46 (right), 52, 54 (bottom), 55, 60 (right), 61, 63 (bottom), 64, 70, 82, 87, 88, 93 (left), 93, 97, 101, 102, 103, 104, 105, 117 (bottom), 119, 124, 127, 128, 131 (top), 133, 134, 135 (top), 138, 139 (top), 147 (bottom left), 150 (left), 157 (top), 164 (left), 165, 166, 182; CORBIS/Arte & Immagini srl: 17 (bottom), 31, 34, 35 (top), 35 (bottom), 40, 58, 140–141, 142, 144 (left), 167; CORBIS/Yann Arthus-Bertrand: 111, 147 (bottom right); CORBIS/Austrian Archives: 69, 131 (bottom); CORBIS/Bettman: 1, 36, 46 (left), 47, 56 (top), 73, 80, 84 (bottom), 110 (left), 116, 117 (top), 118, 120, 132, 159, 162, 163, 170 (left), 173 (bottom), 176, 177, 180; CORBIS/Stefano Bianchetti: 171; CORBIS/Tibor Bognár: 148 (right); CORBIS/Christie's Images: 66–67, 99 (top), 130 (right), 144 (right), 145 (top), 179; CORBIS/Elio Ciol: 20 (bottom), 29, 151; CORBIS/Geoffrey Clements: 129; CORBIS: 19 (top). 96. 139 (bottom); CORBIS/Chrstopher Cormack: 149 (center); CORBIS/Gianni Dagli Orti: 65, 99 (bottom), 113 (left), 126, 135 (bottom); CORBIS/Gillian Darley: 148 (left), 149 (bottom); CORBIS/Edimédia: 37 (bottom); Thalamus/Oliver Frey: 86; CORBIS/John van Hasselt: 90; CORBIS/Dalas & John Heaton: 71; CORBIS/Chris Hellier: 68; CORBIS/Historical Picture Archive: 27 (bottom), 81, 92, 98, 160, 161; CORBIS/Angelo Hornak: 108, 115 (top); CORBIS/Lanz von Horsten: 79; CORBIS/George H.H. Huey: 84 (top); CORBIS/Wolfgang Kaehler: 156; CORBIS/Bob Krist: 30; CORBIS/Michael S. Lewis: 18 (top); CORBIS/Chris Lisle: 45; CORBIS/Massimo Listri: 2–3; CORBIS/William Manning: 10–11; CORBIS/Francis G. Mayer: 22, 109, 114, 144 (center), 164 (right), 175; CORBIS/Ali Meyer: 60 (left), 72, 89, 154, 155; CORBIS/Michael Nicholson: 115 (bottom); CORBIS/Philadelphia Museum of Art: 63(top); Thalamus Publishing: 6–7, 20 (top), 48, 78, 79 (left), 85 (both), 150 (right), 170 (right); CORBIS/Leonard de Selva: 172; CORBIS/ML Sinibaldi: 100; CORBIS/Ted Spiegel: 27 (top), 41, 51, 53, 56 (bottom); CORBIS/Philip Spruyt: 21; CORBIS/Stapleton Collection: 83, 110 (right), 173 (top); Thalamus Studios: 18 (bottom), 19 (bottom), 38, 74–75 (all); CORBIS/Keren Su: 76–77; CORBIS/Graham Tim: 112; CORBIS/Gustavo Tomisch: 113 (right); CORBIS/Vanni Archive: 19 (center); CORBIS/Sandro Vannini: 13, 125, 147 (top), 149 (top); CORBIS/Nik Wheeler: 121

Page 1: God gives Adam the spark of life from Michelangelo's Sistine Chapel ceiling fresco (pre-restoration).

Title page: *The Procession of the Magi* (c.1460) by Benozzo Gozzoli (1420–97). Gozzoli was inspired by the remains of ancient classical buildings, and included many in his paintings. He was also one of the first artists to convey the illusion of three-dimensional space through perspective, and one of the first to include portraits of his patrons in his work. Here, Lorenzo de' Medici, who ruled Florence from 1469 until his death, is shown as one of the Magi.

CONTENTS

The Flowering of the Renaissance

The Renaissance was essentially a revival of classical tradition which—with its pagan iconography—seemed to be in conflict with the Catholic Church. Yet very few scholars became so absorbed in pagan themes as to reject Christianity. Throughout the Renaissance, artists continued to undertake commissions from the Church and, when necessary, blend classical and religious elements. One of the most striking examples of this is Sandro Botticelli's *Primavera* (c.1478), also called *The Allegory of Spring*. Painted for Lorenzo de' Medici's villa on the edge of Florence, it has a dreamy, classical antiquity, and yet has been shown to contain elaborate Christian iconography.

Some revisionist historians have described the Renaissance as an indistinct period of transition from medieval to modern times. This is like describing a concert without music, or a garden without flowers. Even stripped to its bare bones, it is a unique period of European history, two centuries when modern civilization was founded and our political, cultural, religious, and economic landscape was defined.

While it is widely accepted that the Renaissance had its roots in late 14th century Florence, it received its cultural inspiration from the revival of classical learning, the humanist study of ancient text in an attempt to better understand nature and mankind. The term "Renaissance" (from rebirth) refers to the awakening of European culture after the gap of a thousand years, lost since the collapse of the great civilizations of the ancient world.

Outside Italy, the tendency has been to acknowledge the historical legacy of the Middle Ages in shaping what was to follow. However, the rebirth that was first coined as an idle boast by contemporary scholars developed into something far greater than even the most optimistic 14th-century humanist could have imagined. Today the term has come to represent a remarkable range of cultural, political, economic, theological, and social achievements in Europe, arguably the high point of Western civilization.

The Renaissance developed its full potential amid the city-states of 15th century Italy, benefiting from the flourishing cosmopolitan communities that provided a haven for scholars and artists through cultural patronage. This phenomenon gathered momentum with each work of humanist scholarship, and each fresco, sculpture, building, and painting. Despite political and military upheavals, this rebirth of culture thrived, constantly developing to reach new horizons.

By the end of the century it began to encompass the rest of Europe. At the same time, a similar phenomenon was developing independently in northern Europe with Flemish artists, German humanists, and French scholars. As these two cultural forces met, they created new artistic and scholastic endeavors, playing a part in the development of national identity, religious divergence, and vernacular expression

The humanist quest for knowledge that first inspired the Renaissance also encouraged merchants and explorers to probe the unknown, and before the end of the 15th century European sailors had discovered both the Americas and a sea route to the Orient. These explorers expanded the boundaries of the known world, extending the Renaissance worldwide by the early 16th century.

The Renaissance ended in different places at different times. By the time it had run its course in Italy in the early 16th century, it was in full spate elsewhere in Europe. While the effects of the Reformation were having a detrimental

effect on culture in central and western Europe, the Renaissance was continuing in the Atlantic fringes of Europe, in Britain and Spain. In general terms it can be said to span the two eventful centuries from the mid-14th century until the middle of the 16th.

This book traces the historical development of the Renaissance from its origins in late medieval Florence, through its period of maturity in the rest of Italy, then its spread through the rest of Europe. To describe the Renaissance is like trying to paint a beautiful wild bird; it is impossible to capture its full glory from only one angle, thus the subject should be viewed from several aspects to encompass its full vibrant beauty. Although the Renaissance is considered a predominantly cultural phenomenon, it took place within a historical framework, when cities and states traded with each other, waged war, and shared the commonalities of art and scholarship.

In the same two centuries, the political landscape was transformed through war, exploration, and dynastic union, and the dramatic development of commerce, banking, and international trade. Religious divisions would result in the Reformation, dividing Europe by the end of the era.

Above all, it was a time of optimism, shared cultural experiences, and intellectual expression. If this spirit of cross-fertilization of events, places, cultures, and ideas has been captured by this work, it has achieved its end.

CHRONOLOGICAL TABLE

	1400	1420	1440	1460	1480
IDEAS	**Salutati** dies, 1406 Council of Pisa, 1409 Council of Constance begins, 1414 **Jan Huss** burnt at stake, 1415	**Poggio** discovers a copy of Petronius, 1423 **Guarino da Verona** teaches Greek at Ferrara, 1429 Council of Basel, 1431	**Nebrija** born, 1442 **Leonardo Bruni** dies, 1444 Freiburg University founded, 1457	**Erasmus** born, 1466 **Machiavelli** born, 1469 Universities founded: Ingolstadt, 1472; **Trier**, 1473; **Mainz**, 1476; **Tübingen**, 1476	**Luther** born, 1483 Translation of Plato by **Ficino**, 1485 **Guarino da Verona's** *Grammar* printed, 1488 **Paracelsus** born, 1493
LITERATURE	**Boccaccio** *Decameron*, 1338–53 **Chaucer** dies, 1400 **Froissart** completes *Chronicles*, c.1400 **Bruni** begins his history of Florence, 1404	First modern-language version of *Aeneid*, 1427 Plays of **Plautus** rediscovered, 1429 **Biondo's** *Decades*, 1437 **Valla's** *Disputatione dialectiae*, 1439	**Gutenberg** invents moveable type, c.1440 *De gramaticus* by **Suetonius** discovered, 1455 First printed book, **Gutenberg** Bible, 1455	First printing presses: Italy, 1465; Switzerland, 1468; France, 1469; Caxton in England, 1474 First printed edition of **Dante's** *Divine Comedy*, 1472	**Nebrija** *Latin Introductions*, 1481 Birth of **Aretino**, 1492 **Sebastian Brandt** *Ship of Fools*, 1494 **Rabelias** born, 1495
ART	**Fra Angelico** *Annunciation*, c.1400 Births: **Rogier van der Weyden**, 1400 **Masaccio**, 1401 **Fra Filippo Lipi**, 1406 **Limbourg Brothers** *Duc de Berry Book of Hours*, c.1413	**Donatello** *St. George*, 1420 **Masaccio** *Holy Trinity*, c.1426 **Masaccio** dies, 1428 **Giovanni Bellini** born, 1430 **Jan van Eyck's** *Ghent Altarpiece*, 1432	Births: **Botticelli**, 1445 **Perugino**, 1446 **Ghirlandaio**, 1448 **Leonardo da Vinci**, 1452 **Van Eyck** dies, 1441 **Donatello** *Gattamelata*, 1444	Births: **Tilman Riemenschneider**, 1460 **Piero di Cosimo**, 1462 **Dürer**, 1471 **Michelangelo**, 1475 Deaths: **Donatello**, 1466; **Fra Filippo Lippi**, 1469 **Botticelli** *Primavera*, 1478	Births: **Raphael**, 1483 **Sebastiano del Piombo**, 1485 **Pontormo** and **Corregio**, 1494 **Titian**, 1490 **Holbein**, 1497 **Botticelli** *The Birth of Venus*, 1485 **Leonardo da Vinci** *The Last Supper*, 1497
ARCHITECTURE	**Filarete** born, 1400 **Brunelleschi's** Foundling Hospital, Florence, 1418; S. Lorenzo, 1418; and dome of the Florence cathedral begun, 1420	**Brunelleschi's** Pazzi Chapel, Florence, begun, 1429 **Brunelleschi's** S. Spirito, Florence, begun 1436	**Bramante** born, 1444 **Brunelleschi** dies, 1446 Palazzo Pitti, Florence, 1451 *De re aedificatoria* by **Alberti** written, 1452 **Alberti's** façade of S. Maria Novella, Florence, begun, 1456	**Alberti** S. Sebastiano, Mantua, 1460 **Filarete** dies, 1469 Alberti begins S. Andrea, Mantua, 1470 Deaths of **Alberti** and **Michelozzo**, 1472 **Bramante** begins S. Maria presso S. Satiro, Milan, 1478	**Peruzzi** born, 1481 **Alberti's** *De re aedificatoria* published, 1485 **Giuliano da Sangallo** S. Maria delle Carceri and Villa Medici begun, 1485 **Bramante** S. Maria delle Grazie, Milan begun, 1492
POLITICS and HISTORY	Popes elected: **Innocent VII**, 1404 **Gregory XII**, 1406 **Alexander V**, 1409 **Martin V**, 1417 **Gian Galeozzo** unites Visconti lands in northern Italy, 1385 First Lollard martyr, 1401 **Ladislas II** of Poland defeats Teutonic Knights at Tannenberg, 1410 **Sigismund** elected HR Emperor, 1411 **Henry V** king of England, 1413 English defeat French at Battle of Agincourt, 1415 Portuguese capture Ceuta, 1415 Election of **Martin V** as pope ends Great Schism, 1417 Outbreak of Hussite Wars in Bohemia, 1419	Popes elected: **Eugenius IV**, 1431 **Felix V** (at Basel), 1439 **Henry V** made heir to French throne at Treaty of Troyes, 1420 **Charles VII** king of France, 1422 **Henry VI** king of England, 1422 **Leonardo Bruni** elected Chancellor of Florence, 1427 Siege of Orléans lifted, 1429 **Joan of Arc** burned at stake, 1431 Pope **Eugenius IV** flees to Florence after revolt in Rome, 1434 Congress of Arras allies France and Burgundy, 1435 **Albert II** elected HR Emperor, 1438	Popes elected: **Nicholas V**, 1447 **Calistus III**, 1455 **Pius II**, 1458 **Alfonso V** of Aragon becomes **Alfonso I** of Naples, 1442 Papacy returns to Rome, 1443 Battle of Kossovo, 1448 **Lorenzo de' Medici** born, 1449 French take Rouen, 1449 **Francesco Sforza** first Sforza duke of Milan, 1450 **Frederick III** elected HR Emperor, 1452 Defeat of English ends Hundred Years' War, 1453 Turks capture Constantinople, 1453 **Matthias Corvinus** king of Hungary, 1458	Popes elected: **Paul II**, 1464 **Sixtus IV**, 1471 Death of **Henry the Navigator**, 1460 **Edward IV** king of England 1461 **Louis XI** king of France, 1461 Castilians capture Gibraltar from Arabs, 1462 **Cosimo de' Medici** dies, 1464 **Charles the Bold** duke of Burgundy, 1467 Marriage of **Ferdinand** and **Isabella**, 1469 Swiss forces defeat **Charles the Bold** at Murten/Morat, 1476 Pazzi Conspiracy in Florence, 1478 Spanish Inquisition established, 1478	Popes elected: **Innocent VIII**, 1484 **Alexander VI**, 1492 **Matthias Corvinus** takes Vienna from **Frederick III**, 1485 **Diaz** rounds Cape of Good Hope, 1487 Treaty of Pressburg recognizes Habsburg rights to Bohemia and Hungary, 1491 Moorish Granada falls to Spanish, 1492 **Columbus** lands in New World, 1492 **Maximilian I** elected HR Emperor, 1493 **Charles VIII** of France invades Italy; Treaty of Tordesillas 1494 **Louis XII** king of France, 1498 **Vasco da Gama** reaches India, 1498 **Savonarola** burned, 1498

1500	1520	1540	1560	1580	1600
Calvin born, 1509 **Luther** posts 95 theses, Wittenburg, 1517 **Zwingli** begins preaching Reformation, Zurich, 1519	*Complutensian Polyglot Bible* published in Spain, 1522 Deaths of **Nebrija** and **Reuchlin**, 1522 **Tyndale** English New Testament, 1525	**Copernicus** *De revolutionibus*, 1543 Council of Trent starts, 1545 **Luther** dies, 1546 **Ignatius Loyola** dies, 1556	Deaths: **Melancthon**, 1560; **Calvin**, 1564; **John Knox**, 1572 **Galileo** born, 1564 **Plantin** Polyglot Bible, 1568	**Edmund Campion** executed, 1581 **George Buchanan** dies, 1582 Remains of Pompeii discovered, 1592	**Bacon** The *Advancement of Learning*, 1605 **Galileo** uses telescope to observe the Moon's mountains, 1610
Erasmus's *Enchiridon* published, 1501; *Adagia*, 1508; *Greek New Testament*, 1516 **Machiavelli** *The Prince*, 1513	**Reuchlin** *On the Art of the Cabbala*, 1517 **Erasmus** *Colloquia*, 1522 **Machiavelli** dies, 1527 **Rabelais** *Pantagruel*, 1532	**Marot** dies, 1544 **Tasso** born, 1544 **Cervantes** born, 1547 **Bandello** *Novelle*, 1554; *Lazarillo de Tormes*, 1556	**Guicciardini** *History of Italy*, posthumously, 1561 **Shakespeare** born, 1564 **Ascham** *The Schoolmaster*, posthumously, 1570	**Marlowe** *Dr. Faustus*, 1585 **Spenser** *Faery Queene*, 1590 **Shakespeare** *Henry V, Twelfth Night, As You Like It*, 1599	**Shakespeare** *Hamlet*, c.1601 **de Thou** *History of His Own Time*, 1603 **Cervantes** *Don Quixote*, 1605–15
Michelangelo *Pietà*, 1499 **Bosch** *Garden of Earthly Delights*, c.1500 **Leonardo** *Mona Lisa*, 1502 **Michelangelo** Sistine ceiling, 1508–12 **Grünewald** *Isenheim Altarpiece*, 1510–15	**Leonardo da Vinci** dies, 1519 **Raphael** dies, 1520 **Altdorfer** *St. George*, 1525 **Veronese** born 1528 **Holbein** settles in England, 1532 **Michelangelo** *The Last Judgment*, 1536–41	**Cellini** salt-cellar for Francis I, 1540 **Holbein** dies, 1543 **Titian** *Charles V at Mühlberg*, 1549 **Vasari's** *Lives*, first edition, 1550 **Lucas Cranach the Elder** dies, 1553	**Tintoretto** *Susanna and the Elders*, 1560 **Veronese** *The Marriage at Cana*, 1562 Deaths of **Michelangelo**, 1564; **Cellini**, 1571; **Vasari**, 1574; **Titian**, 1576 **Caravaggio** born, 1571 **Rubens** born, 1577	**El Greco** *Burial of Count Orgaz*, 1586 **Hilliard** *An Unknown Youth*, c.1588 **Veronese** dies, 1588 **Tintoretto** *The Last Supper*, 1592–94 **Poussin** born, 1593 **Tintoretto** dies, 1594	**Caravaggio** *St. Matthew*, 1600 **Rembrandt** born, 1606
Bramante begins work on St. Peter's, 1506 **Vignola** born, 1507 **Palladio** born, 1508 **Bramante** dies, 1514 Hampton Court Palace, 1515–30 Château Chambord, 1519	**Michelangelo** Medici Chapel, 1520; Laurentian Library begun, 1523 Segovia Cathedral begun, 1523 **Peruzzi** dies, 1536 **Serlio's** first of *Six Books of Architecture* published, 1537	**Sansovino** St. Mark's Library, Venice, 1540 **Michelangelo** takes over St. Peter's, 1546 **Palladio** Basilica, Vicenza, 1546–50 **De l'Orme** Château of Anet, 1550 **Palladio** Palazzo Chiericati and Villa Rotunda, begun 1550	**Herrera** Escorial begun, 1563 **Palladio** S. Giorgio Maggiore, Venice, 1565 **Vignola** Gesù, Rome begun, 1568 **Inigo Jones** born, 1573 **Palladio** Il Redentore, Venice, 1576; Teatro Olympico, Vicenza, 1579	**Palladio** dies, 1580 **Smythson** Wollaton Hall, England, 1580 **Pirro Ligorio** dies, 1583 **Jean Le Mercier** born, 1584 **Herrera** dies, 1597 **François Mansart** born, 1598	**Inigo Jones** Queen's House, Greenwich, 1616
Popes elected: **Pius III**, 1503 **Leo X**, 1513 **Cabral** discovers Brazil, 1500 Basel join Swiss Confederation, 1502 Naples to Spain, 1504 League of Cambrai, 1508 **Henry VIII** king of England, 1509 Portuguese capture Goa, 1510 Medici restored in Florence, 1512 English defeat Scots at Flodden, 1513 **Francis I** king of France, 1515 **Charles V** king of Spain, 1516, HR Emperor, 1519 **Cortés** lands in Mexico, 1519 **Magellan** starts circumnavigation, 1519	Popes elected: **Hadrian VI**, 1522 **Clement VII**, 1523 **Paul III**, 1535 **Luther** excommunicated, 1520 Field of the Cloth of Gold, 1520 Diet of Worms, 1521 Turks expell Knights Hospitaler from Rhodes, 1522 Battle of Pavia, 1525 Peasants' Revolt, Germany, 1525 Sack of Rome, 1527 Confession of Augsburg, 1530 **Pizarro** leads expedition to Peru, 1531 **Henry VIII's** Act of Supremacy, 1534 Supression of the Anabaptists of Münster, 1535 **Thomas More** executed, 1535	Popes elected: **Julius II**, 1550 **Marcelus II; Paul IV**, 1555 **Pius IV**, 1559 Spaniards discover California, 1540 **Thomas Cromwell** executed, 1540 War of the Schmalkaldic League, 1546 **Edward VI** king of England, 1547 **Henry II** king of France, 1547 Battle of Mühlberg, 1547 **Mary I** queen of England, 1553 **Charles V** abdicates; **Philip II** king of Spain, 1556 **Elizabeth I** queen of England, 1558 **Ferdinand I** elected HR Emperor, 1558 French recover Calais from English, 1558	Popes elected: **Pius V**, 1566; **Gregory XIII**, 1572 **Charles IX** king of France, **Catherine de' Medici** as regent, 1560 Religious Wars in France, 1562 **Maximilian II** elected HR Emperor, 1564 Turks besiege Malta, 1564 **Duke of Alba** sent to Netherlands, 1567 **Elizabeth I** of England excommunicated, 1570 Battle of Lepanto, 1571 St. Bartholemew's Day Massacre, 1572 Dutch war of independence begins, 1572 **Henry III** king of France, 1574 **Rudolf II** elected HR Emperor, 1576	Popes elected: **Sixtus V**, 1585 **Urban VII** and **Gregory XIV**, 1590 **Innocent IX**, 1591 **Clement VIII**, 1592 **Francis Drake** completes circumnavigation, 1580 **Rudolf II** moves HRE capital to Prague, 1583 **William of Orange** assassinated, 1584 First attempt to found colony in Virginia, 1585 **Drake** raids Cadiz, 1587 Spanish Armada, 1588 **Henry IV** king of France, 1589 **Henry IV** defeats Catholic forces at Ivry, 1590 **Henry IV** converts to Catholicism, 1593 Edict of Nantes, 1598 **Philip III** king of Spain, 1598	Popes elected: **Leo XI** and **Paul V**, 1605 English East India Company granted charter, 1600 Dutch East India Company granted charter, 1602 **James I** (VI of Scotland) first Stuart king of England, 1603 Gunpowder Plot, England, 1605 Truce agreed between Spain and Netherlands, 1609 **Louis XIII** king of France, 1610 with **Marie de' Medici** as regent, 1610 War of Kalmar between Denmark and Sweden, 1611

CHAPTER 1

Florence—Cradle of the Renaissance

It is traditionally held that the Renaissance began in Florence in the early 1400s, then spread throughout Italy. This cultural phenomenon was taken north of the Alps following the French invasion of Italy in 1494, allowing it to spread throughout the rest of western Europe. Although this is largely true, it represents a great over-simplification. It ignores the reverse flow of artistic and cultural influences that reached Florence from northern Europe and elsewhere in the Mediterranean.

What made the Florentine republic so special was its embracement of a secular political system that encouraged the patronage of scholarship, architecture, and the arts. That the oligarchs who controlled the city were willing to open their purses is due in turn to the establishment of Florence as a center of the humanist movement during the previous century.

The first great humanist, and often credited with giving the Renaissance its name, had been Petrarch (1304–74), who maintained that Platonic thought and Greek studies provided a new cultural framework separate from scholasticism. He had heavily influenced fellow Italian scholars and poets, including Giovanni Boccaccio di Certaldo (*see also page 150*), the Florentine author of *The Decameron* (written 1348–53), who argued that although the muses had long been banished from Italy, Dante Alighieri (1265–1321), the last great author of the Middle Ages, in his many writings and ultimately with his *Divine Comedy* had opened the way for their return; and Petrarch had restored them with a humanist revival of long-lost culture, civilization, inquiry, and above all, hope for humanity.

In the realm of the visual arts, the Florentine artist Giotto (1266–1337) had experimented with light, realism, and perspective. The artists who followed him combined experimentation with inspiration derived from humanist scholars such as Petrarch: they were no longer painting a devotional work, but trying to capture the essence of humanity. It was a significant difference in outlook, the catalyst for the great artistic outpouring of the period we know as the Renaissance.

In the mid-14th century the humanist writer Coloccio Salutati was the leading exponent of this notion of cultural rebirth, and his

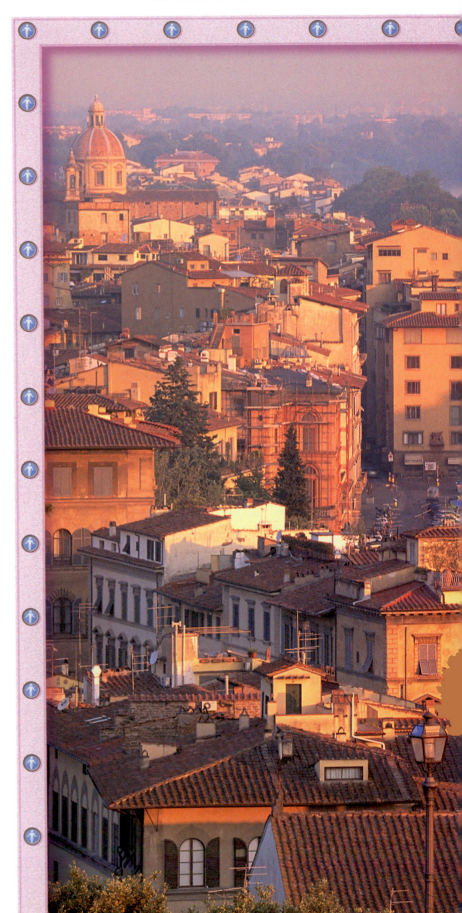

appointment as Chancellor of Florence in 1375 epitomized the establishment of this city as the center of the humanist movement. He saw Florence as the natural political and cultural successor of the ancient Roman Republic, an aspiration that inspired the city's secular leaders, and ushered in the spread of patronage.

The Florentine humanist mantle was taken up by Salutati's disciple Leonardo Bruni following the chancellor's death in 1406, advocating this unique combination of civic pride and municipal patronage. The Republic of Florence transformed into the first great Renaissance center, reborn as the "ideal city" of a new golden age.

The River Arno bisects Florence as it passes under the Ponte Vecchio. Modern Florence still evokes the splendor of the Renaissance.

Breaking the Medieval Mold

At about the start of the 15th century, Florence emerged as the cultural and artistic center of Europe. A celebration of humanity and the natural world emerged from the dry pages of classical texts, developing into a cultural movement that would change the world.

The 14th century had been a time of great uncertainty. Economic stagnation and warfare had cast a shadow over Italy, and bubonic plague had ravaged the entire continent, reaching that country in 1348. Florence's population had dropped from 100,000 to just under half that in a single year. Those who had survived began to question their belief in a God who appeared to have punished them, and a Church that did nothing to help. The pope had been seen to be barely able to control his own destiny, let alone provide spiritual leadership. In 1378 the king of France had decided that he disliked the pope in Rome and had elected one of his own, splitting the Church and secular Europe in a schism that lasted for four decades.

In the 14th century most Italian city-states that had emerged during the 11th century were ruled by *signori* (despots) or oligarchies.

In Florence the situation was a little different, since Florentines had clung to the notion of municipal freedom longer than their neighbors. By the late 1300s the city and its hinterland were governed by republican factions, who—whenever in power—promptly abandoned republicanism to rule in *signoral* (or dictatorial) manner.

This system almost invited political coups and oligarchic in-fighting, but by 1378 a faction headed by one Maso degli Albizzi had seized and retained control of the city. He continued to rule Florence as a relatively benign dictator until his death in 1417, at which point power was shared between his son, Rinaldo de' Albizzi, and Niccolò de' Uzzano, the head of a leading patrician family. They paid lip-service to republican ideals, but to all intents they ruled as *signori*. This encouraged the growth of political opposition, led by the wealthy Florentine banker Giovanni de' Medici and his son Cosimo. The end of civic strife with the seizure of power by the young Medici in 1434 ushered in a new era of political stability, allowing Florence to prosper under the rule of the banking dynasty. While some historians claim it was Medici patronage that established Florence as the cultural center of the Renaissance, they were simply following a long tradition of oligarchic patronage.

Light from the darkness

Florentine Giotto "di Bondone" (1266–1337) is generally recognized to be the pioneer of the artistic renaissance of the 14th century. Giotto was one of the first artists to break the Byzantine-influenced rules of religious art; he preferred a more natural, less stylized approach to religious subjects, combining influences from the High Gothic movement that was sweeping northern Europe with his own perception of realism and perspective—but he would not have achieved recognition without the continued patronage of the Church.

What really transformed Florentine art was the growth of secular patronage during the century after his death. In the 15th century Giotto's innovations were taken a stage further by "Masaccio," Tommaso di Giovanni di Simone Guidi (c.1400–28), a young artist who has been seen as the founder of a Florentine tradition of using light, color, perspective, and a truer

depiction of the human form to reintroduce and achieve a hitherto long-lost level of realism.

By this time Florence was a different place from the pessimistic city that had survived the Black Death. Growing numbers of humanist scholars sought inspiration in the classics, and

encouraged both artists and patrons to do the same.

Humanism was responsible for the view that mankind was experiencing a time of rebirth, a flowering of civilization after a hiatus that had lasted since the fall of ancient Rome. From 1400 onward, a combination of humanist writing, increased secular wealth, and the relative stability of government encouraged the spread of these beliefs, inspiring the leading families who ran the city to undergo their own metamorphoses.

Facing: Giotto's *Lamentation* shows a new awareness of three-dimensional space, but remains medieval in appearance compared to the later Masaccio, **above,** of *St. Paul Giving Alms and The Death of Ananias.*

Humanism—The Intellectual Springboard

"Humanism" was a term used in the 18th century enlightenment to describe an education based on a study of the classics. Later, it came to mean something much larger; summed up by one historian as "the entire intellectual movement of the Renaissance."

Facing: *The School of Athens* by Raphael is one of several frescos in the Vatican executed by the master that combine all the elements of Renaissance techniques with humanist imagery. Painted 1509–11.

Right: Contemporary 14th-century portrait of humanist poet and scholar Francesco Petrarca.

Since the 19th century, humanism has been closely associated with the Renaissance; a blanket term applied to almost every aspect of intellectual or cultural development during this period and associated with the study of classicism. More appropriately, it has been applied to any system of belief that places human affairs at its core, and is a doctrine emphasizing an individual's capacity for self-realization through reason. It is this latter aspect that eventually came into conflict with the Church, since the corollary is to reject established religion along with the supernatural. Humanism was adopted by Renaissance scholars during their rediscovery of the classical world, particularly the surviving works of Greek philosophy, and in this the Church at first failed to see any danger to its medieval interests—for a very short period.

The term "humanism" was first used by Francesco Petrarca, or Petrarch (1304–74), the poet and scholar who, influenced by classical Roman literature, wrote sonnets in the vernacular. Petrarch encouraged the rediscovery and circulation of these ancient texts, inspiring a subsequent generation of scholars, artists, and thinkers. He used the term to express the spirit of intellectual freedom by which man asserted his independence from medieval restrictions, most notably the authority of the Church. This involved questioning existing moral, religious, social, and political values.

However, its original meaning, as coined by classical writers Cicero and Varro, was the search for an intellectual ideal based on knowledge. Petrarch and his successors believed these classic Greek and Roman texts contained the key to knowledge; a blueprint for civilization and the key to understanding the world and humanity. The classics became a guide by which the men of the Renaissance would live.

The Church soon frowned on these notions, and before long humanists became embroiled in theological controversy. By challenging the hierarchical structure of medieval theocracy, humanist thinkers were creating a political weapon; a new ideology that would give hope to those who felt repressed by the strictures imposed on them from above. Humanism grew in the cities and communes of Italy that were fighting for political autonomy from the control of pope or emperor—personifications of fundamentally medieval institutions. The writings of classical Greek philosophers also encouraged the spread of republicanism, leading to the revival of republican forms of government in Florence and Venice.

Studia humanitatis

Popes and emperors had weathered political crises before, and rather than repress these humanist scholars, they attempted to use the new doctrine for their own ends. Humanist scholarship continued to develop during the 15th century, but while many humanists became teachers and classical historians, others served Church and State, adapting these new ideas for secular or religious ends. The more enlightened rulers of the age incorporated elements of

humanism into their systems of government, giving them a veneer of modernity.

For example, the Mass was rewritten along more classical lines, while the papacy employed humanist scholars to act as propagandists, citing classical arguments for the legitimacy of papal primacy. While the humanist movement was generally critical of the Church, the papacy used classical sources to deflect criticism and avoid reform. However, the new spirit of theological inquiry would ultimately lead to a rejection of the Catholic Church—the Reformation.

It has been argued that while "humanism" was a broad intellectual concept rather than a definitive movement, it produced a cultural thread that encompassed all progressive scholars, artists, and leaders of the Renaissance. Modern academics have labeled this *studia humanitatis*, a largely untranslatable term first coined by the Roman philosopher Cicero. It embraced the study of humanity and involved the advocacy of learning, particularly the study of classical writing and language; grammar, rhetoric, moral philosophy, and history. Finally it embraced the study of nature and *studia divinitatis*, or divinity.

Together these disciplines represented a firm belief in classical scholarship, the foundation of a general spread of intellectual inquiry. It led to the establishment of centers of learning, which in turn ensured that future generations would continue the drive toward a new civilization based on humanist learning.

Centers of learning founded before 1400

university founded
- before 1300
- 1301–1400
1289 date of foundation

Scotland

NORTH SEA

Ireland

ENGLAND

Wales

Oxford c.1190

Cambridge 1209

ATLANTIC OCEAN

GERMANY

Cologne 1388

Erfurt 1392

Paris c.1150

Prague 1348

Krakow 1364

Angers 1337

Orléans 1235

Heidelberg 1386

Vienna 1365

Bay of Biscay

FRANCE

Vercelli 1228

Buda 1389

Orange 1364

Pavia 1361

Montpellier 1289

Grenoble 1339

Vicenza 1204

Cahors 1332

Treviso 1318

Valladolid 1208

Toulouse 1229

Avignon 1303

Piacenza 1248

Padua 1222

Ferrara 1391

Coimbra 1308

Salamanca 1227

Huesca 1354

Perpignan 1329

Pisa 1343

Florence 1349

Arezzo 1215

Lérida 1300

Siena 1246

Perugia 1308

Lisbon 1290

SPAIN

Corsica

Rome 1303

Seville 1254

Balearic Islands

Sardinia

Naples 1224

Salerno 1173

MEDITERRANEAN SEA

AFRICA

Sicily

The Medici—Patrons and Princes

For most of the Renaissance, Florence was a republic in name only. True political power rested in the hands of a ruling oligarchy formed by its leading patrician families. By the mid-15th century Florence came to be dominated by one of these: the Medici.

Right: In his superb bust of Cosimo de' Medici, Benvenuto Cellini has portrayed the Florentine banker as an ancient Roman military emperor. It is, perhaps, no coincidence that the bearded Cosimo resembles the Roman emperor Marcus Aurelius, who apart from being a successful soldier was a noted thinker and philosopher. Cellini's career is outlined on page 145.

Facing top: Portrait of Lorenzo de' Medici by Girolamo Macchietti (1535–92). Since the sitter was no longer alive when this portrait was painted, Macchietti must have worked from other paintings or the several busts of Lorenzo that existed.

The Medici rose to prominence in the 14th century, their fortune based on banking and commerce. In 1429 the Albizzi family held power, but a string of military setbacks encouraged the establishment of an opposition, led by Cosimo de' Medici (1389–1464), son of the founder of the Medici bank, Giovanni di Bicci de' Medici (1360–1429). Although banished for a year by his rival Rinaldo Albizzi, Cosimo returned to challenge Rinaldo for electoral control of the city, finally gaining power in 1434. It was then the Albizzis who were exiled from Florence, which remained in Cosimo's hands for three decades.

Unlike the oligarchs who had preceded him, Cosimo had no desire to share power with his peers. He altered the city's constitution to safeguard his position, controlling the selection of candidates for the Signatory (ruling council) and smaller civic bodies. Cosimo ruled Florence indirectly through his supporters, while he continued to run his banking empire. The Medici soon became one of the richest families in Italy, and the city prospered under his leadership.

He created what amounted to a princely court in Florence and, under his patronage, artists, sculptors, and scholars flocked to the city, which by this time was widely regarded as the cultural center of Italy. Cosimo also lavished money on civic and ecclesiastic projects. For example, he ordered the rebuilding of the Convent of San Marco, then furnished it with a magnificent library.

His death in 1464 marked a renewal of the struggle between oligarchs and republicans, but Cosimo's eldest son Piero de' Medici regained the family's control of Florence in 1466, overthrowing a short-lived republican administration. Gout-ridden, Piero proved an inattentive banker and poor administrator, but he arranged a marriage between younger brother Lorenzo and a girl from the Orsini family, the greatest old patrician house in the city. They would no longer be considered *nouveau riche*.

Lorenzo de' Medici (1449–92) became head of the Medici empire on Piero's death in 1469 and, like Cosimo, he elected to control the government from a distance, while continuing his father's program of civic and ecclesiastic building works, and patronage of the arts.

Murder in the duomo

In 1478 members of the Florentine Pazzi family conspired against the Medici, joining forces with Girolamo Riario, a nephew of Pope Sixtus IV (p.1471–84). Assassins struck outside the *duomo* (cathedral) on Easter Sunday, and although Lorenzo escaped, his younger brother Giuliano was killed in front of the high altar. This prompted a popular rising in support of the Medici, and the mob hunted down and killed the conspirators. Sixtus retaliated by excommunicating the entire city, prompting Florence to declare war on the papacy. The pope laid siege, aided by his

Neapolitan allies, but Lorenzo brokered a secret deal with King Ferrante of Naples and the allies returned home. Unable to fight the Florentines alone, Sixtus sued for peace.

After the Pazzi conspiracy Lorenzo changed his policy, ruling Florence directly. Legislation passed in 1480 legitimized hereditary Medici rule. From that point he oversaw all aspects of civic government, which caused irreparable damage to his increasingly neglected banking interests. By the time of Lorenzo's death in 1492, the Medici bank was virtually bankrupt.

A contributory factor was his continued patronage of the arts, commissioning works by Verrocchio, Botticelli, and others, for private and civic works of art. By the time of his death Lorenzo "the Magnificent" was regarded as the leading artistic patron in Europe.

His dynasty did not long survive his death. In 1494 the family were exiled from the city in a French-backed coup. Political power devolved into the hands of the monk Savonarola (*see pages 20–21*), who ruled Florence as a virtual dictator. Although the Medici would return in 1512, they never regained complete control of the city, nor provided further lavish patronage.

Centers of Renaissance artistic activity in Italy as recorded by Giorgio Vasari, 1550

population density per square mile, 1550

150
125
100

– – – state boundary, 1550

% of total art commissions, 1280–1550

● more than 12
● 6–12
● 2–5
● less than 2

Below: Medallion commemorating the defeat of the Pazzi Conspiracy, with Lorenzo de' Medici at the top, by Bertoldo di Giovanni, struck in 1478.

The Flowering of Architecture

Dominated by Filippo Brunelleschi's *duomo* (cathedral), 15th-century Florence became a place where the architect was revered as an artist, and where architectural perfection was the goal of both builders and their patrons.

Above: The *duomo* of Florence. Brunelleschi—who learned mathematics before becoming an apprenticed metalworker—used carefully designed proportions for the drum and dome to rise in fixed mathematical intervals (*see elevation on page 38*).

Right: Francesco di Giorgio's plan for a church illustrates the way Renaissance architects devised a system of measurements based on human proportions (after Vitruvius). Here, the two sets of lines are differently colored to show them clearly.

Inspired by humanist scholars, the Florentines believed in the concept of the "ideal city," and through a combination of civic planning and secular or ecclesiastical patronage, they transformed their environment. These men embraced the notion of architectural harmony during the 15th century, blending in newly commissioned buildings with the rest of the city.

Like other cities in Renaissance Italy, Florence retained its medieval core, centered around the market place, town hall, and central *piazza* (square). At first a handful of buildings were erected around this core, but as the architectural boom got underway, whole sections of the city were transformed.

Just like contemporary scholars, Florentine architects of the 15th century turned to the classics for inspiration. Filippo Brunelleschi (1377–1446) was arguably the first of these humanist architects, since he applied classical theories to the Ospedale degli Innocenti (Foundling Hospital) in Florence, now viewed

as the city's earliest finished Renaissance building. He went on to work on his masterpiece, the redesign of the *duomo*, a structure which had taken a century to build—and internal work continued for another half-century.

The cathedral's design was changed in line with the latest architectural ideas, and Brunelleschi was called in to supervise the completion of this great project, begun by Arnolfo di Cambio. Rejecting the Gothic style of roof construction, which he saw as representative of the Germanic barbarians who had destroyed Rome, he sought inspiration in the ruins of classical Italy and in the treatise *De architectura* written by first-century BC architect Vitruvius. The Roman writer emphasized the balance of unity, strength, and beauty, and the creation of a symmetrical and harmonious design that combined aesthetic appeal with practicality.

After examining the construction of late Roman basilicas, Brunelleschi engineered the great dome (and from which Florence's and other Italian cathedrals received their common appellation *duomo*—even if they lacked a dome) that still surmounts the premier cathedral of Florence, erected in 1420–34. His philosophy was typical of the humanist approach that resulted in the return to a classical sense of proportion and style. For these men, Imperial Rome represented an architectural golden age, thus their work was heavily influenced by classical examples.

Past transforms the present

In the 15th century Florence's increasingly wealthy leading families commissioned ambitious houses, municipal buildings, and country retreats, all built along classical lines. For the most part they were designed to blend in with their surroundings, having a basic simplicity that was both elegant and in keeping with the earlier buildings around them. In effect they were larger versions of medieval structures, but designed to create the impression of space and light.

Even the most modest of new buildings had frontages pierced with stylish windows, archways, and balconies. More elaborate structures incorporated magnificent entranceways and porticos, grand staircases, and supporting columns that allowed larger internal spaces. In almost all cases, the arches and columns of antiquity inspired the design of these features.

The best examples are probably Taddeo Gaddi's Ponte Vecchio, the Palazzo Strozzi designed by Benedetto da Maiano, and Michelangelo's Laurentian Library. After his triumph with the *duomo*, Brunelleschi received a series of non-secular commissions, and almost single-handedly rebuilt the spiritual centers of the city. The Florentine churches of San Lorenzo, Santa Maria degli Angeli, San Spirito, and the Pazzi chapel were all designed by him.

Another church architect, the Genoese Leon Battista Alberti, wrote *De pictura* (1435) and *De re aedificatoria* (1450), the latter one of the most influential architectural manuals in history. Unlike Vitruvius, he described the practice as well as the theory of architecture. These men were not simply copying classical architecture; they were drawing on ancient examples to create architecture relevant to the world in which they

Left: Architects of the Early Renaissance drew inspiration from *De architectura libri decem* (the ten books of architecture) by Marcus Pollio Vitruvius, who worked in Rome in the 1st century BC. His books were translated and published in the 16th century; this is a page from the famous 1556 edition.

lived. While the Florentine style of humanist architecture spread across Italy and eventually into northern Europe, Florence remained the epicenter of Renaissance architectural design.

Left: Although the arched windows of the Palazzo Strozzi still contain Gothic elements, the architect Benedetto da Maiano arranged the three floors in strict classical order and proportions. The ground floor is now ruined with modern shop fronts.

Below: Mathematical harmony—Brunelleschi's Foundling Hospital uses ratios of 1:2, 1:5, and 2:5 to achieve a lucid and elegant design.

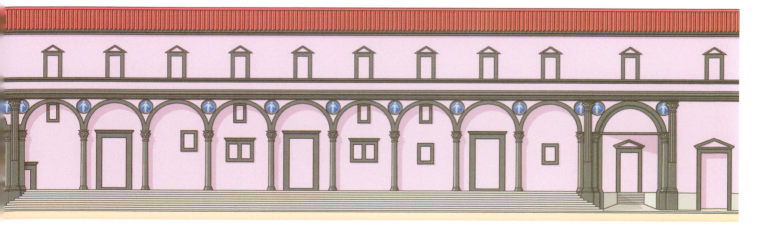

Savonarola and Social Reform

While Florence remained a free city, its citizens were divided into well-defined social strata. Civic power remained in the hands of the *grandi*, the city's elite, epitomized by the Medici. While the city remained relatively stable, a revolt led to social upheaval and a change in the balance of power.

Right: Portrait of the radical preacher Girolamo Savonarola by the painter Fra Bartolomeo.

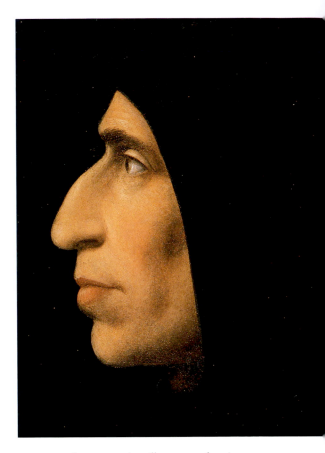

Like most Italian cities of the period, Florence was free of a feudal overlord and run by its own elected government. Encouraged by its establishment as a banking center, Florence's wealth increased and its financial influence extended far beyond the Italian peninsula. While the city benefited as a whole in the form of grand municipal buildings and a buoyant economy, the mass of the wealth remained in the hands of a few powerful families, the patrician oligarchy who maintained a firm grip on government.

The *grandi*, nicknamed the *popolo grasso* (fat people), included nobles, bankers, and even the leading manufacturers in the city, and constituted about five percent of the Florentine population during the 15th and 16th centuries. The greatest patrician families, such as the Medici, behaved more like princes than citizens of a republic.

Below this social elite were the heavily taxed *mediocri*, an urban middle class of small merchants,

Below: Fresco depicting a group of Florentine nobles with falcons, by Gianfrancesco da Tolmezzo, 1498.

master craftsmen, and well respected artisans. To a large extent social mobility was linked to wealth. Men of commerce could join the ruling elite, although for the most part the ranks of the oligarchy remained tightly closed to the rising stars of the *mediocri*. It was a matter of maintaining the *status quo* and being accepted by the right people.

The bulk of the population (some 70 percent in 1500) comprised the *popolo minuto* (little people), who had small hope of advancement. As the population increased, the exclusivity of both the *grandi* and the trade guilds meant that the proportion of urban poor increased steadily, kept in their place by the merchants, artisans, and producers who employed them.

A shamed theocracy

The poor had no say in government, since only those rich enough to pay taxes were elligible to vote in council elections. They were excluded from the most lucrative trades, which remained tightly controlled by the guilds. The threat of revolt remained ever-present, and the *grandi* recalled the bloody revolt of the *ciompi* (wooden shoes) of 1378, when cloth-workers rose in insurrection. The poor were kept in a position of subservience but given occasional treats, such as free food and drink during festivals, financed by the *grandi*.

In the 15th century the Medici established then maintained tight control over the city, ruthlessly suppressing any hint of rebellion. During the last decade, the Dominican monk Girolamo Savonarola (1452–98) became the focal point of resistance to the Medici, whom he saw as corrupt. He leveled the same criticism at the papacy, which did little to endear him to any of his superiors.

When the Medici were exiled in 1494 (*see page 17*), Savonarola temporarily seized control of the government, thanks to the support of the *mediocri*. However, his anti-papal views and reliance on support from the lower strata of society eventually earned the disapproval of both the Florentine nobility and the middle class.

Worse still, he dabbled in external politics. Savonarola supported Charles VIII's invasion of Italy in 1494, calling the French king "an instrument in the hands of the Lord who has sent you to cure the ills of Italy." This coincided with Savonarola's excommunication by Pope Alexander VI (p.1492–1503), on the grounds of his continual criticism of the papacy. Savonarola was seized by his enemies and publicly executed in Florence's main square, a lesson to anyone who threatened to upset the *status quo*.

Above: Charles VIII the Courteous of France was not so polite when he invaded Italy in 1494. Savonarola's support for the French king contributed to the Florentine ruler's downfall.

The town center of Florence during the 15th century was dominated by the important civic buildings, the *duomo* to the north and the Palazzo della Signoria (town hall, later called the Palazzo Vecchio) to the south. On the south bank, one of the most important Renaissance churches was nearing completion, Brunelleschi's Santo Spirito (18). During the 15th century, almost 100 palaces of the *grandi* were built or "modernized," as wealthy families sought to outdo each other in imitation of the Medici.

Florence in 1500

1 San Marco (museum)
2 SS. Annunziata
3 Ospedale degli Innocenti (Foundling Hospital)
4 Palazzo Medici
5 San Lorenzo, Laurentian Library
6 Santa Maria Novella
7 *Duomo* (cathedral)
8 Giotto's campanile
9 Baptistry
10 Santa Croce, Pazzi Chapel
11 Bargello (national museum)
12 Orsanmichele
13 Palazzo Vecchio, Palazzo della Signoria (town hall)
14 Palazzo Strozzi
15 Santa Trinitá
16 Palazzo Spini
17 Palazzo Pitti (museum)
18 Santo Spirito
19 Santa Maria del Carmine, Brancacci chapel
20 Palazzo Uffizi (1560, now galleries)

—— approximate line of Early Renaissance city wall

Machiavelli and the Florentine State

Florentine political theorist Niccolò Machiavelli served as a diplomat and military advisor until dismissed by the mid-1480s. He then devoted his time to writing, producing works on state craft that transformed the outlook of the Renaissance ruler.

Below: Tapestry with a prince and maiden in courtly Renaissance dress. Machiavelli viewed princes as visionary reformers, and many of the Florentine *grandi* preferred their image as chivalric men rather than grasping bankers and politicians.

Machiavelli (1469–1527) entered the Florentine civil service in 1498 as a secretary to the city's main bureaucrat, and was soon promoted to chancellor, one of the city's senior administrators. While his duties involved administrative and military work, Machiavelli's growing role was that of diplomat. He led several important diplomatic missions, including embassies to the court of Holy Roman Emperor Maximilian I, and to the Vatican, ruled by Pope Julius II (p.1503–13), where he met Cesare

Borgia (*see pages 52–53*), the man believed to be his political model for *Il Principe* (The Prince), his controversial treatise on statesmanship. Machiavelli was a natural statesman, able to analyze the political realities of the states and courts he visited and apply this knowledge to benefit Florence.

In 1505 he reorganized the Florentine army,

using the army of the ancient Roman Republic as a model. Under his guidance, military service became a civic duty for the city's youth. A militia force was created based on compulsory conscription for a limited term, foreshadowing the national conscription system used in most Western countries some 400 years later.

Machiavelli's citizen army proved less successful than he hoped, faring badly against the Pisans, then soundly defeated by the Spanish in 1512. That said, the Spanish usually won every battle they fought during this period. His military doctrines were later enshrined in his *Art of War*, a work that influenced later military commanders, including Henry of Navarre and Gustavus Adolphus.

Machiavelli was a staunch advocate of republicanism, therefore when the Medici returned to power in 1512 he was interrogated on suspicion of subversion and ousted from office. He retired to his farm outside the city and, condemned to life as a bystander in Italian politics rather than an active participant, devoted the rest of his life to writing about state craft.

The misuse of power

His first and most famous work was written as a means of regaining the political stage. In *Il Principe*, he couched his treatise on what he saw as the reality of Italian politics in a manner he considered would appeal to Lorenzo de' Medici, to whom he dedicated the book. Machiavelli removed state craft from confines of morality; what remained was an uncompromising manual for the modern political world.

He drew on his own experiences of Florentine government, and relied on his shrewd and often highly accurate observations of the workings of other states. As such it outlined the realities of the political scene in Renaissance Europe, but did so in a way that shocked many of those who shrank from admitting the ruthlessness of those in power. Many readers were outraged by what most regarded as an advocacy of despotism, and an affront to all "men of goodwill." Some even linked Machiavelli to Satan.

Machiavelli, the ardent republican, was not betraying his beliefs but returning to the classics

1266–1337	1304–74	1375	1378	1386–1466	1413	1434	c.1444
Giotto di Bondone adds naturalism to religious painting, beginning the artistic renaissance	Life of Petrarch (Francesco Petrarca), the Italian humanist credited with naming the Renaissance	Coloccio Salutati is appointed Chancellor of Florence, helps the city become a humanist center	Maso degli Albizzi seizes control of Florence, ruling until 1417	Life of Florentine sculptor Donatello (Donato di Betto Bardi)	Florence cathedral is completed with Filippo Brunelleschi's dome	Political stability and cultivation of cultural patronage with the rise of the Medici banking dynasty	Michelozzo builds the Palazzo Medici Riccardi, a Roman-style villa retreat for the banking family

to seek inspiration for the present. His view of the Renaissance prince was as a reformer and visionary, not a despot, and he argued that his guidelines were simply the stripped-down path to power. A true prince would add his own charisma and morality to these bare bones. Machiavelli's beliefs were better represented in his pro-republican *Discourses on Livy*, but he was forever linked to the "Machiavellian" politics

outlined in his earlier work.

Even after the removal of the Medici, Machiavelli was unable to return to Florentine political life, since after the publication of *Il Principe* his fellow republicans viewed him with suspicion. His health deteriorated steadily during his years in the political wilderness and he died in 1527, a patriot and loyal republican who remained a misunderstood outcast.

c.1445–51	1466	1478	1494	1495–97	1498	1501–02	1513
Construction of the Palazzo Rucellai in Florence, designed by Leon Battista Alberti	Piero de' Medici, overthrows republican administration to restore oligarchic control of Florence	The papacy excommunicates Florence, triggering a short-lived war with the city	Bankrupted by Lorenzo's neglect of banking interests, the Medici are ousted in a French-led coup	Artist, philosopher, engineer, and scientist Leonardo da Vinci paints *The Last Supper*	Continuing to preach against the Florentine government's wishes, Girolamo Savonarola is burned for heresy	Michelangelo (di Lodovico Buonnarroti-Simoni) sculpts *David*	Machiavelli publishes *Il Principe*, a study of Italian politics that mistakenly brands him as a despot

Italy in the 15th century

DUCHY OF SAVOY

DUCHY OF MILAN

TRENTO

REPUBLIC OF VENICE

Lake Geneva
• Geneva
Rhône
• Aosta
Isère
• Ivrea
• Vercelli
• Susa
• Turin
Durance
Dauphine

FRANCE

SALUZZO
• Saluzzo
• Mondovi
• Tenda
Provence
• Monaco
• Nice

MONTFERRAT
• Asti
• Alessandria
• Tortona

Lake Maggiore
• Como
• Novara
Milan
VISCONTI
1450 SFORZA
• Pavia
• Lodi
Ticino
Po
Adda
• Cremona
• Piacenza
• Bobbio
• Parma

Lake Como
• Bergamo
• Brescia
• Crema

Trento •
• Belluno
Cividale •
• Gorizia

Lake Garda
• Vicenza
Treviso •
Aquileia •
• Grado
• Trieste

Verona •
Adige
Piave
Padua •
• Este
Veneto
• Venice
Chioggia •

Gulf of Venice

Istria

• Mantua
GONZAGA
MANTUA

Po
• Reggio
Modena •
ESTE
Ferrara •
ESTE
DUCHY OF FERRARA
claimed by the papacy

DUCHY OF MODENA

• Bologna
BENTIVOGLIO
• Imola
• Ravenna

Emilia Romagna
• Faenza
• Forli
• Cesena
• Rimini
MALATESTA

REPUBLIC OF GENOA
• Genoa
Gulf of Genoa

• Massa
LUCCA
Lucca •
• Pistoia
Arno
• Pisa
• Florence
MEDICI
REPUBLIC OF FLORENCE
• Livorno
• Volterra
• Arezzo
• Siena
• Cortona
• Urbino
MONTEFELTRO
• Ancona

Umbria
Ancona
PAPAL STATES
Perugia **BAGLIONI**
• Assisi
• Fermo

LIGURIAN SEA

Isola di Capraia

• Piombino
Portoferraio •
Portoferraio PIOMBINO
Elba

• Massa
• Chiusi
REPUBLIC OF SIENA

Tiber
• Orvieto
• Spoleto
Spoleto
• Aquila
• Pescara

Abruzzi

• Talamone
• Viterbo
• Sutri
Tevere (Tiber)

Corsica
to Genoa
• Bastia

Isola del Giglio

TYRRHENIAN SEA

• Ajaccio

• Rome

Patrimony
of St. Peter

Terra di Lavoro
• Pontecorvo
• Terracina

Isola Ponziane

• Naples

Isola d'Ischia

Sardinia
to Aragon
• Olbja
• Sassari

• Oristano

Legend:
- Duchy of Savoy
- Duchy of Milan
- Republic of Genoa
- Papal States
- Republic of Venice
- Republic of Florence
- Republic of Sienna
- Spanish Aragonese empire
- other Italian states
- lands of the Colonna family
- lands of the Orsini family
- lands of the Conti family
- **BAGLIONI** ruling family

• Cagliari

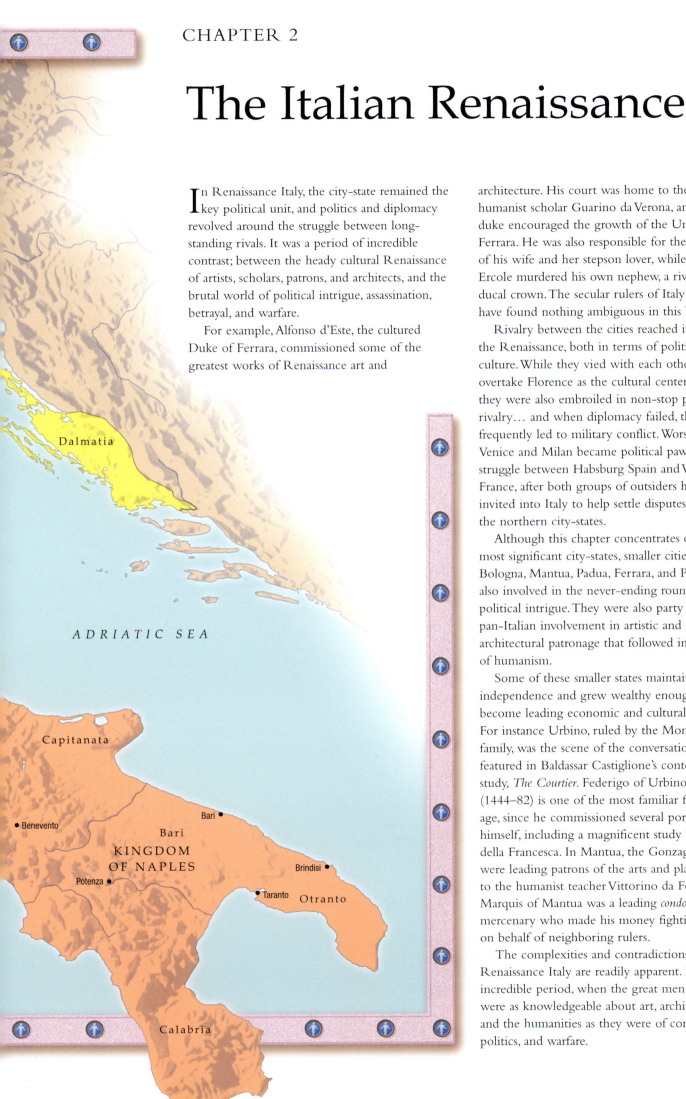

CHAPTER 2

The Italian Renaissance

In Renaissance Italy, the city-state remained the key political unit, and politics and diplomacy revolved around the struggle between long-standing rivals. It was a period of incredible contrast; between the heady cultural Renaissance of artists, scholars, patrons, and architects, and the brutal world of political intrigue, assassination, betrayal, and warfare.

For example, Alfonso d'Este, the cultured Duke of Ferrara, commissioned some of the greatest works of Renaissance art and architecture. His court was home to the great humanist scholar Guarino da Verona, and the duke encouraged the growth of the University of Ferrara. He was also responsible for the murder of his wife and her stepson lover, while his father Ercole murdered his own nephew, a rival for the ducal crown. The secular rulers of Italy would have found nothing ambiguous in this behavior.

Rivalry between the cities reached its peak in the Renaissance, both in terms of politics and culture. While they vied with each other to overtake Florence as the cultural center of Italy, they were also embroiled in non-stop political rivalry… and when diplomacy failed, this frequently led to military conflict. Worse still, Venice and Milan became political pawns in the struggle between Habsburg Spain and Valois France, after both groups of outsiders had been invited into Italy to help settle disputes between the northern city-states.

Although this chapter concentrates on the most significant city-states, smaller cities such as Bologna, Mantua, Padua, Ferrara, and Pisa were also involved in the never-ending rounds of political intrigue. They were also party to the pan-Italian involvement in artistic and architectural patronage that followed in the wake of humanism.

Some of these smaller states maintained their independence and grew wealthy enough to become leading economic and cultural centers. For instance Urbino, ruled by the Montefeltro family, was the scene of the conversations featured in Baldassar Castiglione's contemporary study, *The Courtier*. Federigo of Urbino (1444–82) is one of the most familiar faces of the age, since he commissioned several portraits of himself, including a magnificent study by Piero della Francesca. In Mantua, the Gonzaga family were leading patrons of the arts and played host to the humanist teacher Vittorino da Feltre. The Marquis of Mantua was a leading *condottiere* mercenary who made his money fighting wars on behalf of neighboring rulers.

The complexities and contradictions of Renaissance Italy are readily apparent. It was an incredible period, when the great men of Italy were as knowledgeable about art, architecture, and the humanities as they were of commerce, politics, and warfare.

The Italian City-States

Throughout the Renaissance, Italy remained a political patchwork of independent city-states, each jealous of its neighbors and wary of outsiders. By the 15th century they were highly developed and prosperous communities, the perfect breeding ground for humanist ideas and culture.

Below: Influenced by his friend Leonardo da Vinici and patronized by Ludovico Sforza, who ruled Milan (1494–99), Donato Bramante became the founding father of the High Renaissance. He played with fictive spaces, such as pretend windows and artificial perspective. The dome of Santa Maria delle Grazie is a fine example of his work.

For much of the Middle Ages, Italy was the most urbanized corner of Europe, with a tradition of city-states stretching back to the 11th century. Once a battleground between pope and Holy Roman Empire, by the 14th century these cities had largely freed themselves from their spiritual and temporal overlords, maintaining their own government and defending themselves without the assistance of outsiders.

Some of the Italian cities became great centers of commerce, banking, and production. The ports of Venice, Genoa, and Pisa depended on maritime trade, while Florence relied on banking and the wool trade. By the 15th century Venice, Milan, and Naples were among the most populous cities in Europe, where political power belonged to the possessors of urban wealth: the bankers and merchants. The political life of each city centered around power struggles between these magnates and other members of the ruling city oligarchies, usually members of the older patrician families.

The rise of a new mercantile class as a result of economic growth changed the power structure of most Italian cities during the 15th century. The patricians had ties with the land and the feudal nobility, although they might also involve themselves in business. Increasingly, the wealthier members of guilds demanded a greater share in government, and generally they got their way. Families like the Medici were bankers who later joined the patrician ranks through marriage, showing a degree of social mobility during the 15th century that was largely absent a century later, when admittance to the ruling oligarchy was tightly controlled.

Once a political leader and his faction had gained control of the local government he usually became head of state, or at least placed a reliable subordinate in the position. In some cases this was followed by a bid for absolute power, suppressing all other forms of authority. If this was achieved, the *signore* (despot or tyrant) was then in a position to make his rule hereditary. In broad terms this was how all the Italian ruling families came to power: the Medici in Florence, Sforza in Milan, Este in Ferrara, and several others.

A brief balance

The tendency toward hereditary despotism was universal in Italy, whatever course it took on the route from urban commune to tyranny. The stakes were high. To seize power, members of the leading families resorted to assassination, military coups, terror, mob rule, and invasion. Defeat could mean exile or death.

Sometimes the city-states' attempts to dominate their neighbors threatened the stability of the region—Milan seeking control of the Po valley, Florence dominating Siena, Pisa, and Lucca, and the Papal States coveting the Romagna created conflict in the Italian peninsula in the mid-15th century. A decade or so later the expansionist policy of Venice caused concern as far afield as France and Germany.

By the late 15th century a delicate equilibrium was reached, a balance of power

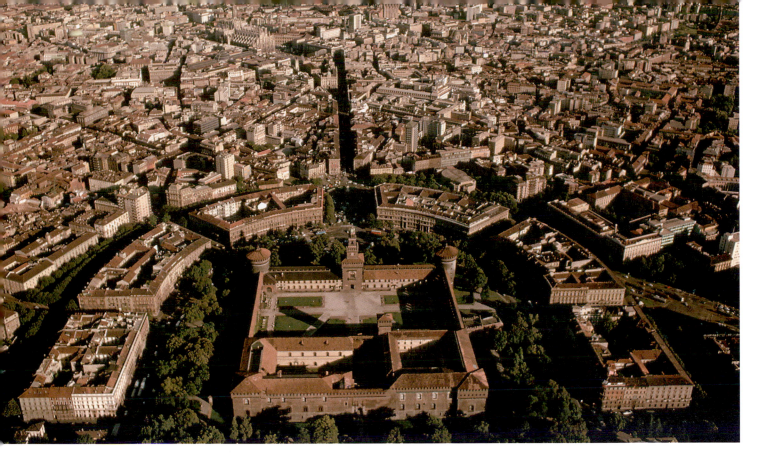

maintained by constant diplomacy, until the *status quo* was shattered by the French invasion of 1494, which transformed the political landscape. From that point, the Italian city-states became little more than pawns in the struggle between Habsburg Spain and Valois France.

By this stage many of the smaller elements of the Italian patchwork of states had been amalgamated with larger ones. Although the small city-states of Ferrara, Mantua, and Siena retained their independence, the five most powerful Italian states—Venice, Florence, Milan, Naples, and the Papal States centered on Rome—dominated the political map. Control of these provinces became a key element in the pan-European struggle between the Habsburgs and the Valois, making Italy one of the most war-torn areas of the continent for over half a century.

Above: In Florence the great families built palaces, but elsewhere the continual state of war required stronger fortifications. The modern city of Milan built itself around the design of the Castello Sforzesca.

Left: This woodcut, which appeared in the *Liber Chronicarum* of 1493 by Michael Wohlgemuth and compiled by Hartmann Schedel, shows the city of Pisa on the River Arno as it was at the time before the visible effects of the Renaissance on its architecture changed its still medieval appearance. The compilation also indicates the interest shown by Germans in 15th-century Italy and the emergent artistic disciplines.

Milan–Pawn and Prize

For centuries, Milan was caught in the middle of a territorial struggle between the papacy and the Holy Roman Empire; factional fighting within the city became a hallmark of Milanese politics. By the 14th century the pro-imperial Visconti family ruled the city and embarked on two centuries of expansion.

One of the first Italian communes, Milan developed a unique form of government involving all three land-owning classes: the patrician nobles, the lesser nobility and knights, and the plebeian majority of merchants, artisans, and manufacturers. Elected officials of the plebians became the real rulers, as certain families came to dominate politics.

Rule became increasingly tyrannical during the 14th century, when the Guelf (pro-papal) faction, led by the Della Tore family, and the Ghibelline (pro-imperial) faction, led by the Visconti, struggled for control. In 1277 Archbishop Ottone Visconti became Lord of Milan, beginning a two-century period of intermittent tyrannical rule by the family. The Visconti gradually improved the prosperity and security of Milan while ensuring the support of the plebians, thereby maintaining their grip on the city. By the middle of the 14th century Visconti rule had become hereditary.

Early in the 14th century the Visconti embarked on a policy of territorial aggression that brought them into conflict with the papacy. Despite excommunication and the preaching of crusades, they remained defiant and continued to expand their territory. Among the most important acquisitions were Pavia, Piacenza, Bergamo, Brescia, and Parma, most acquired voluntarily, or by purchase rather than by invasion. Ambitious attempts to dominate Genoa and Bologna were less successful.

The great Visconti period began in 1354 when brothers Galeazzo II and Bernabò became joint rulers. They added Pavia and Bologna to Milanese territory (the acqustion for which the family was excommunicated). In 1385 Galeazzo's son Gian Galeazzo Visconti seized power, buying the title Duke of Milan from the emperor. He married Isabella, daughter of the French Valois king John II, and also married his own daughter into the French royal family. This latter union lay at the

Above: Portrait of Gian Galeazzo Visconti by Pisanello (1395–1455).

root of France's later claim to Milan. Gian Galeazzo was soon regarded as one of Italy's leading tyrannical princes. A great patron of the arts, he sponsored work on Milan's cathedral (a *duomo* without a dome) and the *certosa* (monastery) of Pavia, and commissioned paintings and sculptures. Humanist scholars were hired as propagandists for the family, who enhanced their profile within Italy and helped overcome the antipathy of the papacy to their Ghibelline stance.

An unfortunate marriage

Gian Galeazzo continued his family's policy of territorial expansion, and apart from Venice and Florence, controlled all of northern Italy by the time of his death in 1402. Many of his subject cities then regained their independence or fell under Venetian control.

In 1412 Filippo Maria Visconti became the last Visconti duke and devoted himself to regaining his father's territories. He employed the best mercenary captains available, including Francesco Sforza, whose success was rewarded with the hand of the duke's daughter. When Filippo died in 1447 the Milanese proclaimed the foundation of a republic and hired Sforza to defend it. Instead, he seized the city in 1450 and became its ruler, establishing his own dynasty. Sforza ruled Milan as duke until his death in 1466, maintaining good relations with Florence and France, who granted him control of Genoa.

In Milan, Francesco was careful to ensure popular support, but his successors proved less able. His son Galeazzo Sforza was an absolutist ruler whose extravagance irritated his subjects. He was assassinated in 1476, leaving his seven-year-old son Gian Galeazzo as duke. Galeazzo's brother Ludovico il Moro ("the Moor") ruled as regent, establishing a glittering court filled with some of the most prominent artists and scholars of the age, including Leonardo da Vinci.

The Peace of Lodi had ended a century of conflict in 1454 and became the basis for a league of Italian city-states, which ensured precarious peace based on diplomacy. This was upset in 1488 when Ludovico Sforza married a princess of Naples, who encouraged him to intervene in Neapolitan politics. Florence, Venice, and even the Neapolitans sided against Milan, and war threatened. In need of allies, Ludovico Sforza made the fateful decision to ask King Charles VIII of France (1483–98) for assistance.

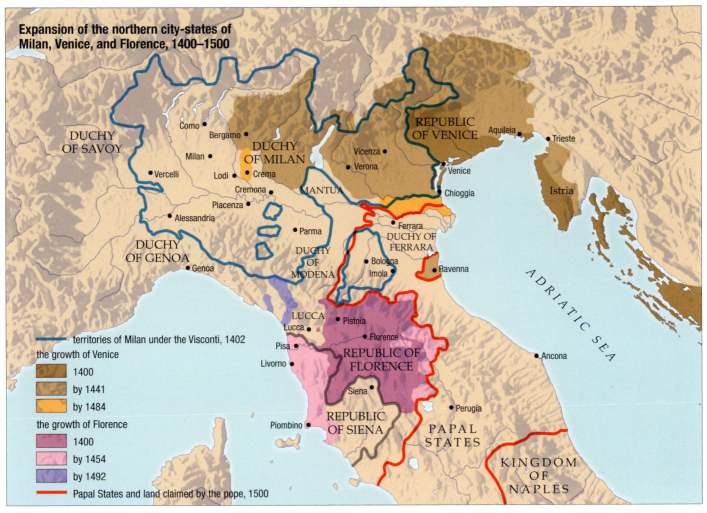

Expansion of the northern city-states of Milan, Venice, and Florence, 1400–1500

DUCHY OF SAVOY

Como
Bergamo
DUCHY OF MILAN
Milan
Vercelli
Lodi · Crema
Cremona
Piacenza
MANTUA
Alessandria

Vicenza
Verona

REPUBLIC OF VENICE
Aquileia
Trieste
Venice
Chioggia
Istria

DUCHY OF GENOA
Parma
DUCHY OF MODENA
Genoa
Ferrara
DUCHY OF FERRARA
Bologna
Imola
Ravenna

ADRIATIC SEA

LUCCA
Lucca
Pisa
Livorno
Pistoia
Florence
REPUBLIC OF FLORENCE
Siena
Ancona

Piombino
REPUBLIC OF SIENA
Perugia
PAPAL STATES

KINGDOM OF NAPLES

— territories of Milan under the Visconti, 1402

the growth of Venice
- 1400
- by 1441
- by 1484

the growth of Florence
- 1400
- by 1454
- by 1492

— Papal States and land claimed by the pope, 1500

Left: Milan's *duomo*, which started building in 1386 under the patronage of Gian Galeazzo, was still conceived in the Lombard Gothic style. The impact of the Renaissance had little effect on its design. Building continued for several centuries, completion only taking place in 1887.

The Maritime Republic of Venice

The only Italian city-state to have an overseas empire, Venice grew into the richest port in Europe during the Middle Ages. By the Renaissance the Venetians had acquired territory in mainland Italy, and so became embroiled in clashes with their neighbors.

Amid a lagoon at the northern tip of the Adriatic, Venice was settled by Roman refugees fleeing barbarian invaders in the fifth century AD, and from its inception the inhabitants looked to the sea for their livelihood. The Venetians traded with the Frankish kingdoms of western Europe, the Byzantines to the east, and later the Arab invaders who swept around the Mediterranean in the seventh century.

A merchant oligarchy ran the city through two assemblies, the Great Council and the Council of Ten, with the doge as the titular head of the Republic. The Council of Ten was a permanent ruling body, while a larger senate was formed from selected members of the Great Council, a closed body of over two thousand members, recruited exclusively from the most powerful mercantile families. The Great Council voted on major issues, while the senate handled the day-to-day business of government. However, the exclusive and non-elected Council of Ten was

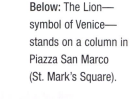

Below: The Lion— symbol of Venice— stands on a column in Piazza San Marco (St. Mark's Square).

the real power in Venice and maintained a firm grip, executing or banishing any opposition, for instance, in 1355 the doge Marino Faliero was executed after plotting a conspiracy. Above all, Venice was a trading port. Merchants maintained extensive mercantile links and clashed with rivals such as Genoa, a city that challenged Venetian maritime influence in the central Mediterranean in a war that lasted for much of the 14th century.

By 1450 Venice was at the height of its power, the richest city in Italy and the center of a sprawling seaborne empire that extended down the Adriatic coast to Greece, then into the Aegean. Its currency, based on the gold *ducat*, was considered the most stable in Europe, her population made Venice the largest city in Renaissance Italy, and her citizens enjoyed the bountiful fruits of trade in the busiest marketplace in the Mediterranean. A decade later the Venetian empire was shrinking, the economy in shreds, while enemies threatened on both land and sea.

Fighting for land and trade

The change occurred following the fall of Constantinople in 1453, freeing the Ottoman Turks to expand through Greece and the Balkans toward the shores of the Adriatic. Although it took almost a century for Venice to lose most of its colonies in Greek waters, the economic effect was felt far more rapidly, since many hitherto lucrative ports in the eastern Mediterranean were closed to Venetian trade. By the early 16th century the Portuguese

Left: *Fishermen Presenting the Ring of St. Mark to the Doge*, by Cavaliere Paris Bordone, c.1545. Bordone (1500–70) was an eminent painter of the Venetian school who studied under Titian and Giorgione (*see pages 142–43*). In his early career he worked in Venice, Vicenza, and Treviso, but later traveled to France at the invitation of either Francis I or II, where he was knighted. On his return to Venice he paused in Augst and Milan, where he painted many portraits. This, his best known work, shows all the brilliance of color and light effects for which the Venetian school became celebrated.

development of a maritime trade route between Europe and India ended the Venetian monopoly on eastern trade. The Venetians responded to these reverses with an aggressive military and naval campaign to limit Turkish expansion, while merchants sought alternative trading partners.

Another solution was to find ways of expanding Venice's toehold on the Italian mainland. From 1380 the Venetians intervened in Italian affairs, expanding the borders of their mainland possessions at the extent of her neighbors, especially Milan. By the late 15th century Venice was a threat to peace in Italy, having seized Padua, Verona, and other city-states, uniting the remainder in a loose anti-Venetian coalition, resulting in intermittent fighting.

Despite several setbacks, these conflicts never threatened the city itself. Apart from the Ottoman Turks, no Mediterranean power could rival Venice for the size and efficiency of its navy, making it all but impervious to attack.

While the city prospered, merchants spent their money on civic improvements and patronage of the arts. Despite its relatively conservative government, the wealth of Venice attracted a range of artists and scholars who helped transform the city into one of the most dynamic cultural centers in Italy; the home of Bellini, Titian, Giorgione, and Tintoretto. As this artistic excellence reached its peak in the 16th century, Venice became the successor to Florence and Rome as the cultural hub of the Late Renaissance.

Naples—The Spanish Toehold

With its largely agrarian economy, southern Italy was the poor relative to the more urbanized north. A secular vassal of the pope, the king of feudal Naples was unable to separate the destiny of his kingdom from that of the Papal States to the north.

Below: *Ferdinand of Aragon's Fleet in Naples Harbor* by Francesco Pagano, a Neapolitan painter working in the latter half of the 15th century.

For centuries, southern Italy had been a battleground between pope and emperor, Norman adventurers, Byzantines, and Turks. In 1265 Pope Clement IV (p.1265–8) asked Charles of Anjou, brother of the French king, to help secure southern Italy for the papacy. Charles drove out German garrisons established by the Holy Roman Emperor and, as a reward, was named King of Naples and Sicily. His French followers were granted feudal territories in the kingdom, while French officials were brought in to govern the country.

The Neapolitans saw this as foreign occupation, and in 1282 revolted against French rule. Although the "Sicilian Vespers" revolt was crushed on the mainland, the Spanish king of Aragon decided to use the distraction to seize Sicily for himself. For the next two centuries the houses of Aragon and Anjou fought for the kingdom's territories, until it was finally reunited by King Alfonso V "the Magnanimous" of Aragon, who conquered Naples in 1442, becoming Alfonso I of Naples (1395–1458). From that point, southern Italy was firmly within the Spanish political sphere.

A keen classicist, Alfonso was considered one of Italy's leading patrons of humanist scholarship, his court attracting leading scholars of the age, including Lorenzo Valla, author of *The Donation of Constantine*, a treatise re-examining the role of the Church in the light of humanist teaching. He encouraged a fusion between Spanish and Italian artists and scholars, while the University of Naples founded by Emperor Frederick II in 1224 was enlarged and became a leading humanist center of learning. Other schools sprang up during the 15th century, together with several printing businesses and a conservatory of music. This cultural tradition lasted into the 16th century; the theologian Juan de Valdes studied in Naples during the 1530s, while toward the end of the century Carravagio painted for court patrons.

A static kingdom

Above all, King Alfonso was a Spaniard. Like Charles of Anjou, Alfonso allocated fiefdoms to his supporters and made fellow countrymen his administrators. He was largely unsuccessful in his attempt to establish Naples as a leading mercantile city—Spanish merchants preferred to use their Catalonian port of Barcelona, which was becoming a major trade center in the western Mediterranean. Naples' prosperity continued to rely on the patronage of the court and the agrarian production of its hinterland.

The kingdom's close links with the papacy to the north prevented further territorial expansion on the Italian mainland, although Alfonso tried to acquire several Adriatic and Ionian ports through diplomatic maneuvering, with little success. He held his throne as a feudal vassal of the pontiff, so the two states remained closely linked during the 15th century. Neapolitans occasionally intervened in Italian affairs on the pontiff's behalf; although Alfonso tried to follow his own political course, he was unable to break his links with the pope. He died in battle against Genoa in 1453, fighting at the head of a papal-Neapolitan army.

The kingdom was divided between his brother John, who gained Sicily, Sardinia, and Spanish possessions, while Naples itself was inherited by Alfonso's middle-aged illegitimate son Ferrante, or Ferdinand I (r.1458–94). He inherited his father's enlightened attitude toward artistic and scholastic patronage, but was otherwise remembered as an oppressive and merciless ruler, who massacred many of his nobles following a rebellion in 1485.

Ferdinand was troubled by Pope Pius II (p.1458–64) and his successors, who refused to recognize Ferdinand's accession due to his illegitimacy, until the selection of a Spanish Borgia pope, Alexander VI in 1492. Another continuing problem was the French Anjou claim to the Neapolitan throne. He was succeeded by his son Alfonso II (r.1494–95), linked by marriage to the Sforzas in Milan. The marriage of Alfonso's daughter Isabella to the Duke of Milan helped precipitate the crisis that led to the French invasion of Italy in 1494.

Spanish holdings in the Mediterranean

Aragonese territory, 1430

kingdom of Aragon & Castile, 1492

Venetian territory, 1441

Papal States, 1492

Early Development of Renaissance Art

When humanism revived interest in classical philosophy and literature, it also encouraged observation of nature and humanity, and the portrayal of life with hitherto unimagined realism. The Italian Renaissance art movement lasted for two centuries, producing some of the greatest works in history.

Below: *The Birth of Venus*, by Alessandro di Mariano Filipepi, better known as Botticelli. The artist, who has come to epitomize the Early Renaissance, spent all his life in Florence except for a visit to Rome in 1481–2, when he painted frescoes in the Vatican's Sistine Chapel. His best known paintings are the *Adoration of the Magi, Primavera* or *Allegory of Spring* (*pages 6–7*), and *The Birth of Venus*, completed in 1485.

The new-found artistic freedom provided through the patronage of secular rulers led to the commissioning of a range of subjects, from classically inspired scenes to portraits, landscapes, and exercises in perspective and color unimaginable before the rise of humanism. The artist became a creative being, respected as much for his vision and imagination as for his technical skill.

Although the evolution of Italian Renaissance art was a continuous process, historians have traditionally divided it into three phases: the Early, High, and Late Renaissance periods. Some scholars regard Florentine artist Giotto di Bondone (c.1267–1337) as the true father of Renaissance art, although his work was a move toward a more natural form of expression, a precursor to what followed rather than a new style in its own right. His work inspired the next generation of Florentine artists, who created a new movement during the late 14th and early 15th centuries.

The first leading Renaissance artists—painter Tommaso di Giovanni di Simone Guidi (nicknamed "Masaccio," 1401–28), sculptor Donatello or Donato di Betto Bardi (1386–1466),

Taming space—perspective

The lasting achievement of the Renaissance was the perfection of linear perspective, the mathematical representation of a three-dimensional space on a two-dimensional surface. The architect Brunelleschi is credited with the first physical experiments in the subject, and his success was such that the sculptor Donatello took up the quest for perspective in his low-relief marble and bronze panels. The painter Masaccio also employed Brunelleschi's ideas in his fresco of the *Holy Trinity* in Santa Maria Novella (*see Florence plan, page 21*) in c.1426. In 1436 the humanist Leon Battista Alberti wrote a treatise on perspective, which influenced the Italian Renaissance artists who followed, and led the way to the High Renaissance period.

and architect Filippo Brunelleschi (1377–1446) —were all Florentines who shared the vision that art should develop as a reflection of humanity and the natural world, not remain a static discipline constrained by dogma and convention.

The art of antiquity inspired rather than provided a template for these men, who desired to learn for themselves by trial and error rather than copy existing styles or methods. Early Renaissance artists sought to create art that reflected the world around them, whether it be the accurate portrayal of the human body in art or sculpture, the incorporation of light and color, or the use of natural proportion in architecture.

Capturing perfection

Observation and inquiry became vital to the artist, skills that manifested in an almost scientific manner. Artists tried to incorporate perspective, anatomical perfection, or keenly observed representations of natural phenomena into their work, sometimes relying on ideal forms rather than on literal appearance to capture true beauty. To many, the physical world was an imperfect embodiment of spiritual beauty, and they sought to improve on nature, not just capture its essence.

Early Renaissance is closely associated with 15th-century Florence, the cradle of artistic thought. By the mid-15th century a new generation of artists came to the fore in the city; Sandro (Alessandro) Botticelli (1445–1510), Antonio and Piero del Pollaiuolo (1432–98 and c.1441–96), and others inherited the traditions of their predecessors. The spread of humanist-inspired patronage to cities such as Venice, Milan, and Naples led to a widening of the artistic circle, as more patrons and artists embraced the cultural phenomenon. For example, architect Leon Battista Alberti (1404–72) in Rimini, Andrea Mantegna's painting and engraving (1431–1506) in Padua, and the painter Jacopo Bellini (c.1400–71) and his son Giovanni (c.1430–1516) from Venice captured the spirit of this humanist-inspired art revival and helped establish their cities as centers of artistic excellence.

By the late 15th century the exceptional had become normal, the technical work on proportion, perspective, light, color, and motion perfected by great artists setting the standard for others to follow. The Italian humanist artists of the 15th century were innovators, prepared to flaunt existing conventions in the search for natural beauty. In the artistic phases that followed, this quest for perfection would be taken a stage further.

Above: *David* by Donatello, the most influential sculptor of his age. Donatello's output during his life was prodigious, and Vasari said of him that: "he left behind him so much work through the world that it may rightly be asserted that no artist worked so hard as he."

Left: *The Court of Ludovico Gonzaga* by Andrea Mantegna. He painted numerous religious works, but the influence of wealthy patrons provided plenty of secular work too.

35

Da Vinci and the Birth of Natural Philosophy

If any one artist personifies the quest for knowledge of Renaissance man, it is Leonardo da Vinci, who spanned the Early and High Renaissance periods. Although primarily thought of as an artist, his inquiring mind led him to study a range of sciences, from architecture to anatomy and military technology to zoology.

Above: Leonardo da Vinci (1452–1519), self portrait. **Facing top:** Drawing of a revolutionary flying machine with standing man (da Vinci used mirror writing to deter spies). **Facing bottom:** Poor formulation of experimental materials led to extensive damage to *The Last Supper* during da Vinci's lifetime.

Born in 1452 the illegitimate son of a Tuscan country notary and a local peasant woman, Leonardo da Vinci received a rudimentary education in his village school but was noted for his artistic skill. Following his father's move to Florence in 1469, he was apprenticed to the studio of Verrocchio, where the young Leonardo learned his trade. He joined the artists' Guild of St. Luke in 1472, marking his transition from apprentice to artisan, although he still worked for Verrocchio. Leonardo's hand is seen in a number of his master's paintings, including *The Baptism of Christ* and *The Annunciation*.

According to the art historian Giorgio Vasari (1511–74), the period known as the High Renaissance began in 1490—although there is no clear demarcation as to when it ended. By this date Leonardo was a mature artist, but his hand is detected by Vasari in the making of the High Renaissance, in particular in the search for ever greater perfection in the rendering of the human form. While today Leonardo's paintings are revered, to Vasari they were only a part of the route map to the exquisite perfection of Raphael and—especially—the divine Michelangelo.

Leonardo's first major commission as an independent artist was the *Adoration of the Magi*, a work begun in 1481 for a monastery on the outskirts of Florence. The composition featured a pyramid-shaped grouping of the Virgin Mary, the Christ child, and the three Magi, surrounded by well-wishers. This reveals Leonardo's fascination for mathematics and geometry, which he claimed embraces everything in the universe. Although the work was unfinished, it was the first true display of the genius that was to follow.

Even while painting this work, Leonardo was experimenting with a less rigid style, where his figures captured the energy of movement. Although this was not a departure for Renaissance artists, Leonardo based his figures on well observed sketches drawn from real life, a growing knowledge of anatomy, and an understanding of human movement.

Leonardo left Florence in or around 1482 and sought employment at the Court of Ludovico Sforza in Milan. In his letter of introduction, he cited his expertise in engineering, architecture, military technology, and sculpture, as well as painting. He was duly hired, and worked on architectural projects in Milan while continuing his anatomical studies and painting. His work from this period includes a painting of Ludovico Sforza's mistress, now known as *The Lady with an Ermine* (c.1483), the *Madonna of the Rocks* (1484), and *The Last Supper* (1495–7).

Thirst for knowledge

During this time he developed a growing interest in science, filling notebooks with his observations on a wide variety of phenomena, from anatomy, architecture, astrology, engineering, philosophy, sculpture, perspective, military inventions, town planning, and numerous other, often unrelated subjects. It was as if his mind required continual challenge, moving from project to project and discipline to discipline in the search for knowledge and perfection.

When the French occupied Milan in 1499 and deposed Ludovico Sforza, Leonardo left Milan and was back in Florence by the next year. The following period included some of his best work, and his ability to capture human anatomy and expression ensured a steady stream of patrons. The pieces include *The Virgin and Christ Child with St. Anne* (1500–5), complete with superb preliminary sketches, and his most famous painting, the *Mona Lisa* (1506), a subject tentatively identified as the wife of the prominent Florentine official Francesco del Giocondo. His later works included the *Battle of Anghiari* (c.1510) and *St. John the Baptist* (1515).

Increasingly, Leonardo devoted time to natural philosophy and engineering, and his observations made him the most celebrated inventor of his day. In 1516 he was invited to France by Francis I, who established him in a manor at Cos-Luce, on the Loire. Leonardo worked on several projects for his French patron, including designs for the Château Chambord, a scheme to regulate the flow of the Loire, and a hydro-dynamic project designed to provide irrigation for the entire region. He died before these plans reached fruition.

While science only emerged as a discipline in the 17th century, Leonardo da Vinci and his contemporaries relied on scientific investigation of nature to achieve scientific results. Others followed his example, and natural philosophers such as Copernicus, Kepler, and Galileo continued to observe and record their natural surroundings to advance their knowledge of the world.

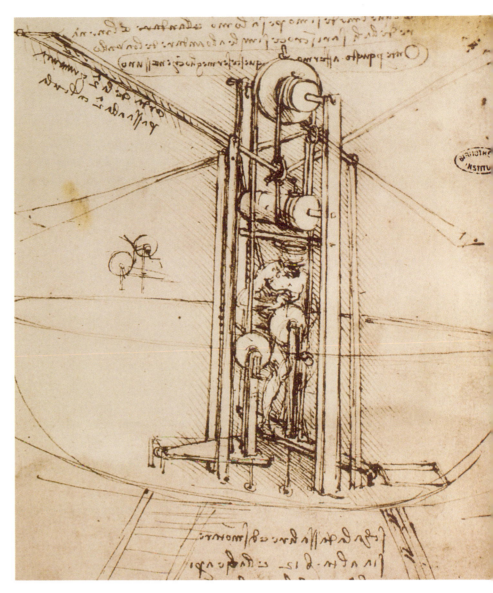

Architectural Patronage in Renaissance Italy

Painter, architect, and the first Renaissance art historian Giorgio Vasari said of architect Filippo Brunelleschi, "He was given to us by Heaven to invest architecture with new forms." He was followed by a stream of architects who incorporated humanist ideas into the palazzos of wealthy Italian rulers.

Facing top: View of Santa Maria del Fiore (the *duomo*) in Florence. In the foreground the façade of the Palazzo Pitti and the greenery of the Boboli Gardens are visible.

Facing bottom: It was a time of civil unrest, and the great palazzi were constructed like fortresses around pleasant courtyards, like this fine example in the Palazzo Medici.

Filippo Brunelleschi (1377–1446) was inspired by the writings of the classical Roman engineer and architect Vitruvius, whose treatise *De architectura libri decem* was re-written by Poggio Bracciolini in 1414. Between 1420 and 1446 the Florentine architect "modernized" several existing churches, but his greatest achievement was the construction of the dome of the cathedral (the *duomo*) which dominated the city. His new look was a humanist remodeling of a medieval style, but one which emphasized the Vitruvian cornerstones of strength, unity, and beauty. The result was a breathtaking reworking of classical examples to suit the environment of a working city.

While this great Florentine worked primarily on churches, secular architecture gave the greatest scope for expression to a new breed of architects who followed Brunelleschi. Designs for public spaces such as theaters, civic buildings, or the *palazzi* (palaces) of wealthy merchants were all influenced by the examples of Roman antiquity, adapted to suit the Renaissance Italians who commissioned them.

The notion of the "ideal city" was a humanist concept graphically illustrated by Pierro della Franchesca in the mid-15th century. Urban planning was a reflection of civic pride, and architects such as Leon Battista Alberti (1404–72) pursued designs for a hierarchy of buildings, distinguishing designs by function (civic, ecclesiastic, or domestic) and proportioning them to fit a cohesive urban plan. By the 16th century this movement was in full flow, and artists such as Michelangelo and Vasari were called on to redesign the heart of many Italian cities.

While civic leaders were reappraising the appearance of their cities, they were also redefining the way they lived. At first, residences for the urban elite were built in the heart of the existing city. For example, the urban *palazzo* was usually built near the center, amid the medieval buildings, but its external, often fortress-like simplicity belied sumptuous interior décor.

Integration to segregation

Increasingly, *palazzi* were built by architects who sought inspiration from the classical buildings of antiquity. Some were based on the city blocks or *insulae* of ancient Rome, where shops and workshops at street level were sited beneath the grander living quarters of the floors above, providing security to the urban residents while making the best use of limited space. Alberti designed the Palazzo Rucellai in Florence (c.1445–51) along the lines of the *insula* but incorporated a modern sense of light and space, augmented by a classical façade.

Michelozzo (1396–1472) set a new trend with the enormous Palazzo Medici Riccardi (c.1444) at Fiesole outside Florence for the banking family, based on the layout of a rural Roman patrician villa. The ancient Roman weekend retreat described by Pliny had inspired a new way of life. When Raffaelo Sanzio, or Raphael (1483–1520) was commissioned to design the Villa Madama in Rome (c.1518), he sought inspiration from the Medici villas in Tuscany, particularly the Poggio a Caiano *palazzo* built by Giuliano da Sangallo (c.1485). These two palaces then became the blueprint for the country residences of most of

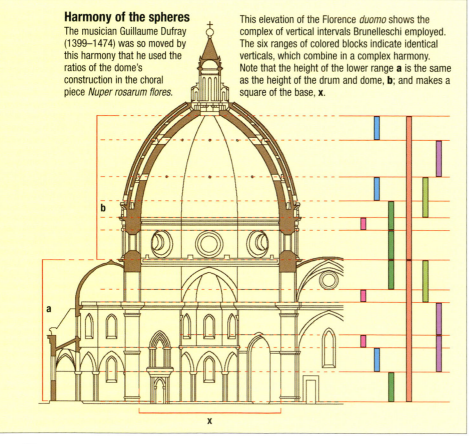

Harmony of the spheres
The musician Guillaume Dufray (1399–1474) was so moved by this harmony that he used the ratios of the dome's construction in the choral piece *Nuper rosarum flores.*

This elevation of the Florence *duomo* shows the complex of vertical intervals Brunelleschi employed. The six ranges of colored blocks indicate identical verticals, which combine in a complex harmony. Note that the height of the lower range **a** is the same as the height of the drum and dome, **b**; and makes a square of the base, **x**.

the elite of 16th century Italy. After Florence, the chief center for dignified rural living was Venice, where wealthy merchants sought escape from the overcrowded city in rural *palazzi* built by Andrea Palladio (*see page 149*). The Medici family had redefined the way Italian rulers lived, creating a lifestyle that set these families apart from the rest of Italian society for the first time.

The Condottieri–Warfare in Italy

Italian warfare during the late Medieval and Renaissance periods is traditionally associated with *condottieri* mercenaries. Although portrayed as anachronistic, they were a perfect reflection of the way Renaissance Italians dealt with disputes among themselves.

Facing: Detail of the equestrian statue of Venice's captain general mercenary, Bartolomeo Colleoni of Bergamo (1400–75) by Andrea del Verrochio. The authorities were obliged to cast the statue after his death because the warrior had left funds expressly for the purpose. He wanted it erected in Piazza San Marco, but the Venetians cleverly misunderstood and hid the statue away before the remote Scuola di San Marco. Verrochio died before completion, which was undertaken by the bronze caster Alessandro Leopardi, who signed it.

During the centuries before the French invasion of Italy in 1494, condottieri were considered the military backbone of Italy. *Condottiere* (plural, *condottieri*) is an Italian term derived from the Latin *conducere*, meaning either to conduct or to hire. It originally referred to the leader of a band of mercenaries, but was later extended to include the mercenary soldiers as well as the leader of a company. Most cities relied on militia for everyday security and defense. The ranks were usually filled by a levy, men mustered for a set period of military service, and the standard of training and military prowess was considered low. Even military innovators such as Niccolò Machiavelli, who drew on the examples of

antiquity, were unable to do much with city militia. Instead, the core of any Italian army was a force of *condottieri*.

The use of *condottieri* began during the 14th century, when adventurers left the feudal killing grounds of northern Europe to seek employment amid the rich cities of Italy. Whichever faction controlled a city—usually supporters of pope or emperor—they were reluctant to arm the entire populace, which would inevitably include supporters of the rival faction; the solution was to hire mercenaries.

Once employed, *condottieri* were able to seize control of the city, or could support one faction against another. Machiavelli was thus opposed to the use of mercenaries. In his *Art of War*, he argued that if *condottieri* lost a battle, the city would have no means of defense and be at the mercy of the enemy. If the *condottieri* won, the city would be in their debt, in danger of being at the mercy of their mercenary! This happened to the Visconti in 1450 (*see page 28*).

Below: *Naval and Land Battle* by Niccolò dell' Abate (1509/12–71), a native of Modena who introduced landscape painting to the French Fontainebleu school.

1265	1282	c.1300	1354	1380	1385	c.1400	1402
Charles of Anjou drives the Holy Roman Empire from southern Italy and is made King of Naples & Sicily	Neapolitans rebel against French rule; Pedro of Aragon wars with Anjou over Sicily and is made its king	Most Italian cities are free from the Holy Roman Empire and papacy that previously dominated them	Milan's key period of Visconti rule begins with the election of brothers Galeazzo and Bernab	Venice begins aggressive expansion, at the expense of neighboring city-states	Gian Galeazzo Visconti takes Milanese power and marries his daughter to brother of Charles VI of France	Milan, Naples, and Venice are among the richest cities in Europe; their bankers gain great influence	The Visconti rule of northern Italy falters after the death of Gian Galeazzo

disputes. In addition to internecine fighting, these states sometimes formed alliances or leagues to stand firm against foreign invasion, or when faced with military action by pope or emperor. Cities fought for control of border territories or towns, fought for commercial domination (the root of the war between Venice and Genoa), and fought for control of centers of production, such as wool-producing provinces. Some conflicts seemed never-ending, like the century-long fight for supremacy between Florence and Pisa, a war that often sucked in the neighboring states of Siena and Lucca.

War without death

Uniquely, warfare in Italy during this period aimed to be bloodless. Campaigns consisted mainly of maneuver, where objectives could be won with a minimum of casualties. Military power—and therefore revenue—was based on the size of a mercenary band, and casualties could reduce a *condottieri* captain's prestige and income.

In the rest of Europe, warfare was a bloody business, with mounted knights dominating the battlefield, their supremacy then shaken first by bowmen, then by infantry armed with pikes. The advent of gunpowder was gradually influencing warfare, particularly in the way sieges were fought and the ability of fortifications to withstand attack. While new ideas were incorporated in Italian battles, tactics that involved unnecessary slaughter were avoided. Warfare became a stylized game, fought between celebrated *condottieri* captains in a manner that had more in common with sport than battle.

This changed in 1494. The French invaders were trained in the style of warfare fought in northern Europe, where the shock of mounted knights, firepower of archers or artillery, and the steadiness of veteran pikemen were the arbiters of victory. The *condottieri* did not stand a chance, and within a year their civilized style of combat was gone forever, replaced by the harsh realities of modern warfare.

There was much scope for *condottieri* employment in Renaissance Italy. Despite the best diplomatic efforts of city-state representatives, warfare was readily used to settle

CHAPTER 3

Rome–The Papal Bastion

The Renaissance was not an easy period for the Church. The schisms and papal exiles of the previous century had severely weakened the institution, and although healed by the early 15th century, the legacy of these rifts was the introduction of a new style of Church government. Decisions were now expected to be made by committee rather than by the pontiff alone. Of course, this "conciliar" approach was unacceptable to the papacy, and for most of the 15th century a series of popes struggled against the conciliarists to impose their supremacy over Church and State.

The perception had arisen that the Church and the papacy were flawed bodies, given to avarice, corruption, and non-spiritual worldliness. The papacy was the only multi-national business of its day; immense profits were made from enterprises such as the sale of indulgences and the rental of monastic or ecclesiastical land. While many senior clerics realized that major reform was necessary, little was done to curb the profiteering that seemed endemic within the late Medieval and Renaissance Church.

Renaissance popes struggled to improve their image and tried to extend their control over Rome and the adjacent Papal States. By the end of the 15th century the pope had effectively become a secular prince as well as a spiritual leader, and was embroiled in politics as the ruler of the territory that dominated central Italy. This inevitably meant that the pope was a party to war, the incitement of rebellion and foreign invasion, and the subjection of rebel factions within his own secular territory; a far cry from his spiritual role as God's representative.

Of all the Renaissance popes, none was more notorious than the Borgia pope, Alexander VI. The pope and his family were masters at the art of secular rule, while using their ecclesiastical offices to further the power and wealth of the Borgia dynasty. They tried to make Rome and the Papal States part of a hereditary monarchy, with a Borgia patriarch as its unchallenged leader.

For all their machinations, the Borgias were unable to make a lasting impression on the political landscape, and Alexander's successor Pope Pius III (p.1503) dismantled the last vestiges of Borgia rule. While the secular legacy was transitory, the damage done to the Church was far more extensive. The corruption and worldliness of Alexander VI gave reformers the ammunition they needed to call for drastic change. The seeds of the Protestant Reformation had been sown.

Alexander and his successors saw the need to improve their position by turning Rome into a cultural center, with the Vatican at its heart. They achieved this through artistic patronage; the commissioning of works by artists such as Michelangelo and Raphael, and the architectural transformation of Rome to reflect some of its former classical glory. This was the High Renaissance period, when the likes of Pope Julius II (p.1503–13) and Michelangelo conferred over the decoration of the Sistine Chapel, and popes were known for their humanist scholarship. While cultural achievements improved the image of Rome and the position of the pope, they did little to address the issues that threatened to tear Christendom apart.

The Rome of Giorgio Vasari

This birds' eye view reconstruction of Rome is based on the map by the artist and art historian Giorgio Vasari (1511–74). The Rome of the popes is mainly located in the area between the seven hills on which Rome was originally built and the river. This was due to the destruction of the ancient Roman aqueducts by barbarians in the sixth century, which forced the inhabitants to move closer to the river, although this area was unhealthy and subject to flooding. When Rome was at its peak In the fourth century the area contained within the Aurelian Wall (marked A) was completely built up. After the fall of the western Roman empire, the city's population contracted dramatically. At this point in the Renaissance the city was beginining its recovery and expansion after the slump centuries of the medieval era.

Porta Solara
(*Porta Salaria*)

Porta Pinciana

Via Flaminia

Fiume Tevere

VATICAN STATE

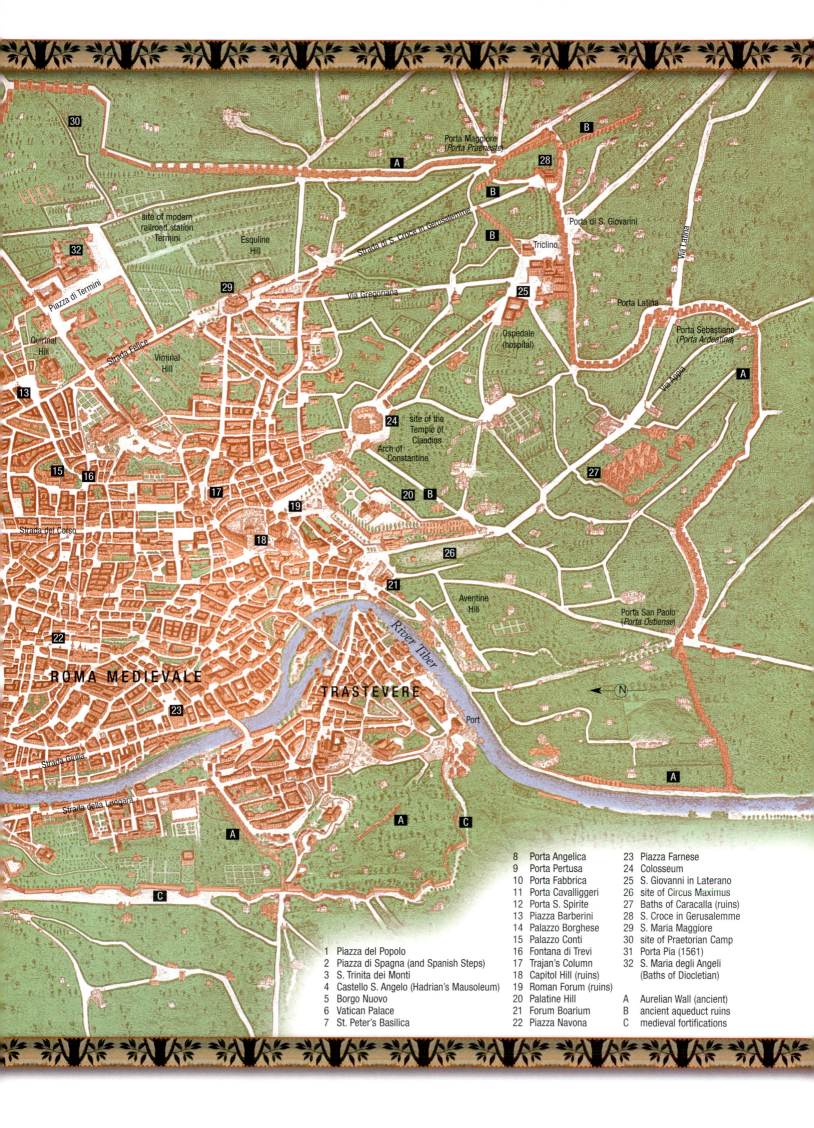

30

site of modern
railroad station
Termini

32

Esquine
Hill

29

Piazza di Termini

Quirinal
Hill

Strada Felice

Viminal
Hill

Via Gregoriana

Strada di S. Croce in Gerusalemme

A

Porta Maggiore
(Porta Praeneste)

B

28

B

Porta di S. Giovanni

Via Latina

B

Triclino

25

Ospedale
(hospital)

Porta Latina

Porta Sebastiano
(Porta Ardeatina)

Via Appia

A

13

15

16

17

19

18

24

site of the
Temple of
Claudius

Arch of
Constantine

20

B

27

26

A

Strada del Corso

21

22

ROMA MEDIEVALE

23

Strada Giulia

Strada della Lungara

A

TRASTEVERE

C

Aventine
Hill

River Tiber

Port

Porta San Paolo
(Porta Ostiense)

N

A

C

8	Porta Angelica	23 Piazza Farnese
9	Porta Pertusa	24 Colosseum
10	Porta Fabbrica	25 S. Giovanni in Laterano
11	Porta Cavalliggeri	26 site of Circus Maximus
12	Porta S. Spirite	27 Baths of Caracalla (ruins)
13	Piazza Barberini	28 S. Croce in Gerusalemme
14	Palazzo Borghese	29 S. Maria Maggiore
15	Palazzo Conti	30 site of Praetorian Camp
16	Fontana di Trevi	31 Porta Pia (1561)
17	Trajan's Column	32 S. Maria degli Angeli
18	Capitol Hill (ruins)	(Baths of Diocletian)
19	Roman Forum (ruins)	
1	Piazza del Popolo	20 Palatine Hill
2	Piazza di Spagna (and Spanish Steps)	21 Forum Boarium
3	S. Trinita dei Monti	22 Piazza Navona
4	Castello S. Angelo (Hadrian's Mausoleum)	A Aurelian Wall (ancient)
5	Borgo Nuovo	B ancient aqueduct ruins
6	Vatican Palace	C medieval fortifications
7	St. Peter's Basilica	

Ripe for Reform–The Late Medieval Church

The Church was in crisis for much of the late Middle Ages. Internal schism and clashes with secular powers in Europe had weakened the papacy. When the spread of humanism encouraged the questioning of long-held beliefs, Renaissance popes were forced to reform or risk the Church's collapse.

During the 14th and 15th centuries, Europe experienced a decline characterized by a drastic population decrease across the continent, reduced trade and agricultural production, the withering of central authority, an increase in warfare, and an acute economic depression. This was particularly apparent in Germany, where the

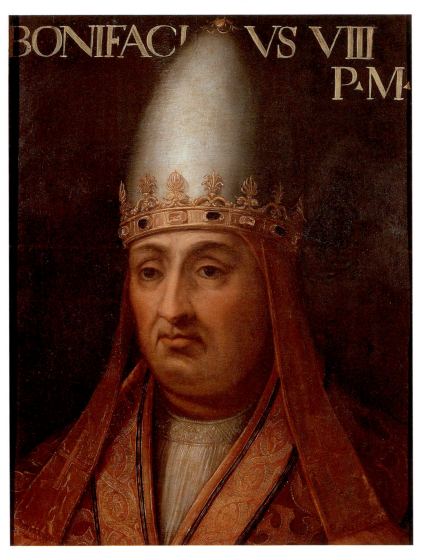

lack of central control encouraged petty rivalry and warfare.

During this period the Church should have provided the laity with spiritual guidance, but instead was virtually paralyzed by a series of internal disputes. In 1303 Pope Boniface VIII

(p.1294–1303) died in mysterious circumstances after an attempted kidnapping by French agents. He was followed by Benedict XI, then the College of Cardinals elected the Archbishop of Bordeaux as Pope Clement V (p.1305–14). Rather than remain amid the political turmoil of Rome, he established a seat in the southern French town of Avignon, where he was accused of being a puppet of the French king, Philip IV.

Clement and the six pontiffs who succeeded him remained in France until 1377, when Pope Gregory XI (p.1370–78) moved the papacy back to Rome. Urban VI (p.1378–89) was an Italian who refused to return to Avignon, so the French cardinals returned home and elected their own pope, Clement VII (p.1378–94). The Church now had two papal sees.

This Great Schism split the Church, each group claiming legitimacy. The division continued until the Council of Constance (1414–18), a gathering of senior churchmen that ended the schism by selecting Pope Martin V (p.1417–31), a member of the leading Roman Colonna family. Although the Church was reunified, a loss of faith undermined authority its at a time when only a strong papal hand could stay the spread of anti-clericalism—yet the papacy seemed to revert to its worldly ways.

Buying independence

During the 15th century the papacy was accused of greed, nepotism, a lack of celibate restraint, absenteeism, and pluralism, but worse still, the growing trend of 15th-century Italian popes was to pursue material goals. Abuses of the sacraments (baptism, marriage, penance, ordination, and last rites) led to accusations of profiteering, while a revived medieval practice, the sale of indulgences to expurgate sin, became a hugely lucrative industry.

A growing number of dissidents questioned the authority of the Church and demanded a more representative and accountable form of Church government. Disagreements between Pope Eugenius IV (p.1431–47) and the conciliarists led to the adoption at Basel of an anti-pope, Felix V (p.1439–49), a rebellion against the authority of Rome that found vocal support in northern Europe and Switzerland.

The Pragmatic Sanction of Bourges (1438) limiting the pope's influence on French affairs was typical of a move toward decentralization, as

Left: Such was the perilous state of affairs during the Great Schism that the Papal Palace in Avignon was constructed more along the lines of a medieval castle than a gracious home suitable to the head of the Church. The internal dispute was sparked when Pope Boniface VIII, **pictured on the facing page**, died after being kidnapped by agents of the French king, who had become frustrated by Boniface's reassertion of papal supremacy. Known to history as the last medieval pope, Boniface heralded the popes of the Renaissance by using his position to enrich his family and pursue a feud against the powerful Colonnas.

regional ecclesiastical centers sought the protection of secular rulers. A similar arrangement known as the Pragmatic Sanction of Mainz followed in Germany the next year, forcing the pope to agree to secular interference in return for guaranteed income.

The growth of humanism encouraged this dissent. The scholarship of Christian humanists helped expose the shortcomings of the Latin Vulgate (Latin "common version") Bible, the one approved credo of the Church. They helped focus the laity away from their belief in divine mysteries to the potential for human good, ushering in a more practical form of Christianity. The writing of Desiderius Erasmus (c.1466–1536) encapsulated this new emphasis on redefining Christianity. He and his fellow scholars railed against the abuse of papal power and corruption that was hidden behind a screen of mysticism, but above all they encouraged the laity to question their spiritual leaders.

The Great Schism in the Catholic Church

allegiances between 1378–1409

- to Avignon
- to Rome
- Portugal changes from Avignon to Rome; Germany, varies in different states

The Renaissance Popes

During the century following the Great Schism, a series of strong-willed pontiffs re-established their authority over the Church and increased the political power of the papacy, while turning Rome into a center of artistic patronage.

Below right: Pius II was a humanist, but a pope who kept the reins of power firmly in his hands. Portrait by Justo de Gante.

As Pope Martin V (p.1417–31), Cardinal Otto Colonna set about establishing post-schism papal authority, in Rome and across Europe. His political astuteness showed he was no puppet of the secular rulers who supported his appointment. Similarly, Martin's obstruction of the conciliar movement enhanced the authority of his office at the expense of Church reform.

His successor Eugenius IV (p.1431–47) was unable to avoid convening the Council of Basel (1431–49), but his continued obstruction led to the appointment of a rival or anti-pope in 1439. This did little to strengthen the conciliarists, and ultimately led to their isolation from ecclesiastic power.

Nicholas V (p.1447–55) and the first Borgia pope Callistus III (p.1455–58) continued the policy of sidelining conciliar reformers and established direct links with regional churches. Italian-born humanist Pope Pius II (p.1458–64) repudiated the conciliarists at the Congress of Mantua, ensuring that power remained firmly in the hands of the papacy.

Above: Sixtus IV brought planning to Rome's streets and the famous library to the Vatican, but his expansionist policies resulted in neighborly conflict with the Italian city-states.

Safe from internal pressure, the late 15th-century popes turned their attention to enlarging their secular fiefdom in Italy. Venetian Pope Paul II (p.1464–71) built the ostentatious Palazzo Venezia, ushering in a new era of architectural commissions designed to dignify the papacy with buildings worthy of its reaffirmed status.

Paul II was later criticized for his opposition to the Roman Academy, a group of Roman-based humanist scholars including Giulio Pomponio Leto (1425–c.98), but his anti-humanism was the exception among Renaissance popes. Later popes saw the humanist movement as a means to redefine the image of the Church.

Pope Sixtus IV (p.1471–84) embarked on a policy of territorial expansion that brought the Papal States into conflict with the surrounding cities; first Florence and then Venice and Naples. His diplomatic and military endeavors achieved little, but back in Rome his program of architectural improvements would have a lasting effect. He was responsible for the construction of the Sistine Chapel and the establishment of the Vatican Library.

The Lutheran movement

Innocent VIII (p.1484–92) was less successful. The rival Roman houses of Orsini and Colonna temporarily wrested control of Rome from a pontiff who appeared more concerned with artistic patronage than temporal politics. His successor was altogether more worldly. Alexander VI (p.1492–1503) ushered in a new era, and for a

decade the papacy came to symbolize corruption, immorality, and nepotism (*see following page*). He gave strong leadership and established the Papal States as a clearly defined secular region, providing the Church with much-needed revenue and political influence.

Alexander VI was also a leading patron of the arts, a trait shared by the man who succeeded him, Pope Julius II (p.1503–13). As well as commissioning work by Michelangelo, Raphael, and Donato Bramante, Julius oversaw the rebuilding of St. Peter's Basilica and the expansion of the Vatican Library. More than any other pope of this period, Julius II helped to define Rome as a cultural center. He was also a skilled administrator, politician, and military commander, expanding the Papal States to include Bologna and Perugia, and participating in anti-Venetian

and anti-French alliances to protect his northern borders.

After Julius's death the papacy suffered a decline. Leo X (p.1513–21) was a lavish artistic patron but did little to discourage Martin Luther's split from the Church; the ineffective Dutch Pope Hadrian VI (p.1522–23) was notably miserly. Pope Clement VII (p.1523–34) endured the sack of Rome by an Imperialist army in 1527, and was party to the growing division between the papacy and Lutheran supporters in Germany. Although Pope Paul III (p.1534–49) restored a degree of prosperity to Rome and supervised Church reform, he too was unable to halt the Lutherans. A century of inspired, gifted, and cultured popes had helped to create Renaissance Rome, but also paved the way for the Reformation.

Above: Detail of a painting by Raphael of Pope Leo X with the Cardinals Medici and Rossi, c.1517–19. Raphael's unflattering portrait depicts the pope as corpulent—he was known to perspiration continually from his brow—however, Leo had an agreeable nature. He was born in Florence in 1475, the second son of Lorenzo de' Medici the Magnificent, and inherited the Medici love of artistic patronage.

Alexander VI, the Borgia Pope

The most notorious family in Renaissance Italy, the Borgias symbolize the extremes of the age. Rodrigo Borgia, who became Pope Alexander VI, and his children Lucrezia and Cesare proved to be as brilliant as they were duplicitous, treacherous, and immoral.

Below: Borgia piety was mostly for show—Pope Alexander VI praying.

The scion of the Spanish-Italian family who first rose to prominence was Alfonso Borgia (1378–1458), who became Pope Callistus III (p.1455–58). His main papal policy was the call for a crusade against the Ottoman Turks as a response to their capture of Constantinople in

1453. He regarded this as a tool with which to unite the Church and Europe's secular powers under the leadership of the papacy, so ostracizing the conciliarists. However, he was best remembered for his nepotism, electing his 25-year-old Spanish-born nephew Rodrigo (1431–1503) to the College of Cardinals in 1456.

Two years later, Rodrigo became Vice-Chancellor of the Holy See, a position he used to amass a fortune. He flouted the rules of celibacy, leading a life of "unbridled sensuality," maintaining a mistress (Vannozza de Catanei) and siring seven children while serving the Vatican, including Cesare (1475–1507) and Lucrezia (1480–1519). His uncle's successor, Pope Pius II, even had to order his subordinate to cease holding "unseemly" orgies within the grounds of the Holy See.

In 1492 he was elected pope, allegedly because his widespread bribery secured the votes of 17 of the 22 members of the College of Cardinals. Although simoniacal dealings probably took place, Rodrigo Borgia's diplomatic skills won the vote of Cardinal Sforza, a key member of the elective college, in the face of widespread opposition from cardinals from leading Italian families such as the Medicis, Caraffas, and Roveres.

Rodrigo selected the title Pope Alexander VI, and so began a decade of unrestrained corruption, avarice, manipulation, and treachery. He began by replacing his mistress with a younger woman, Guilia Faranese, who produced two children while he was pope. His other forms of patronage were equally fruitful. He supported the University of Rome and made substantial improvements to the Vatican and to Rome.

An undesirable patriarch

One of his first official acts was to issue a Papal Bull in 1493 recognizing the division of the New World into Portuguese and Spanish spheres of influence. The ratification of this diplomatic deal came in 1494, known as the Treaty of Tordesillas. Alexander was well aware of the potential of the new lands, and wanted to ensure the Church could exert its influence there. He then imposed tighter control over Rome, ostensibly to combat lawlessness, but more likely for his own political

757	1378	1417	1438	1439	1460	1473	1492
The pope is given central Italian territories by Frankish King Pepin II as the Papal States	French cardinals elect Clement VII, creating their own papacy in Avignon, beginning the Great Schism	The Council of Constance elects a single pope, Martin V, ending the Great Schism	Led by Charles VII of France, the Pragmatic Sanction of Bourges restricts papal powers	Felix V becomes the first anti-pope, created by conciliarists against Pope Eugenius IV	Pius II asserts papal authority over the conciliarists	Pope Sixtus IV commissions Sistine Chapel, famed for Michelangelo's series of biblical paintings	Spanish Borgia pope, Alexander VI, recognizes Alfonso's son Ferdinand I as King of Naples

and fiscal ends.

His principal advisor was the papal vice-chancellor Ascanio Sforza, brother of Ludovico Sforza of Milan. He encouraged Alexander to join an alliance with Milan and Venice, a pact sealed in April 1493 by the marriage of Lucrezia Borgia to Giovanni Sforza, the ruler of Pesaro. The papacy was now firmly embroiled in Italian politics, as both Milan and Venice were threatened by French and German imperial claims to their territories.

A month later, an envoy of King Charles VIII (r.1483-98) of France arrived in Rome, requesting papal support for the king's claim to the Neapolitan throne. Alexander refused, and instead acknowledged the succession of Alfonso, son of the late King Ferrante I of Naples, as Alfonso II of Naples.

Alexander feared Charles himself more than foreign powers holding sway within Italy. He was well aware that several cardinals and senior clerics led by Cardinal della Rovere had corresponded with the French king, asking for help in deposing a pope charged with simony, corruption, and lasciviousness. Alexander's respite was short-lived. In September 1494 Charles crossed the Alps into Italy at the head of an overwhelmingly powerful French army.

Today the Vatican City is an autonomous state independent of Italy. Although it is considerably smaller than in the Renaissance, the heart of the Vatican within its medieval fortifications is still essentially the same as it is shown in Vasari's map on page 42.

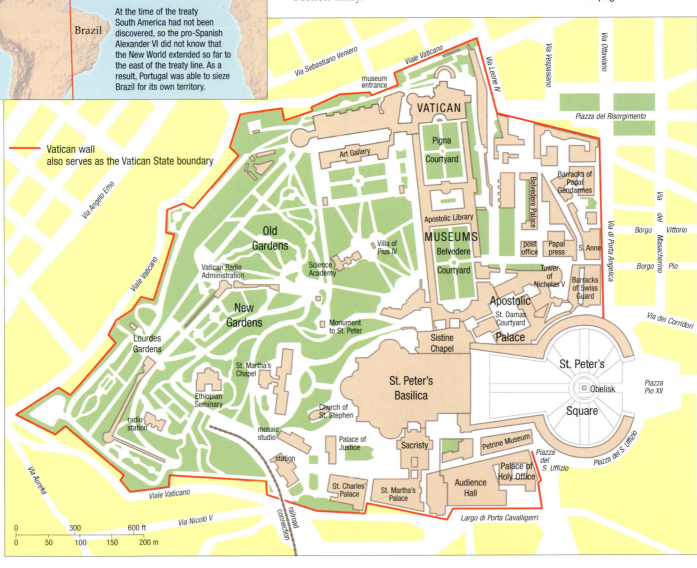

The Treaty of Tordesillas, 1494

ATLANTIC OCEAN

Spanish | Portuguese

Brazil

At the time of the treaty South America had not been discovered, so the pro-Spanish Alexander VI did not know that the New World extended so far to the east of the treaty line. As a result, Portugal was able to sieze Brazil for its own territory.

— Vatican wall also serves as the Vatican State boundary

1495	1495–1520	1497	1503–13	1507	1514	1517–20	1527
Alexander VI breaks a truce with Charles VIII and forms an alliance against France's claim on Naples	High Renaissance period; Rome is considered the artistic capital of Italy	The Borgia family is forced to return territory to the rival Orsinis after defeat at Soriano	Golden era of patronage under Julius II, who also expanded the Papal States	In a second offensive, a papal army kills Cesare Borgia, ending the dynasty	Raphael (Raffaello Sanzio) is appointed chief architect of the Vatican by Pope Leo X	Leo X fails to contain Martin Luther and his supporters, allowing the Reformation to develop	Habsburg Holy Roman Emperor Charles V sacks Rome, which was allied with France

The Rome of Pope Alexander VI

As patrons of the arts, the Borgia court attracted the most gifted men of the age, and provided the background for the greatest scandals of the Renaissance. Meanwhile, Alexander gradually gained complete control of the Church and the Papal States, becoming a secular dictator in all but name.

King Charles VIII's army entered Rome in late December 1494. Abandoned by all but his closest supporters and immediate family, Alexander sought refuge in the papal fortress of Castel Sant' Angelo. The French laid siege, but Charles was reluctant to openly oppose the supreme head of the Church. He agreed to a compromise, accepting Alexander VI as the true pope and in return requesting papal support for his claim to the throne of Naples. Alexander refused, and when the French marched south to Naples in February he formed an anti-French alliance that involved the papacy, the Holy Roman Empire, Spain, Venice, and Milan.

Italy became the main battleground in a struggle between the French Valois kings and the Spanish-Austrian Habsburgs. By the end of the year the French had returned across the Alps, having soundly defeated a Venetian and Allied army at Fornovo on July 6, 1495. The Italian *condottieri* were no match for the *gendarmes*

(knights) supported by professional mercenary pikemen, firearm troops, and artillery.

Alexander set about strengthening his position, rooting out his opponents and placing greater trust in his family and loyal supporters. His first target was the Orsini family, who had consistently opposed him in the political arena. Financed by the sale of ecclesiastical offices, Alexander's youngest son Juan Borgia, Duke of Gandia, led a military campaign against them, capturing several Orsini castles near Rome before laying siege to the main Orsini stronghold of Bracciano (*see the map on page 24 for lands of the leading Roman families*). On January 25, 1497 the garrison sallied out and defeated Juan at Soriano, forcing the pope to accept an unfavorable peace settlement that allowed the return of most Orsini bases.

The plots multiply

Alexander sought help, and Gonsalvo de Cordoba, "The Great Captain," and his small, veteran Spanish army came to his aid. Cordoba laid siege to the Roman port of Ostia, held by French troops on behalf of Cardinal della Rovere, the pope's main opponent. Ostia fell within two weeks, allowing the transfer of several nearby towns held by untrustworthy cardinals to the secure demesne of Juan's Duchy of Gandia.

The Borgia triumph was short-lived, since a week later in July 1497 Juan's body was found in the Tiber, the victim of an assassin's dagger. The perpetrator was never caught. Pope Alexander emerged from mourning and a brief period of guilt-ridden piety with renewed belief in the importance of familial ties. He gave Juan's elder brother Cesare Borgia free rein in Rome and the Papal States, which he held for just over five years.

The power of the College of Cardinals was curbed by filling its ranks with Spaniards and Borgia favorites, so there was no risk of a collegial insurrection. The pope was safe from formal castigation, while Cesare safeguarded his secular interests and protected him from attack. Numerous plots were recorded, suggesting an undercurrent of resentment to Borgia rule in Rome.

In early August 1503, Pope Alexander, Cesare, and a handful of loyal followers dined with Cardinal Adriano da Corneto in a villa outside Rome. The following day Alexander took ill and within a week was on his deathbed. He died on August 18 from an unidentifiable illness, although the rapid decomposition of his corpse hinted at the use of poison. The great papal tyrant was dead, and Cesare would not survive him for long, since without the support of the pontiff his secular ambitions had little chance of success.

The Borgia dynasty was a unique period in Rome, when the cultural achievements of the Renaissance became entwined in Machiavellian intrigues of Italian politics. Never again would a pope wield so much secular power or stray so far from his spiritual path.

Cesare Borgia—Renaissance Prince

The illegitimate son of Cardinal Rodrigo Borgia, Cesare Borgia was groomed from birth to hold high ecclesiastical office. He quickly denounced this role to become a strong ruler and commander with the thirst for power and wealth characteristic of the family.

Above: Portrait of Cesare Borgia by Giorgione (1477–1510). While flattering, the impression of ruthlessness is clear in the steely expression and far-seeing eyes.

The young Cesare Borgia (1475–1507) left his native Rome to receive a humanist education in Perugia and Pisa, and as a teenager was named the bishop-elect of Pamplona. When his father became Pope Alexander VI in 1492, Cesare first became the Archbishop of Valencia, then a cardinal, which brought him immense wealth. Cesare was not interested in spiritual matters, and probably his only action as a cardinal was the investiture of King Federigo of Naples in 1497. Shortly afterward he renounced the cardinalate to become Captain General of the Church on the death of his brother Juan. While numerous critics accused Cesare of his half-brother's murder, no tangible evidence was produced.

With the blessing of his father, Cesare imposed his will on Rome, enhanced by the title of Duke of Valentinous. He traveled to France in late 1498 to give the new king, Louis XII, a papal annulment of his marriage. The following year Louis invaded Italy, leading French troops back over the Alps to seize Milan from his enemies the Sforzas. Cesare accompanied him; the Sforzas' opposition to the Borgias had become a vendetta following the annulment of the marriage between Lucrezia Borgia and Giovanni Sforza. This marked the end of Sforza influence in Rome, allowing Cesare to become his father's principal lieutenant.

Cesare waged a highly successful campaign in the Romagna (1499–1500), ensuring that papal power extended from Bologna in the north down to the Adriatic coast at Rimini and Pesaro. His father rewarded him with the title of Duke of the Romagna, *de-facto* ruler of the Papal States on behalf of the pope. At the same time he extorted whatever he could from his offices, and was accused of involvement in an assassination attempt against the Duke of Biseglia, Lucrezia's new husband.

Rivals share a fate

Plans to force Tuscany into the papal fold had to be laid aside when Cesare was sent south to negotiate a secret treaty that divided Naples between Spain and France, a clear reversal of

Alexander's previous policy of supporting his southern neighbor. On his return Cesare faced widespread insurrection in the Romagna, allegedly encouraged by the Orsinis and Colonnas. The new treaty stripped these patrimonial families of their erstwhile Spanish and French supporters, allowing Cesare to wage brutal campaigns (1500–01 and 1502–03) and seize Orsini and Colonna lands, which were turned over to the pope's grandchildren, the offspring of Juan and Lucrezia Borgia. While Lucrezia went on to marry Alfonso, heir of Ferrara (thereby enhancing Borgia prestige in Italy), Cesare relied on his military abilities to further his family's position.

The leading opponent to Borgia power, Cardinal Orsini, was captured by Cesare in October 1502, and thrown into the dungeon of Castel Sant' Angelo in Rome. Two weeks later he was dead, probably murdered on Cesare's orders. By judicious use of assassination, counter-espionage, extortion, and political chicanery, Cesare gained complete control over the Papal States. He used this power to further his position, allegedly looting art treasures, estates, and land virtually at will.

Alexander's successor, Pope Julius II, was determined to curb Cesare's power. He led the papal army into battle against its former commander in 1504. Cesare was defeated, captured, and himself imprisoned in Castel Sant' Angelo, languishing there for a year before being released and exiled to Spain, where he was imprisoned again. He escaped in 1506, reaching the safety of Pamplona.

"Il Pamplona" was planning his return to the Italian stage supported by his new-found Navarrese allies when a papal army besieged Cesare's base at Viana, overlooking the River Ebro. On March 11, 1507 Cesare was killed in a skirmish outside the town and the Borgia dynasty came to an end, its passing mourned by none save Machiavelli, who saw Cesare as the epitome of the Renaissance prince; a master of war, diplomacy, and intrigue.

Above: Detail of the Swiss Guard from *The Mass of Bolsena*. This is the right-hand section of a Raphael fresco that spans a doorway in the Vatican. It depicts a miracle that took place in 1263 in Bolsena, near Orvieto, when—during mass—Christ's blood trickled from the host. Raphael painted Pope Julius II witnessing the miracle in the left-hand panel, with four of his cardinals—all relatives, with whose support he defeated Cesare Borgia. As mercenaries, the Swiss Guard were devoted to whichever pope was in power.

Art of the High Renaissance

The High Renaissance was dominated by a handful of great artists such as Michelangelo, Leonardo da Vinci, Raphael, Donato Bramante, and Titian, the acknowledged masters of technical and aesthetic perfection.

Right: *Christ at the Column* by Donato Bramante (1444–1514), painted about 1490. In his mature painting style, Bramante discarded unneccessry decoration and concentrated on the force of a simple image, the essence of the High Renaissance. However, he is better known as an architect, and his greatest achievement was the design for St. Peter's Basilica. Pope Julius II felt that the ruinous condition of the old church was unsuited to his planned mausoleum, and commissioned Bramante to build him a new church. Many architects eventually worked on St. Peter's, but Bramante's basic design survived.

Right: The 19th-century neo-classicist artist Horace Vernet created this fanciful picture of Pope Julius II sitting in the Vatican Palace ordering work on Bramante's plan of St. Peter's from the architect himself, and Raphael and Michelangelo. Vernet's portrait of the pope is accurately based on a contemporary painting by Raphael (or more likely by members of his studio).

Some art historians described the High Renaissance style as "the gathering of artistic energy and the formation of a controlled equilibrium." For the first time, technical and aesthetic perfection, a unity of color, composition, and perspective, combined to make a painting come alive to the viewer. During this period, from about 1495 to 1520, Rome rather than Florence or Venice was considered the artistic capital of Italy, and there the painter was elevated to a hitherto unimagined position as the premier artisan.

The patronage of popes such as Alexander VI, Julius II, and Leo X did much to encourage a revision of religious art through humanist eyes. This resulted in masterpieces that helped transform the image of Rome and the papacy; art as a form of spiritual propaganda.

While Leonardo da Vinci—symbol of the restlessness of Renaissance thinkers—was constantly engaged in artistic, anatomical, and scientific experiments that expanded human

understanding, in turn encouraging contemporaries to examine the natural world and apply their observations to art, Michelangelo approached it a different way. A man who has come to typify the artistic genius of the High Renaissance, Michelangelo (*see following page*) applied his multiple talents to architectural design, sculpture, painting, and even poetry. He created works that met the sought-after balance between aesthetic beauty, natural perfection, and innovative design. His statue of *David*, the Sistine Chapel, the tomb of Julius II, the cupola of St. Peter's Basilica, and his *Pietà*s all contain that balance and artistic perfection.

Harmony of spirit

Raphael (Raffaello Sanzio, 1483–1520) demonstrated a different type of passion. While Michelangelo portrayed the power and spirit of humanity, the young artist from Urbino sought to capture its graceful beauty, emphasized the sublimity of light, proportion, and unity. He combined this approach with a simplicity of form that is breathtakingly effective. Works such as *Madonna del Granduca* (c.1505) and *Maddalena Doni* (c.1507), both now in the Palazzo Pitti, Florence, earned him a deserved reputation as an artist with the ability to encapsulate "the harmony of the human spirit," as one contemporary described his work.

In 1508 Raphael entered the service of Julius II and worked on frescos in the Vatican Palace, including his acclaimed *Disputa* (1509), which emphasized the importance of divine intervention on behalf of the pontiff as God's representative on earth. In 1514 Pope Leo X appointed Raphael as the architect of St. Peter's, and in the designs that followed he demonstrated complete affinity with classical proportion and technique, a humanist building a new Rome to reflect the city's former glory.

His building projects included the Chigi Stables (1514–18), noted for their elegant classical appearance. In his final years Raphael explored darker realms, and his last work, *Transfiguration* (1518–20, now in the Vatican) contained scenes of violence and disharmony, reflecting a change in the artist's sense of balance.

The sack of Rome by the Imperialist (German) army in May 1527 brought the patronage of the High Renaissance to a close. The artists who had enjoyed papal patronage dispersed to other Italian cities, and as far afield as France and Spain. It would be a decade before they could be compelled to return, by which time the artistic world had moved on. Late Renaissance painting saw the development of anti-classical tendencies, and the beginning of Mannerism, a movement founded by Raphael's pupil Giulio Romano (1492-1546). The artistic diaspora and subsequent reinvention of art marked the end of an era, a period now seen as the cultural pinnacle of the Renaissance.

Above: To many, Raphael is the exemplar of High Renaissance painting (Michelangelo is accused of already slipping into Mannerism). But to some art critics, his undoubted abilities with light, shade, and form are spoiled by a sickly sentimentality in his major paintings, clearly observed in the child-lamb symbolism of *The Holy Family with Lamb* (1507).

Michelangelo–Renaissance Genius

Michelangelo typifies the incredibly gifted artists of the High Renaissance. Contemporary historian Vasari saw him as the "perfect exemplar" of Italian art, since he was multi-talented, combining architecture, poetry, sculpture, and painting almost at will.

Above: Few images evoke the core of humanist thought as much as Michelangelo's Adam receiving the ignitive spark of life from God on the ceiling of the Sistine Chapel (pre-restoration). His innocent pose and expression symbolize mankind's innate goodness before Eve ate of the fruit of the Tree of Knowledge. Michelangelo's *Moses*, right, has the stature to bear the burden of the Israelites in their Exodus, and rarely has the patriarch been so monumentally portrayed.

Florentine-born Michelangelo di Lodovico Buonnarroti-Simoni (1475–1564) began his career in 1488 as an apprentice to Domenico Ghirlandaio (1449–94), the best fresco painter of his generation. Some of Michelangelo's earliest surviving sketches show a precocious talent, which in about 1490 earned him the patronage of Lorenzo de' Medici.

Following his patron's death, Michelangelo continued to work in Florence until the city was threatened by Charles VIII, when he departed for the safety of Bologna and Venice. Two years later he arrived in Borgia-dominated Rome. During his five-year sojourn there, his works for the pope included a *Pietà* for St. Peter's Basilica (1498–99), widely regarded as a masterpiece in the sculptural encapsulation of the human anatomy.

When he headed back to Florence in 1501, Michelangelo used his skill to produce his best-known sculptural work, *David* (1501–04). It was given a place of honor in the Palazzo Vecchio, a potent symbol of the quiet determination of the

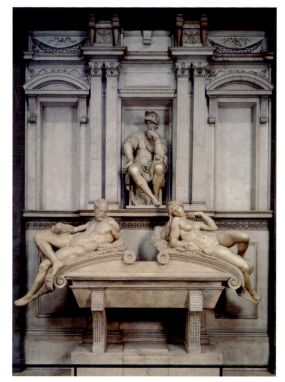

Left: Forgiven for his republican sentiments as expressed in the monumental statue of *David*, Michelangelo was welcomed back to Florence by the ruling Medici family in 1516. Among his many projects there, he showed his flair for combining architectural elements with sculpture, as seen here on the tomb for Giuliano de' Medici, executed in 1526–31.

Florentine republic, defying the Medici goliaths. In 1505 he was summoned to Rome by Julius II, who commissioned several projects designed to reflect greater glory on the Vatican and the papacy.

Although the sequence of work is debatable, Michelangelo almost certainly began by carving a statue of *Moses* for the Church of San Pietro ad Vincoli, then began work on a tomb for his patron. This project was commissioned in 1510 and completed five years later, two years after Julius's death. In 1553 Michelangelo's biographer Condivi recalled that the artist found the project burdensome, calling it "the tragic tomb."

Work on the tomb was concurrent with the Sistine Chapel (1508–12), another commission from Pope Julius. His decorated ceiling told the story of the Creation, a sweeping panorama of Genesis that exalts the human figure and its beauty, and emphasizes the munificence of God as the Creator, the benefactor of human grace.

The Last Judgment

Michelangelo only returned to complete the tomb of Julius II after the completion of the chapel ceiling. He also worked on two dynamic sculptures, *The Dying Slave* and *The Rebellious Slave* (both now in the Louvre, Paris), the works capturing pent-up energy and pathos.

By 1516 Michelangelo was back in Florence,

probably because Leo X was a less enthusiastic patron. The city was back in the hands of the Medici, who showed there was no ill-feeling over his republican statue of *David* by commissioning Michelangelo to work on their private chapel. The Medici chapel in Florence occupied him for 15 years (1519–33), although it was frequently set aside for more interesting forms of artistic expression, including the sculpture *Victory* (c.1527) and the design of the Medici's Bibliotheca Laurenziana (1523) for Pope Clement VII. The completed chapel was deemed a work of genius, incorporating human figures into the supports, Herculean titans bearing the weight of the heavens, a link from God to man.

Michelangelo returned to Rome in 1533 at the invitation of Clement VII, to work on *The Last Judgment*, covering the altar (western) wall of the Sistine Chapel. Filled with depictions of humanity in all its forms, the fresco encouraged Condivi to remark that the artist "expressed all the art of painting can do with the human figure." It was completed in 1541, by which time Michelangelo was in his mid-sixties and revered as a genius.

A string of projects followed, including taking over the design of St. Peter's in 1546, of which the most striking feature is the extraordinary dome that shows how far Michelangelo's vision had extended beyond the classicism of the High Renaissance toward Mannerism. One of his last works, a *Pietà* intended for his own tomb, he allegedly tried to destroy due to spiritual qualms. With only the drum of his great dome completed, he was working on a third *Pietà* when he died in 1564. His death was met with an outpouring of grief in both Rome and his final resting place of Florence.

CHAPTER 4

Imperial Destiny— Habsburg-Valois Rivalry

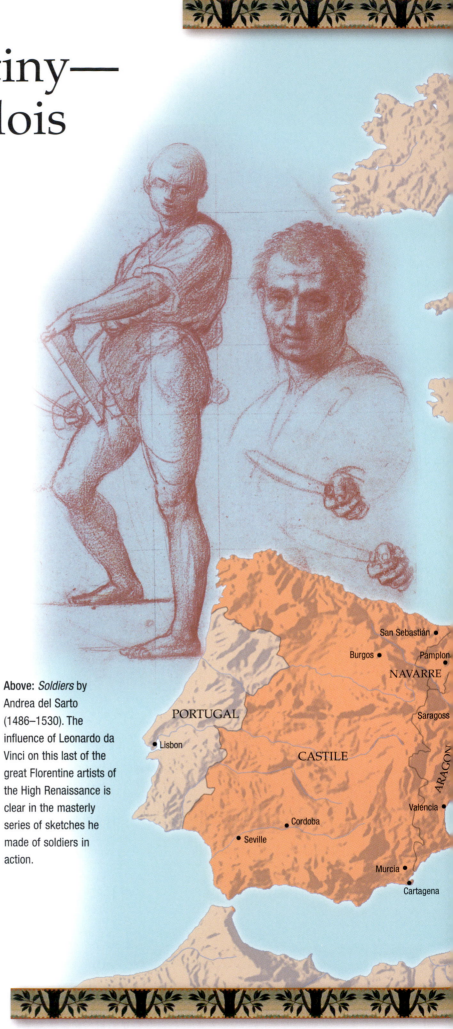

In 1494 Charles VIII, Valois King of France, invaded Italy, starting a conflict that would rage for half a century. Begun as an attempt to reinforce a minor dynastic claim, it became a struggle between France and Imperial Spain, the two superpowers of the 16th century. His successor Louis XII (r.1498–1515) continued the fight, but increasingly the Italian Wars (1494–1529) were fought not between France and various Italian states, but between the Valois domain and the Habsburg territories of Spain and the Germanic Holy Roman Empire.

Two years after the French invasion of Italy, a marriage alliance was forged between a Habsburg prince and the daughter of the Spanish monarchs Ferdinand and Isabella. This was dangerous for the French, since the Spanish were well-placed to interfere in southern France while the German armies of the Holy Roman Empire could march into northern Italy. France also shared common borders with both increasingly hostile regions.

What had become a minor dynastic claim had become a fight for supremacy. For the French, the Italian Wars were a fight for survival against a superpower that threatened to encompass them. To the Habsburgs the conflict was esential to consolidate their disjointed empire and restore their influence in the Italian peninsula.

Renaissance Italy was a battleground, and the vibrant cultural development of the city-states was arrested if not halted by the political upheavals that followed in the wake of the wars. Military successes on both sides were followed by equally critical defeats, and the fortunes of war remained in the balance until 1525, when the Imperialists inflicted a decisive defeat on the French army of Francis I. The process of Imperialist consolidation continued until 1527, when, in an unnecessary finale, the Imperialist army sacked Rome, an act that caused widespread outrage in Europe and marked the end of the political and military upheavals that had devastated Italy—and ended its renaissance.

Above: *Soldiers* by Andrea del Sarto (1486–1530). The influence of Leonardo da Vinci on this last of the great Florentine artists of the High Renaissance is clear in the masterly series of sketches he made of soldiers in action.

Growth of the Habsbug empire and the Habsburg-Valois Wars

- territory of King Philip II of Spain
- territory of Emperor Ferdinand
- Habsburg empire of Charles V
- Republic of Venice
- boundary of Holy Roman Empire
- ✗ Habsburg victory
- ✗ Valois victory

SWEDEN

DENMARK

BALTIC SEA

DUCHY OF PRUSSIA

TUDOR ENGLAND

- Lübeck
- Hamburg
- Stettin

BRANDENBURG

- Berlin

KINGDOM OF POLAND

- Amsterdam
- Utrecht

Spanish Netherlands

- Calais
- Antwerp
- Brussels
- Münster

Berg

Hessen Kassel

HOLY ROMAN EMPIRE

- Breslau

SILESIA

- Prague

BOHEMIA

- Luxemburg

Rhine Palatinate

- Paris

Upper Palatinate

MORAVIA

- Nantes
- Orléans

Württem-berg

Bavaria

- Augsburg
- Munich

Austria

- Vienna
- Pressburg

Lorraine

VALOIS FRANCE

Franche Comté
- Besançon
- Basel

ARCHDUCHY OF AUSTRIA

- Buda

Charolais

SWISS CONFEDERACY

- Bugey
- Geneva

Tyrol

Styria

Carniola

KINGDOM OF HUNGARY

- Bordeaux

Bicocca 1522

DUCHY OF SAVOY

Milan

Agnadello 1509

REPUBLIC OF VENICE

- Venice

- Mohacs

Ceresole 1544

Pavia 1525

Marignano 1515

OTTOMAN EMPIRE

- Toulouse

Novara 1513

Genoa

Fornovoo 1495

Landriano 1529

Ravenna 1512

- Marseilles

DUCHY OF MILAN

Siena

REP. OF FLORENCE

CATALUÑA

- Barcelona

REP. OF SIENA

PAPAL STATES

ADRIATIC SEA

Corsica (to Genoa)

- Rome

TYRRHENIAN SEA

- Palma

Balearic islands

Sardinia (to Spain)

The Garigliano 1503

✗ *Cerignola 1503*

- Naples

KINGDOM OF NAPLES

- Algiers

MEDITERRANEAN SEA

- Bugia

- Palermo

Sicily

Spain and Austria–The Habsburg Empire

During the 16th century Europe was dominated by two dynastic powers, the Valois kings of France and the Habsburgs. Habsburg power reached its peak during the reign of Charles V (r.1519–56), when the family's German possessions were combined with those of Spain to create a superpower.

Right: Ferdinand of Aragon and Isabella of Castile, with daughter Joanna the Mad, mother of Emperor Charles V.

Above: Mary of Burgundy was a prize when she married the son of the Holy Roman Emperor, bringing most Burgundian territory under Habsburg dominion.

The Habsburg (or Hapsburg) dynasty originated in southern Germany and Austria, the house named after their family castle near Aargau in Switzerland. A Habsburg, Rudolf I, became Holy Roman Emperor in 1273, and in the centuries that followed the family increased its holdings in Austria and Styria until they controlled most of southern Germany. As their power grew, so did the level of recognition afforded them, their titles including the crowns of Austria, Bohemia, and Hungary. The elective position of Holy Roman Emperor was held by the Habsburg family for much of the late 13th century, and then again from 1438 onward. Apart from 1740–45, the crown remained in Habsburg hands until 1806, when the empire was abolished on the orders of Napoleon Bonaparte. The Habsburgs continued to rule Austria until the end of the First World War.

In 1477 the death in battle of Charles the Bold (also known as Charles the Rash), Duke of Burgundy (r.1467–77), created a political vacuum in western Europe. The subsequent marriage of Maximilian, son of Emperor Frederick III (r.1452–93) to Charles's heir, Mary of Burgundy, secured most of the Burgundian territories for the Habsburg family, making them one of the most wealthy and powerful houses in Europe.

It also brought conflict with Louis XI of France (r.1461–83), who was envious of this dynastic expansion and claimed some of these territories for his own house of Valois. Despite this war, Maximilian maintained control of Flanders, the Netherlands, Artois, and the Franche Comté. By 1489 the French kings had given up the attempt to reconquer these territories, allowing Maximilian to concentrate on driving the Turks from the gates of his capital of Vienna.

Keys to power

Meanwhile in Spain, the death of Henry IV in 1474 resulted in brief stuggle for succession, but by 1476 his sister Isabella (r.1474–1504) had secured the throne of Castile. In 1469 she had married Prince Ferdinand of Aragon, who duly inherited the Aragonese throne to become Ferdinand II (r.1479–1516), and two principal kingdoms in Spain were thus united. They extended the authority of their government by limiting the power of the nobility, and by campaigning against the Moors of southern Spain, thus unifying their people in a common cause.

When Isabella died in 1504 without producing a male heir, the throne of Castile

| **1273** Rudolf I becomes the first Habsburg Holy Roman Emperor | **1461–83** Louis XI of France extends royal authority over previously independent provinces | **1468** England allies with Charles the Bold, Duke of Burgundy, against France | **1477** Emperor Frederick's son Maximilian marries Mary of Burgundy | **1482** Maximilian secures the Low Countries, Franche-Comté, and county of Artois | **1494** Charles VIII of France invades Italy to claim Naples, beginning the Italian Wars | **1495** Aided by allies from Florence and Milan, Charles VIII reaches Milan without conflict (February) | **1495** Charles VIII's battle with Francesco Gonzaga of Mantua at Fornovo is a stalemate but he retreats (July) |

passed to her daughter Joanna the Mad, who had been married to Prince Philip the Handsome of Burgundy eight years before. Philip was the son of Emperor Maximilian I and Mary of Burgundy, and thus the heir to the Habsburg empire in Germany.

Joanna of Castile produced a son, Charles, born in 1500, the grandson of both Ferdinand and Isabella, and of Emperor Maximilian, therefore the most eligible bachelor in Europe. Although Ferdinand II of Aragon remarried, his second wife also failed to produce a male heir, so when he died in 1516, his grandson Charles inherited the Aragonese throne from his father and the Castilian throne from his mother, which

had been held in trust by Ferdinand until his death. Already Archduke of Austria and Duke of Burgundy, the young Habsburg heir was crowned Charles I of Spain in 1516.

This power increased markedly three years later when his grandfather Maximilian died, and Charles succeeded him as Holy Roman Emperor Charles V (r.1519–58). Like his great rival Francis I of France, he was a young ruler with the energy to make his mark on the European stage. Since his territories now included Spain, Germany, the Low Countries, various Italian states, and Spanish colonies in North Africa, the Caribbean, and Central and South America, Charles V had the resources to do almost anything he wanted.

Above: Emperor Maximilian I and his family, probably painted by Bernard Strigel (1460–1528), a member of the Swabish school of artists. The work was originally painted as a single picture, but later became the left half of a diptych.

1499	c.1500–c.1562	1510	1512	1513	1519	1525	1544
Louis XII of France takes Milan; he agrees to co-rule Naples with Ferdinand of Aragon in the following year	Expansion of French trade under King Francis I	The League of Cambrai (Maximilian I, France, and Aragon) dissolves after failing to secure Venice	France defeats Venice and Spain at Ravenna	French ally James IV of Scotland is killed by the English at Flodden, who are allied with the Holy Roman Empire	Maximilian I dies and Charles I of Spain becomes Holy Roman Emperor Charles V	The French army is devastated by the Holy Roman Empire at Pavia and Francis I is captured	Victory at Ceresole secures France's Alpine borders

Renaissance France

When Francis I inherited the throne in 1515, France was not unified, lacking clearly defined frontiers, and divided by feudal magnates. National consciousness was raised by a consolidation of royal power, a growth in prosperity and by a cultural revolution that transformed France into a European power.

France during the early Renaissance was a patchwork of ducal provinces, Church lands, and royal fiefdoms. Until 1430, most French territory north of the Loire was in the hands of England or Burgundy. In the south, the Royal Demesne was significantly smaller than the lands

held and ruled directly by the French nobles. For the remainder of the 15th century the monarchy struggled to reunify France and increase the crown's holdings.

By the close of the Hundred Years War in 1453, royal control was restored to Gascony, Champagne, and Normandy, giving the monarchy a more stable political and economic base from which it could expand. During the reign of Louis XI (r.1461–83) royal authority was extended into provinces that had hitherto been ruled directly by members of the leading nobility, ending the political anarchy that had divided France earlier in the century.

French expansion, 1430–1559

By the close of the Hundred Years War, England had lost the remainder of its French possessions between 1430–53, with the exception of Calais. Burgundy's collapse in 1476 gave the French opportunities for further expansion.

Legend:
- area held by England until c.1430
- England, 1453
- France, 1453
- annexed by France, with date
- bishopric annexed, 1559
- Habsburg territory, 1559
- Habsburg territory annexed by France and retaken, with dates
- Holy Roman Empire, 1559
- boundary of France, 1559
- city with parliament and foundation date

The collapse of Burgundy in 1476–77 gave Louis the opportunity to expand his borders by annexing the counties of Burgundy, Picardy, and Artois, creating a stable eastern border from the Atlantic to the Mediterranean. This was further extended in 1481 when the lands of Rene of Anjou were annexed by the crown, giving Louis control of Provence, Maine, and Anjou.

A decade later Louis XII (r.1498–1515) attempted to annex the demesne of the dukes of Brittany, but legal wrangles delayed this addition to royal lands until the mid-16th century. The process would be continued by both Francis I (r.1515–47) and his son Henry II (r.1547–59).

Although France contained some of the most thriving urban centers in Europe, its economy was dominated by agriculture. Forests gave way to fields as the late medieval population grew, and the growth of towns increased the demand for agrarian produce. This development reached its peak in the mid-16th century, after which the population grew faster than the level of agricultural production, leading to inflation, and consequently poverty and famine.

Blossoming of trade

Paris was the largest city in northern Europe, with a population in excess of 200,000. Other cities also thrived; the population of Lyon quadrupled to 80,000 between 1450 and 1550; Rouen, Tolouse, Bordeaux, and Marseilles grew at a similar rate. Most served as administrative and ecclesiastical centers as well as marketplaces.

Historians have dubbed the reign of Francis I —the early 16th century—as "the springtime of French trade" because of the rapid expansion in overseas trading, the development of French Mediterranean and Atlantic ports, and the

expansion of river traffic. Trade would continue to thrive until halted by the effects of the French Wars of Religion later in the 16th century, which would impact on the country's economic life.

The Italian Renaissance of the 15th century influenced France by the end of the century, but her full Renaissance flowering would take place a few decades later, during the reigns of Francis I and Henry II. Both monarchs embraced humanism and patronage, and the French noblemen of their courts followed their lead. While Francis and Henry may have become engrossed in the beautification of their palaces and châteaux, they also paid heed to the need for urban planning, following the example set in Florence, Rome, and Milan. Paris was transformed during the 16th century as new boulevards were created (enabling the court to parade in their carriages), great squares were laid out by clearing some of the clutter of medieval buildings, and the nobility vied with each other to improve the appearance of their townhouses, or *hôtels*. More important still, French Renaissance monarchs supported the development of colleges and universities, making them leading centers for humanist scholarship and theological discussion.

Above: King Francis I of France had an ambition to become the Holy Roman Emperor, but his Habsburg rival, Charles V, won the election, thus uniting both halves of the Habsburg dynasty in Spain and Austria

Left: French hunting scene of 1526. By the middle of the 16th century the largely untamed French countryside was becoming increasingly given over to agriculture to support the burgeoning towns and cities, and rural activities like hunting were becoming rarer.

Charles VIII's Invasion of Italy

When King Charles VIII of France entered Italy, he altered the political balance in the Italian peninsula. By attempting to claim the Neapolitan throne by force of arms, he invited the participation of his Habsburg rivals in Italian affairs.

Below: French prisoners at Naples being marched toward Aragonese ships to be taken in capitivity to Spain. After an unopposed annexation of Naples, Charles VIII abandoned his garrison to its fate when the Holy League threatened his over-extended position. From the illuminated manuscript *De Majeste*, 1495.

Charles' somewhat tenuous claim to the throne of Naples (*see pages 32–3, 48–9*) was denied, so he decided to take the kingdom by force, as part of a grander plan to launch a crusade against the Ottoman Turks. Some 25,000 men crossed the Alps, including the cream of French chivalry, 8,000 veteran Swiss mercenaries, and Europe's first modern train of artillery. His allies in Milan and Florence ensured that his progress south was unopposed, and the French entered Naples in February 1495 after a bloodless campaign.

Alarmed by the invasion, Pope Alexander VI, Ferdinand of Aragon, Isabella of Castile, and Emperor Maximilian I concluded an anti-French alliance. Their "Holy League" soon embraced Spain, Germany, the Papal States, and even England. But when his erstwhile allies Venice and

Milan changed allegiance and joined the league, they threatened Charles' lines of communications with the Duke of Orléans' small army garrisoned in northern Italy.

Charles VIII marched north to link up with this force, leaving half his army to hold Naples. A *condottieri* army commanded by Giovanni Francesco Gonzaga of Mantua and paid for by Milan and Venice moved to intercept Charles as he crossed the Apennine mountains near Parma. The armies met at Fornovo, on the banks of the Taro, Gonzaga with 20,000 men (including 4,000 Italian men-at-arms), Charles with 12,000 at his disposal (including 1,000 elite French men-at-arms and 3,000 veteran Swiss mercenaries). The battle on July 6 was a stalemate, but Charles withdrew across the Alps, leaving his garrison in Naples to be destroyed by a combination of Neapolitan guerrillas and an invading Spanish army.

Broken alliances

France used diplomacy to break up the anti-French alliance. Venice and the papacy switched sides, allowing the new king, Louis XII, to march into Milan with little resistance in October 1499, after which he marched south to capture Naples. In February 1500 Louis of France and Ferdinand of Aragon signed the Treaty of Granada, agreeing to share control of Naples, freeing Louis to return north, where Ludovico Sforza had reoccupied Milan. In April 1500 Louis crushed Sforza's remaining Milanese at Novara, ensuring that French control over the Duchy of Milan would continue unchallenged. However, the French-Spanish alliance quickly broke down after Ferdinand landed an army to seize control of Naples. Gonsalvo de Cordoba (The Great Captain) took command of this Spanish expedition, whose arrival was welcomed by the Neapolitans. The Spanish inflicted two sharp defeats on the French; at Cerignola in February 1503, when Spanish firepower drove off a French frontal attack, and at the Garigliano in December, when Cordoba outflanked a strong defensive position behind the river. The remaining French garrison surrendered in 1504.

With his ambitions in southern Italy

Left: Portrait of King Charles VIII of France, by an unknown artist.

thwarted, Louis concentrated on strengthening his position in the north. With the help of Pope Julius II (p.1503–13) a second alliance between France and Spain was arranged in December 1508. The resulting League of Cambrai saw the unlikely alliance of Louis XII, Ferdinand of Aragon, and Emperor Maximilian I, ostensibly a reaction to the spread of Ottoman power. In reality it was an attempt to curb the growing influence of the Republic of Venice.

Assisted by the dukes of Mantua and Ferrara, the allies launched a brief invasion of Venetian territory in early summer 1509, crushing the Republican army at Agnadello in May. Although Venetian territory on the Italian mainland was overrun, the allies were unable to threaten the Republic's survival, since the fleet that could challenge Venetian naval supremacy was lacking.

The alliance fell apart as they squabbled over the spoils, growing divisions encouraged by Venetian diplomacy and bribes. Louis's diplomatic position in northern Italy was becoming increasingly isolated, as the former allies then began to prepare for a war between themselves. After 16 years of conflict in Italy, peace was still a distant prospect in the summer of 1510.

Mercenaries and their Masters

A new era of modern warfare dawned in 1494, when Charles VIII invaded Italy at the head of 25,000 French troops and mercenaries. It was marked by the demise of the mounted knight, the temporary supremacy of the pike-armed foot soldier, and the rapid development of firepower.

Charles VIII's army consisted of his aristocratic *gendarmes* (mounted men-at-arms or knights), a bodyguard of veteran mounted archers, a host of French levies, and a core of mercenary Swiss pikemen—the most respected infantrymen of their day. His force was accompanied by a large and modern train of field artillery, guns mobile enough to keep up with the army as it marched.

The Swiss were the first to make effective use of the pike, which allowed well disciplined infantry to stand up to the charge of mounted knights. Their defeat of Charles the Bold, Duke of Burgundy in 1476 demonstrated their effectiveness, and thereafter they became much sought after as mercenaries. Over 6,000 Swiss accompanied Charles VIII in 1494.

Their Habsburg rivals followed a different path. In Germany *landsknecht* mercenaries were

formed along much the same lines as the Swiss, although they never usurped the superiority of the Swiss pikes. In Spain, military reformers placed greater emphasis on the combination of pikemen with missile-armed troops.

This was a time of great technological improvement and therefore of tactical innovation. The old feudal levies of crossbowmen or archers were slowly replaced by more disciplined bands of troops equipped with crossbows or crude firearms. Once again, the Spanish were at the forefront of this, introducing the widespread use of the *arquebus* (an early form of matchlock firearm) to the battlefields of Renaissance Italy.

The term "military revolution" was coined to encompass these innovations, reflecting the willingness of contemporary princes and

mercenary captains to experiment. Inspired by the humanist emphasis on the ancients, many looked for inspiration in the pages of classical Roman and Greek military theories. Although these ideas were not always successful on the Renaissance battlefield, there was widespread reappraisal of existing doctrines.

Mixed success, mixed forces

For example, Machiavelli's reinvention of Roman legionary organization in the Florentine army was a disaster, but the Spanish successfully adopted a Roman approach to the logistical support of their army, creating specialist supply and engineering corps. They also developed the highly effective *colunella*, a balanced pike-and-shot formation, which eventually led to Spanish domination of the Renaissance battlefield. Firepower, shock of pike, and discipline became the factors that won battles, not the romantic charge of the mounted knight.

The *condottieri* who had dominated warfare in Italy for centuries were no match for the Swiss, *landsknecht*, or Spanish troops who fought for control of the region. They were forced to adopt the new, more aggressive, and more deadly form of warfare imported into Renaissance Italy, but still found themselves regarded as second-rate, compared to the veteran pikemen from beyond the Alps. Worse, the Spanish led the way in the creation of standing armies, paid for and controlled by the State, without having to rely on the dubious loyalty of mercenary captains. In 1502–03, the "Great Captain" Gonsalvo de Cordoba demonstrated the superiority of his Spanish troops by defeating the French and their Swiss mercenaries using firepower and entrenchments, both distinctly unchivalric military innovations. The French reappraised their tactics and at Ravenna in 1512 weakened the Spanish with artillery, then threw in Swiss and *landsknecht* pikemen.

Three years later at Marignano the power of the Swiss pikemen was broken when a well-entrenched French army demonstrated the superiority of firepower on the battlefield. From that point, pikemen, cavalry, and firearm troops had to work together to win battles; commanders could no longer rely on a single battle-winning troop type. At Pavia (1525), Imperialist *arquebusiers* were victorious through close support by friendly cavalry, artillery, and pikemen. The French, who had been slow to abandon the mounted *gendarme*, were completely outclassed. For the next century, the Spanish would dominate warfare in Europe.

Left: This battle scene from the school of Federico Zuccaro (1542–1609) clearly shows the power of the Swiss pikemen in battle, a new force in the Renaissance that finally spelled the end of the medieval armored knight. In his time, Zuccaro became one of Europe's most famous draftsmen and painters. He traveled widely, working in the Netherlands, Spain, England (Elizabeth I sat for a portrait), and throughout Italy, especially in Florence cathedral and the Vatican. This particular work is known to have been later retouched by Peter Paul Rubens (1577–1640).

The Habsburg-Valois Wars

The military successes of Louis XII prompted the Spanish, Imperialists, and most of the Italian city-states to view the French with suspicion. A new phase of conflict would rage in Italy and grow into a pan-European war for dynastic supremacy.

In 1511 Pope Julius II and Ferdinand of Aragon broke from the League of Cambrai, siding with Venice against France. The allies were defeated by the French at Ravena in April 1512, but the gifted French general Gaston de Foix was killed in the struggle and the strategic situation remained unaltered. By the end of the year the French position around Milan was increasingly precarious, since with Imperial help the Milanese had revolted against French rule. Louis XII sent a relief army across the Alps, only to lose it in a dawn attack at Novara in June 1513 by France's old comrades the Swiss, whose services had been bought by the Sforzas. Milan fell soon after.

The scope of the war had widened, since Henry VIII of England invaded France as an ally of the Imperialists. Although little was achieved, Louis lost his ally James IV of Scotland to the English at Flodden (1513). Louis was forced to sue for peace.

Louis died on New Year's Day 1515, and his successor Francis I (r.1515–47) wasted no time. In August he led a new army over the Alps, his advance preceded by agents who bribed Swiss mercenaries away from the Sforzas. On September 13 Swiss loyal to the Sforzas advanced against the French at Marignano, but after a two-day battle they were defeated by superior numbers. A month later Francis entered Milan in triumph, having restored France's supremacy in northern Italy.

When Emperor Maximilian died in 1519, the Kingdom of Spain and the Holy Roman Empire were united on the accession of Spain's Charles I, who became the emperor Charles V. France was virtually surrounded by this vast empire, but Italy remained the battleground between Habsburg and Valois rulers. The fighting resumed in 1521, by which time an Imperial army had formed in Italy, combining the predominantly *landsknecht* forces of the German empire with the professional army of Spain. Under the leadership of Prospero Colonna, the Imperialists recaptured Milan.

Struggling to hold Milan

In April 1522 the French commander Odet de Foix launched veteran Swiss pikemen against an entrenched Imperialist position at Bicocca outside Milan. The attackers were scythed down by point-blank *arquebus* and artillery fire. Once again the French were forced to abandon northern Italy.

Francis I was determined to recapture Milan and gathered yet another army, leading it in person. In Pavia, February 1525, the French army was all but destroyed by the Imperialists, who launched a surprise attack in thick mist. The Valois cause was dealt a crushing blow when Francis was captured, and Habsburg control over Italy was assured (*see pages 72–3*).

Below: King Louis XII of France sets out for war, from a contemporary illuminated manuscript.

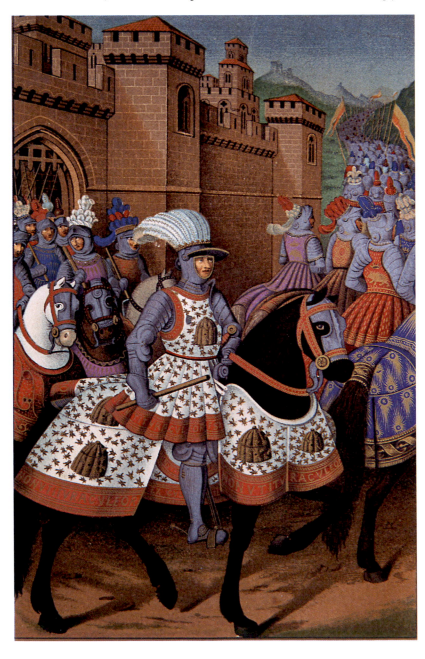

The war continued following the French king's release from captivity. In 1527 a Habsburg army stormed Rome, where Pope Clement VII (p.1523–34) had become an ally of the French. The victorious soldiers sacked the city in one of the most shameful episodes of Renaissance history. It also embarrassed Charles V, who was forced to reach an agreement with the Medici

time the two rulers made extensive use of allies. The French formed an alliance with the Ottoman Turks, who sacked Spanish-occupied Provence in 1543–44. A French victory at Ceresole (1544) secured control of their Alpine border, but no further attempt was made to take the fighting into Italy.

Instead the two sides fought along France's

Above: A military encampment depicted in a medallion from an illuminated manuscript of c.1489–92.

pope, agreeing to sacrifice the Imperial ally of Florence by supporting a papal conquest of the former Medici realm.

In 1536 the armies of Francis and Charles began two years of fruitless campaigning in northern Italy and Provence. After a five-year truce, fighting resumed again in 1543, and this

northern borders, a war that continued until Francis's death in 1547. By that time France was on the verge of a religiously inspired civil war, and the dynastic dispute would take second place to a struggle for supremacy within the country's own borders.

Francis I—Renaissance King

King Francis I was one of the most engaging men of the age; a striking figure who maintained a glittering court, while engaging in a lifelong political and military struggle. The epitome of the Renaissance monarch, he was a superlative patron who forged his country into a leading European power.

Below: Francis I is seen visiting the studio of the sculptor Benvenuto Cellini in Rome; by an unknown painter. Francis became Cellini's patron.

A cousin of his predecessor King Louis XII, Francis I (1494–1547) was only 21 when he succeeded to the French throne after Louis died without an heir in 1515. He inherited the Valois-Habsburg war that would dominate his reign and provide a stage to display his martial prowess.

Like his youthful contemporary Charles I of Spain (1500–56, later Holy Roman Emperor Charles V), Francis represented a new breed of European monarch, determined to project French national interest across Europe, while striving for personal glory on the battlefield and cultural excellence in his court.

Francis experienced the extremes of the fortunes of war. His victory at Marignano (September 1515) caused the collapse of the coalition that opposed him, the capture of the Duchy of Milan, and the signing of a temporary peace between himself and Charles, who became Holy Roman Emperor four years later in 1519.

But Francis found it impossible to control the shifting alliances and loyalties of the Italian city-states, their drift from the French camp encouraged by Habsburg subsidies.

The war resumed in 1521. Francis led his army when it was surprised and routed at Pavia (*see following page*). Francis I was taken to Madrid as a prisoner of the Spanish, where he remained for almost a year, obtaining his release only by agreeing to a humiliating peace treaty, which he repudiated on his return to Paris. Although France remained embroiled in the Italian Wars for the remainder of his reign, Francis would never again risk his life on the battlefield.

His royal dignity was upheld through the maintenance of a glittering court, by the romance and pageantry of the tourney, and becoming the supreme patron of the arts outside Renaissance Italy. It was later seen as the most radiant and creative reign in French history.

Combining the arts

As a patron he encouraged the combination of the Gothic movement with that of Italian Renaissance, which produced a cultural and artistic transformation in France. He brought the aging Leonardo da Vinci to France, and encouraged the budding genius of Andrea del Sarto and the native-born portrait painter Jean Clouet, whose likeness of Francis I remains one of the great depictions of a secular Renaissance ruler. He brought the sculptor and decorative

artist Benvenuto Cellini into his court, and purchased works by Raphael and Michelangelo to decorate his palaces, paintings which would later form part of the Louvre collection.

Francis was also a keen builder, commissioning some of the most impressive architectural projects of the mid-16th century. These included the rebuilding of his Louvre palace in Paris (a project completed by his son Henry II), and the construction of a magnificent hunting lodge in the nearby Bois de Boulogne (the Château de Madrid) and his favorite residence at Fontainbleau. In the latter, Italian architects Rosso Fiorentino and Francesco Primaticcio created a true amalgam of Italian and northern Renaissance styles, advancing an architectural tradition first encountered at the Château de Chambord near Blois.

Francis also encouraged the patronage of scholars, men like Guillaume Bude, the theological scholar Jacques Lefevre d'Etaples, and even the court poet Clement Marot, whose radical religious views eventually led to his fall from favor.

Francis enhanced royal authority in France, containing religious dissent and ensuring the political stability of the kingdom. Although Francis was initially sympathetic to Protestant reformers, increasing religious conservatism marked his later years. On the king's death in 1547 his son Henry II (1519–59) inherited a country politically united but riven by religious intolerance.

Above: The Royal Château at Chambord exemplifies French Renassaince architecture with its distinctive blend of medieval structure and classical Italian form. The largest château in the Loire valley, it was built for Francis I as a hunting lodge. The original design by Domenico da Cortona was altered considerably during the 20-year construction (1519–39). Leonardo da Vinci, a guest of the king, is thought to have also been involved in the original design. When Chambord was almost completed, Francis hosted his old enemy Emperor Charles V here to show off this enormous symbol of his wealth and power.

The Battle of Pavia, 1525

Pavia was the most decisive land battle of the Renaissance, the climactic engagement of the Italian Wars. Hailed as the first modern battle, Pavia witnessed the final demise of the mounted knight and the triumph of firepower.

In late October 1524 Milan fell to the French, but a combination of Francis's over-confidence and the presence of plague encouraged his commanders to move south, undertaking a siege of Pavia, the second-largest city in the duchy. As

Above: Although unattributed, this painting by an unknown artist probably represents the battle of Pavia, with the River Po to the left, and the Ticino running across the center. The event depicted appears to show the collapse of the French defense of the Five Abbeys, after which Francis I was taken prisoner by Charles V.

Despite the defeat of his army and loss of Milan in 1522, Francis I was determined to regain control of the duchy, a state that he regarded as his, through dynastic inheritance. Holy Roman Emperor Charles V was equally determined to prevent the French from regaining a foothold in Italy. A French expedition of 1523 was defeated and forced back across the Alps, allowing the Imperialist commander to take the war into France by invading southern Provence. Despite besieging Marseilles, the Imperialists were forced to pull back into Italy, allowing Francis to lead his army back over the Alps and re-enter Italy, the scene of his last military triumph at Marignano some nine years before.

winter set in, the French settled into their camp and siege lines around Pavia, while to the east the Imperialist army was reinforced by German *landsknecht* and Spanish troops.

In January this army marched to Pavia, where the two sides watched each other behind lines of field fortifications. This lasted for three weeks, during which the siege continued and supplies in the city waned. Imperialist commander Charles de Lannoy needed to attack, but a frontal assault against the well-entrenched French would invite annihilation.

The French siege lines were bisected by the Ticino river and by the high walls of a hunting park that extended northward from the city.

Lannoy decided to attempt to breaking into the park from the north; meanwhile a message was smuggled to Antonio de Leyva, commander of the Imperialist garrison in Pavia, asking him to sortie from his defenses when fighting began.

No escape

During the night of February 23–4 the Imperialist army marched north along the outer wall of the park before turning west along its northern boundary, three miles north of the city. Shortly before daybreak Imperialist engineers demolished part of the wall near the Porta Pescarina gate, allowing a specially selected force of Spanish *arquebusiers* to enter the park.

The Porta Pescarina was opened, and the Imperialists marched into the park. Lannoy's men now lay north and east of the main French camp. These skirmishers forged ahead to capture Mirabello hunting lodge, a key position dominating the wide stream that crossed the park. Simultaneously the Pavia garrison emerged, seizing the lower portion of the park and cutting off the two main sections of the French army from each other.

To the north Francis led his aristocratic *gendarmes* in a series of attacks, but despite early success the men-at-arms were halted by concentrated *arquebus* fire. Pinned by infantry to their front, the horsemen were outflanked and surrounded as more Spanish and German infantry arrived. Unable to escape or use their superior mobility, the elite of the French army were slaughtered on the spot, or else captured to provide a lucrative ransom. Francis I was among the prisoners, spared from death by the arrival of Lannoy's staff.

Further to the south the battle was going equally badly for the French. Isolated from their leaders, the Swiss troops caught between the city and the Imperialist entrenchments to the east met the same fate as the *gendarmes*, although for these mercenaries no quarter was asked for nor given.

As the morning mist cleared, the French survivors were in full retreat southward across pontoon bridges that spanned the river. These flimsy structures collapsed under their weight, and thousands were left to drown in the freezing water, or were stranded and captured by their pursuers. The Imperial triumph was complete. In a single morning the strategic situation in Italy had been reversed, and the French were finally driven from Milan. The duchy would remain firmly in the control of the Habsburgs for 250 years.

Below: A contemporary engraving depicts the final moments of the battle of Pavia after the French army was split, and the power of Swiss mercenary arms was overcome by overwhelming numbers of Imperial infantry.

CHAPTER 5:

A World Beyond–Exploration and Empire

Voyages of exploration, 1432–1522

Magellan was credited with leading the first expedition to circumnavigate the globe, although he never reached home. Soon after arriving in the Philippines (Cebu island), the explorer was killed in April 1521 by warriors of Lapulapu, chief of neighboring Mactan island, when the Filipinos refused to convert to Christianity.

NORTH PACIFIC OCEAN

CHINA

INDIA

Goa
Calicut

Malacca

Sumatra
Borneo
Celebes
Java

Philippines

SOUTH PACIFIC OCEAN

New Guinea

AUSTRALIA

New Zealand

of the Ottomans and the complete change of world view occasioned by the discovery of the new continent, America. A century after its discovery, much of South and Central America had been explored, mapped, conquered, and settled. The new lands provided Europeans with incredible resources, and allowed the Spanish to carve out a prosperous overseas empire.

It is worth examining this world view, since it still influences the way the West perceives the rest of the world. The great voyages of discovery did not actually *discover* anything; Norsemen had reached North America in the tenth century, and the Americas already teemed with indigenous and sometimes sophisticated peoples. Some of these, such as the Maya, Aztec, Inca, and Pueblo cultures, had developed extraordinarily complex civilizations. When the Portuguese reached India, they also discovered nothing new—Arabic and Chinese merchants had plied the same eastern sea lanes for centuries.

What the European explorers found were new trade routes, creating a demand for product, profit, and wealth: all the ideals that bring out the best and the worst in people. For every Francis Xavier, there were hundreds of de Gamas who were prepared to plunder then sink the native vessels they encountered. For every Christopher Columbus, there were many Francisco Pizarros, conquistadors prepared to cheat and murder their way to power and wealth. Within a century of its discovery, much of the population of the New World had died of European diseases or been enslaved, but the coffers of Europe's rulers and merchants were filled with American specie.

For all the brilliance of the Italian Renaissance courts, a shadow hung over the continent. The Muslim empire of the Ottoman Turks had expanded during the late Middle Ages, and took Constantinople in 1453. The growth of the Ottoman empire continued for a further two centuries, until half of the Mediterranean was under Turkish domination. While the political and religious effects were considerable, the Ottoman empire also cut off the ancient trade routes from east to west, forcing Europeans to search for new routes to the lucrative Orient.

Perhaps the best example of the ebullience of the age was the way it coped with the emergence

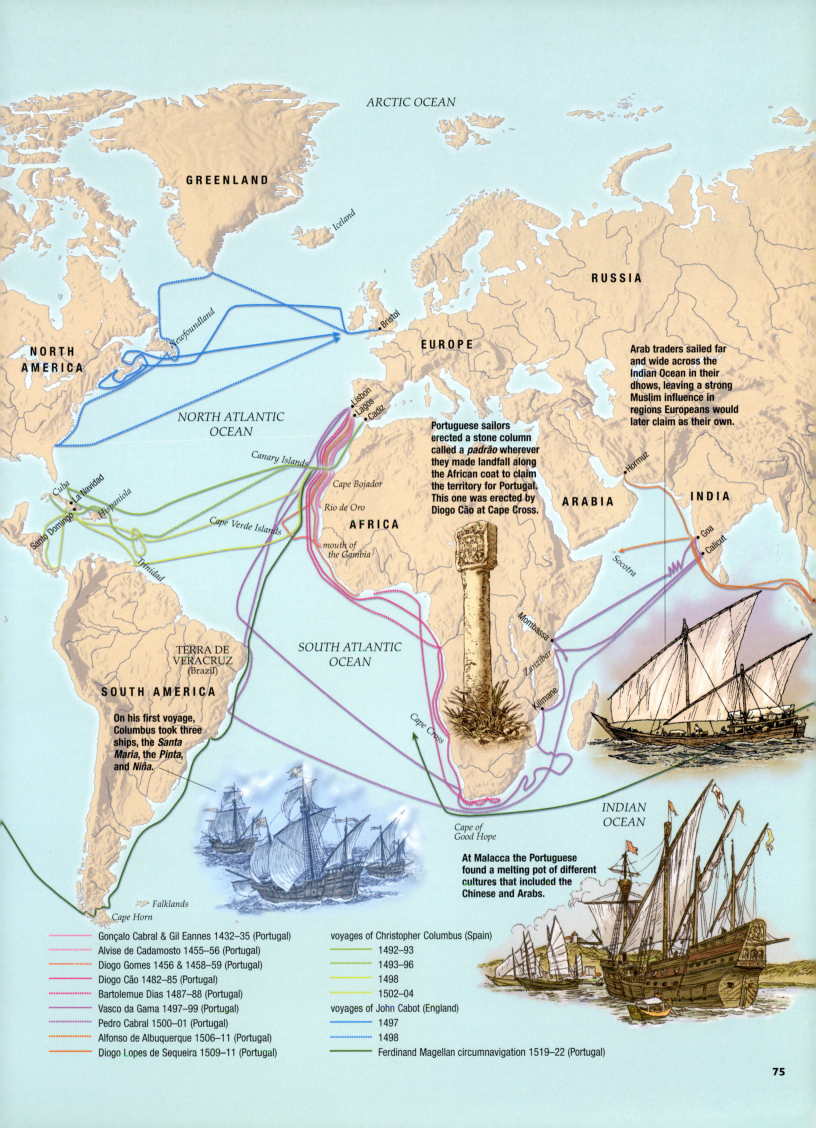

ARCTIC OCEAN

GREENLAND

Iceland

RUSSIA

NORTH
AMERICA

Newfoundland

Bristol

EUROPE

NORTH ATLANTIC
OCEAN

Lisbon
Lagos
Cadiz

Canary Islands

Cape Bojador

Rio de Oro

AFRICA

Arab traders sailed far
and wide across the
Indian Ocean in their
dhows, leaving a strong
Muslim influence in
regions Europeans would
later claim as their own.

Portuguese sailors
erected a stone column
called a *padrão* wherever
they made landfall along
the African coat to claim
the territory for Portugal.
This one was erected by
Diogo Cão at Cape Cross.

Hormuz

ARABIA

INDIA

Goa
Calicut

Socotra

Cuba
La Navidad
Hispaniola

Santo Domingo

Cape Verde Islands

mouth of
the Gambia

Trinidad

TERRA DE
VERACRUZ
(Brazil)

SOUTH AMERICA

On his first voyage,
Columbus took three
ships, the *Santa
Maria*, the *Pinta*,
and *Niña*.

SOUTH ATLANTIC
OCEAN

Mombassa

Zanzibar

Kilimane

Cape Cross

Cape of
Good Hope

INDIAN
OCEAN

At Malacca the Portuguese
found a melting pot of different
cultures that included the
Chinese and Arabs.

Falklands
Cape Horn

Gonçalo Cabral & Gil Eannes 1432–35 (Portugal)
Alvise de Cadamosto 1455–56 (Portugal)
Diogo Gomes 1456 & 1458–59 (Portugal)
Diogo Cão 1482–85 (Portugal)
Bartolemue Dias 1487–88 (Portugal)
Vasco da Gama 1497–99 (Portugal)
Pedro Cabral 1500–01 (Portugal)
Alfonso de Albuquerque 1506–11 (Portugal)
Diogo Lopes de Sequeira 1509–11 (Portugal)

voyages of Christopher Columbus (Spain)
1492–93
1493–96
1498
1502–04
voyages of John Cabot (England)
1497
1498
Ferdinand Magellan circumnavigation 1519–22 (Portugal)

75

The Overland Route to the East

Ottoman expansion was largely furnished by the wealth of trade; goods shipped to the Middle East and Asia Minor from the Orient. While the Portuguese struggled to develop maritime trade routes around Africa, the Turks could rely on land routes that had existed for centuries.

Transporting any commodity over a significant distance had always been an expensive and potentially hazardous enterprise, and this was particularly true in the trade in silks and spices from the Orient. These luxury goods were becoming increasingly popular among the elite of the Ottoman empire. A handful of European merchants braved capture, excessive tariffs, and often the shadow of warfare to trade with the Middle Eastern ports that acted as the termini for this trade. They were pandering to their own new-found markets, encouraged by the rising wealth of Renaissance Europe's nobility and merchant classes. Trade with the Orient was the biggest business venture of the period, and generated the greatest profit.

Europeans were becoming increasingly dependent on spices. Rich and poor, from north and south, everybody wanted the Oriental seasonings that had started to become available— pepper, cinnamon, nutmeg, ginger, cardamom, cloves, and others. The ancient Egyptians and Romans had prized these spices and traded in them, and the demand continued into the Middle Ages, when the Byzantines became the primary importers.

Traditionally, the principal way these spices reached the Mediterranean was by the Silk Road, a trading route that had remained in use for over 1,500 years, taken by Marco Polo when he traveled from Venice to China. The name is relatively modern—it was coined by German geographer Baron Ferdinand von Richthofen (1833–1905) for a collection of routes some 4,000 miles in length, stretching from China to the Mediterranean.

The road stretched for about 2,500 miles through Chinese territory, from the capital of Chang'an (Xian) before splitting to skirt the Taklimakan desert to both north and south. The roads joined before crossing Iran, and either ended on the eastern shores of the Mediterranean at Antioch or curved through Asia

Below: A caravan tracks the wastes of the Taklimakan desert near Dunhuang, China, as they have done for centuries. The rise of the Ottoman empire cut the trade route to the East for Renaissance Europe and prompted a flurry of seaborne exploration to get around the blockade.

The overland trade route between the Far East and Europe

Ottoman empire, 16th century
major components of the Silk Road

The Ottomans controlled the ancient European-Far East trade routes

EUROPE • Antwerp
Genoa • • Venice
MEDITERRANEAN SEA
Constantinople
Aleppo
Damascus
Alexandria
AFRICA
ARABIA
Baghdad
Qum
Nishapur
SAFAVID EMPIRE
Balkh
Bukhara
Samarkand
Tashkent • Kashgar
Balasaghun
Taklimakan Desert
Khotan
Tibetan Plateau
HIMALAYAS
SULTANATE OF DELHI
INDIA
Ürümqi
Ningxia
Datong
Dadu (Beijing)
Chang'an
CHINA
THE GREAT KHANATE

Minor to reach Constantinople (Istanbul). Alternative routes included transport along the Arabian coast to Egypt, then down the River Nile. On its route across Asia it passed through fabled cities such as Samarkand and Kashgar, both made famous by Marco Polo.

Market forces

China kept the secret of silk production from the west until the sixth century, when the Byzantines developed their own silk industry. Italy began silk production in the 13th century, when 2,000 weavers moved from Constantinople in the wake

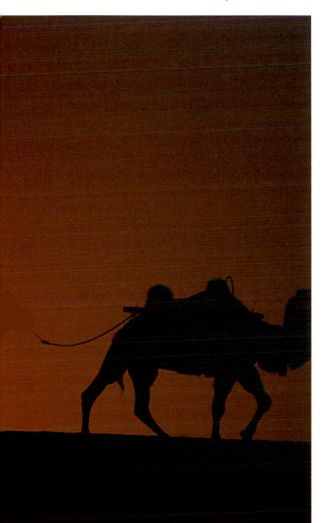

of the sack of the city by crusaders in 1204. Both these new sources undercut the market for Chinese silks, but China maintained a reputation for producing the highest quality textiles.

Trade along the Silk Road reached its peak during the 13th century, when silk, gold, jade, tea, and spices were transported westward. Few of these commodities came directly along it, since many were traded along the route as Chinese merchants sold their goods to Indians, Indians to Persians, Persians to Byzantines, and finally the Byzantines sold the goods to other Europeans. In addition to luxury goods, the Silk Road served as a conduit for ideas; paper, gunpowder, the magnetic compass, the printing press, and mathematics were all stimulated by ideas emmanating from the east.

The rise of the Ottoman Turks and their conquest of the Byzantine empire (*see pages 86–7*) cut the west off from the Orient. It was vital that the West should find an alternative to the now-blocked Silk Road. The new spirit of learning sponsored in the Renaissance and supported by captured Arabic geographic knowlege inspired European princes to fund naval exploration on a scale never before contemplated. The goal—find a sea route to the Indies and the wealth of the Orient.

History accords Christopher Columbus with the first great discoveries, but in fact the Portuguese were well ahead of him, adventuring down the West African coast some 60 years before his "discovery" of America. Portuguese determination to forge a maritime way to the Indies was so successful that by the 16th century the Silk Road was all but finished as an overland trade route; from that point the wealth of the Orient would be transported in the holds of European sailing ships.

A Sea Route to the Indies

In 1477 the publication of Marco Polo's *Book of Marvels* inspired a generation of Europeans with tales of the wonders and riches of the Orient. Together with the breaking of traditional boundaries imposed by feudalism, religion, and geography, it created a wave of explorers.

Above: A man with a true claim to being a Renaissance prince, Henry the Navigator built a school of navigation and commissioned sailors to explore and open up Portugal's trade routes to the Far East.

Venetian merchant Marco Polo (c.1254–1324) traveled to China and gained prominence in the Chinese court of Kublai Khan. He returned to Venice in 1295 and wrote of his experiences two years later, while languishing in a Genoese prison after being captured in a sea battle. The eventual publication of the account came at a time when advances in technology made long-distance voyages possible. The advancement of ship design, improvements in navigation and chart-making, and the perfection of the magnetic compass provided the basic tools of exploration. The astrolabe gave mariners some idea of their latitude, and monarchs were prepared to fund expeditions, inspired by the humanist quest for knowledge and a very ordinary desire for riches.

The first of these patrons was Prince Henry

the Navigator of Portugal (1394–1460). Henry, the youngest of four sons of King John I, had helped organize the invasion fleet when Portugal attacked the Moorish North African port of Ceuta in 1414. The city, which fell after a fierce struggle, lay on the edge of a trading network that spanned much of Muslim Africa. The Portuguese were able to gather valuable economic and geographic information that would help in their effort to extend the Portuguese trading sphere. Prince Henry's contribution to this drive was to found a center of maritime study at Sagres, a peninsula on the southwestern tip of Portugal, which soon became a training ground for a new breed of Portuguese mariners.

In 1432, under Henry's sponsorship, Gonçalo Cabral went west and made a landfall on Santa Maria in the Azores and subsequently discovered the Canary Islands and Madeira, which provided the launch-pad for longer voyages. In 1434 Gil Eannes sailed down the Moroccan coast to the feared Cape Bojador, and went some 200 miles beyond it. A civil war halted exploration until 1455, when a Venetian merchant, Alvise da Cadamosto, made landfall at Cape Blanc, 300 miles south of the Tropic of Cancer. Further to the south he reached the island of Arguim and then the mouth of the Senegal river, before sailing on to Cape Verde and the estuary of the Gambia river. In 1458 Diogo Gomes reached Cape Palmas, which marks the place where the coast curves east into the Gulf of Guinea and the Bight of Benin. When Gomes returned to Portugal Prince Henry was on his deathbed; the royal navigator died in the following year before he saw the greatest Portuguese successes. But he had opened the door to the Indies and after his death Portuguese exploration continued apace. Fernão Gomes was given the monopoly on trade with most of Africa in exchange for exploring a prescribed amount of coastline each year, advancing from Sierra Leone in 1469 to just across the equator by 1474 (a voyage undertaken by Lopo Gonçalves).

Discovery and exploitation

Bartolemeu Dias (c.1450–1500) followed the African coast southward and discovered the Cape of Good Hope, and beyond it the eastern coast of Africa. Vasco da Gama (c.1460–1524) led the first Portuguese expedition to India in 1497–99,

Next Albuquerque sent out the first Portuguese expedition to the Moluccas under Antonio de Abreu. Albuquerque died in 1515, but the expansion of the Portuguese trading empire continued, reaching China in 1517. Borneo and Japan followed (1524 and 1543).

In the wake of the traders came missionaries. One of the first was the Spaniard St. Francis Xavier (1506–52), "the Apostle of the Indies." Sent to Goa as a missionary in 1542, Xavier went on to Malacca, the Moluccas, Ceylon, and eventually Japan.

Left: 16th-century print of Vasco da Gama in his latter years when he served as a colonial administrator.

Below: A statue of Bartolemeu Dias stands at Swellendam in the country he discovered for Portugal—South Africa.

establishing a new sea route from Europe to the Indies via the Cape of Good Hope. It was during a similar trip that Pedro Cabral (c.1467–c.1520) accidentally discovered Brazil (1500) while swinging west into the Atlantic to take advantage of the prevailing Trade Winds.

Francisco de Almeida (c.1450–1510) became the first Portuguese viceroy of India in 1505. Setting up his headquarters in Cochin, he fought the sultan of Egypt and Indian rulers to win Portuguese domination of the area in 1508. Portugal became the dominant European power in the east and would remain so for a century.

The second and greatest Portuguese viceroy of India was Alfonso de Albuquerque (1453–1515). Under his aegis Portugal consolidated the position gained by Almeida. First, he conquered the Arabic island of Socotra and Hormuz in 1507. This gave Portugal some control over the Red Sea and, therefore, the trade route between India and the Mediterranean. In 1510 he took Goa, which would later become a major Portuguese center, and then in 1511 Malacca— the most important port on the route to China.

Columbus–Captain of the Ocean Sea

While the Portuguese tried to find the Orient by sailing east, other explorers reasoned that they could reach the Indies by heading west, since the earth was a sphere, a point demonstrated by both humanist scholars (working from classical texts) and the writings of Marco Polo. The result was the discovery of America, a turning point in world history.

Born into a humble family, Columbus followed the Genoese tradition of seafaring, and in his youth is reputed to have ventured as far afield as West Africa. By 1470–71 he was an experienced mariner and navigator based in Lisbon, and in 1475 he married Doña Felipa Moniz, who bore him a son (Diego) the following year. As early as 1474 Columbus had tried to find a patron to subsidize an exploration to find a passage to the Indies by sailing westward. Unable to find a Portuguese sponsor, he continued lobbying in Spain, while his brother Bartolomeo (who would accompany Columbus on his later voyages) tried to find a patron in France or England.

Columbus's fortunes changed after the capture of Granada from the Moors (1492). He reputedly convinced Father Juan Perez, the confessor of Queen Isabella at the Dominican convent of La Rábida, who lobbied Isabella. By April 1492, Columbus had his royal sponsor. He left Palos in southern Spain on August 3, 1492. He and 50 others sailed in his flagship *Santa Maria*, a lumbering square-sailed merchant carrack of around a hundred tons. She was accompanied by the caravels *Niña* and *Pinta*, faster lateen-rigged vessels of a type used by Portuguese explorers, captained by Andalucian brothers Vicente and Martín Alonso Pinzón.

The first port of call was Spain's most westerly territory, the Canary Islands. On September 6, 1492 they headed west into uncharted waters. As the days passed without sight of land, the crew grew increasingly uneasy. All but Columbus were prepared to give up, when an island was sighted on October 12, part of the group we now know as the Bahamas. In front of incredulous islanders, Columbus claimed the land in the name of Ferdinand and Isabella of Spain.

The first Spanish settlement in the New World was La Isabella on Hispaniola (modern Haiti and the Dominican Republic), named in honor of the Spanish queen. Columbus began to explore the local waters, but his voyage was cut short on Christmas Eve 1492 when the *Santa Maria* ran aground on a reef. She broke up the following day. Salvaging what they could, the crew built a fort from her timbers, which they called La Navidad (Christmas). Columbus left some 40 men there to await his return from Spain, then sailed home with his remaining ships. He reached Lisbon on March 4 and Palos on March 15, 1493.

Diminished returns

This first transatlantic voyage of discovery was an incredible success, and Ferdinand and Isabella happily provided the wherewithal for an even larger expedition; 17 ships, over a thousand men, plus livestock. Columbus left Spain and reached La Navidad on November 28, 1493, only to find that some of his men had been killed by local tribesmen. At La Isabella he fell ill and his captains argued over what to do next. In June 1496 the expedition returned home, having achieving nothing but maintain a fragile colony.

Columbus made two more expeditions to the Americas, a land he still thought was part of the [East] Indies, but neither was successful in finding a passage to the west from the western Caribbean. He returned to Spain in November 1504 and died in Valladolid on May 20, 1506. In death Columbus was as peripatetic as in life, since his body was shipped to Hispaniola. It was later moved to Cuba before returning to Seville in the early 20th century.

John Cabot (c.1450–1499), an Italian who became a naturalized Englishman, was another who sought a western route. He was commissioned by Bristol merchants to search for a northwest passage to the Indies past the newly discovered fishing grounds of Newfoundland. Henry VII commissioned Cabot's son Sebastian to do the same. Others followed, and as it quickly became clear that the New World was not the Indies, merchants exploited this new continent instead. For example, French merchants commissioned the Florentine explorer Giovanni da Verrazano to sail to Newfoundland and lay the foundations for a fur trade, a lucrative business that soon led to French colonization of what would later become Canada.

By the mid-16th century it was clear that the Portuguese were the winners in this race for discovery, and it was they who shipped the spices and silks of the Indies to the growing European marketplaces. However, while most Portuguese explorers and Catholic missionaries were peaceable, other Europeans were more inclined to win overseas territories at the point of a sword in search of new things to trade: land, furs, gold, and silver. The economies of the European maritime states quickly became dependent on this wealth from the New World, beginning the process that would lead to exploitation, colonization, and the birth of new nations in the Americas.

Above: Engraving of Columbus's flagship *Santa Maria*, by the Dutch draftsman and writer Johannes Stradanus (1523–1604).

Facing: Portrait of Christopher Columbus by the renowned mannerist artist Sebastiano del Piombo (1485–1547). This painting depicts Columbus at his peak, the successful explorer fêted by the Spanish court. However, this second of his portraits was probably painted several years after Columbus's death, from studies prepared earlier, since del Piombo painted an earlier one of the older and more gloomy Columbus in about 1504.

Spain's Overseas Empire

On June 7, 1494, Pope Alexander VI divided the New World between Castille and Portugal, thereby recognizing Spain's right to almost all the lands in the New World. While the Portuguese controlled Brazil and the route to the Indies, the Spanish exploited the resources of the new continent.

Below: Made in Antwerp in 1570, this remarkably detailed map shows the islands and seas of the West Indies, with Florida at the top and Cuba at the center. Below it is Jamaica and Hispaniola at the lower right edge.

Pope Alexander's dividing line ran along a meridian passing a hundred leagues to the west of the Cape Verde islands. All new lands to the east belonged to Portugal, while those to the west belonged to Spain, an arrangement ratified by the Treaty of Tordesillas (1494). In 1506, following further discoveries, a new agreement was reached, approving a demarcation line that would run about 50 degrees west of the Greenwich Meridian. This gave Africa and Asia to Portugal, and the New World to Spain (with the exception of Brazil, which still lay to the west of the line).

The Spanish overseas empire left an undying legacy in the form of its Roman Catholic religion and the Spanish language. Already the second language in the USA, Spanish is now spoken by more than 350 million native speakers worldwide, particularly in South and Central America, the heartland of Spain's old overseas empire.

Explored in the wake of Columbus, the first settlers were followed by soldiers and adventurers. Between 1500 and 1700 Spain would conquer most of the lands of South and Central America, and launch forays into the deserts of North America. While north European colonies were struggling for survival on the east coast of America's Atlantic seaboard, Spain established an empire that would last until the independence movements of the early 19th century and the Spanish American War of 1898.

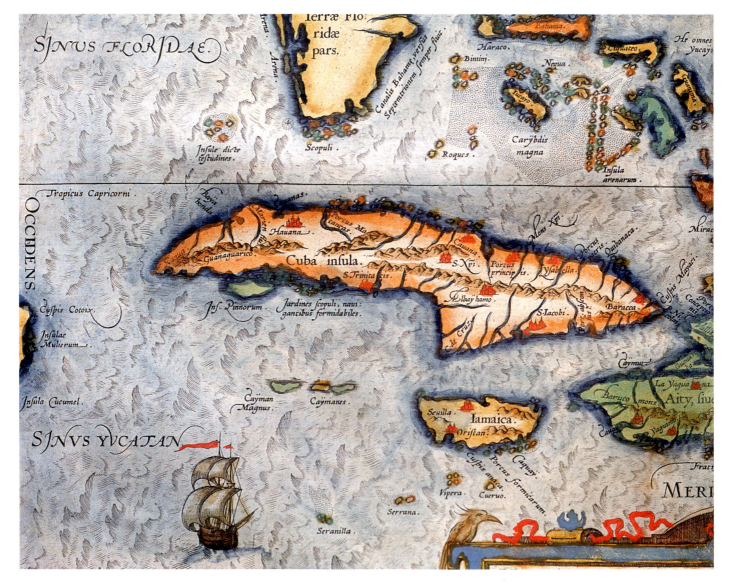

Left: Many of the explorers who followed Columbus were more interested in accruing wealth than in colonization. One of the most infamous was Vasco Núñez de Balboa, whose main achievement was to cross the Isthmus of Panama and, in 1513, become the first European to see the Pacific Ocean. Theodor de Bry's engraving seen here was included in *La Historia del Mondo Nuovo* of 1565, and depicts Balboa extracting a ransom to free Tubanama, a chieftain of the region who the conquistadors seized on their return journey to the Caribbean.

If the driving force for exploration was mercantile, looking for trading opportunities in the east, that for empire was the quest for specie. Columbus searched the Caribbean for gold, while later explorers discovered the metal in New Spain (Mexico) and Ecuador. Even more abundant was silver, cast from mines in Mexico and especially Peru, where whole "silver mountains" were discovered near Potosi (*see map, page 123*). This silver was used to fund the empire and provide the resources and impetus for further exploration, conquest, and colonization.

Funding an empire

The Spanish crown needed silver to pay the bankers who financed their interests in Europe, allowing Spain to play a leading role in European politics and maintain a sizeable army. A fifth of everything produced was sent back to the royal coffers. The Spanish Habsburgs dominated Renaissance Europe, and Spanish hegemony held sway from the Netherlands to Italy, an Old World empire funded by stolen New World wealth.

To ensure that the silver mines produced a regular income, Spanish officials created a well organized bureaucracy in the New World, run by viceroys, who were the crown's representatives with civil and military power. The territories were divided into the Viceroy of New Spain (Central America and the Caribbean islands) and that of Peru (South America). Each viceroy was advised by *audiencias*, councils that also acted as the judiciary of the colonial government. This system was an adjunct of the Council of the Indies based in Seville, the royal body that regulated all production and trade with the Spanish Americas.

The viceroys also controlled the growing Spanish settlements in the New World, whose population of colonists, clerics, and soldiers provided the ruling and entrepreneurial classes in the Americas, while the work was done by native slaves. It has been estimated that over nine million native Americans died in servitude during this period.

The *flota* (fleet) system ensured regular sailings by Spanish treasure galleons from Seville to the New World and back again. Settlers, conquistadors, and European luxuries went out, and specie returned, making Seville one of the richest ports in Europe. Regulated convoys became necessary as European interlopers appeared in the waters of the New World; English, Dutch, and French privateers eager for a share of the riches of the "Spanish Main" (Caribbean basin). This threat increased during the 16th century, as did Spanish dependency on the safe arrival of the annual *flota*.

Age of the Conquistadors

By 1492 the Spanish had cleared the Iberian peninsula of the Moors during the Reconquista, and these conquistadors would transport their crusading zeal to the Americas, where the rewards for their endeavors were immeasurable.

Right: The common conquistador's helemet became a familiar, feared sight to the natives of Central and South America.

Below: A portion of a map of South America, from a Spanish atlas of 1582. Like the map on the previous page, this shows the level of accuracy Renaissance cartography had already achieved with only primitive instruments.

Conquistadors (from the Spanish for "conquerors") were usually *hidalgos*, a term derived from *Hijo de algo* ("son of someone"); gentlemen adventurers and landless nobles who saw military glory as a path to fame and fortune. Most were Castilians whose military laurels were first won during the Reconquista (reconquest). After 1492 they looked to the New World for enrichment.

The first conquest in the New World was the island of Hispaniola. It was from Hispaniola that Juan Ponce de León conquered Puerto Rico in 1508 and Diego Velasquez de Cuellar took Cuba in 1511–19. The first settlement on the mainland was at Darién in the Panama isthmus, settled by Vasco Nuñez de Balboa in 1512, the man who discovered the Pacific Ocean.

The achievements of these early conquistadors were nothing compared to the two titans of New World conquest, Hernán Cortés (1485–1547) and Francisco Pizarro (1471–1541). Born in Medellin, Spain, Cortés studied unsuccessfully to be a lawyer at Salamanca, and took part in the conquest of Hispaniola and Cuba, for which he

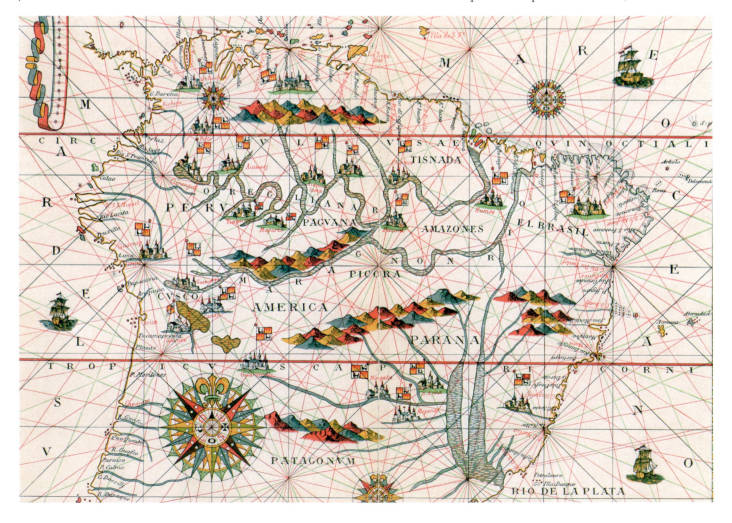

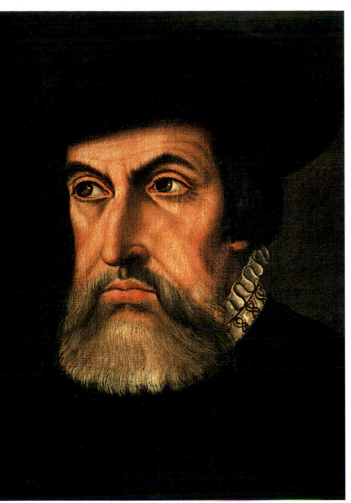

received a large estate. He sold or mortgaged it to buy ships and supplies for an expedition, sanctioned by the island governor, Diego Velasquez de Cuellar.

In 1518 Cortés set out from Cuba with 500 men, ten guns, and 17 horses. He landed on the Yucatán peninsula, took Tabasco, and founded the settlement of Vera Cruz. From there he subdued Tlaxacala, whose inhabitants were forced to become his allies. The Spanish technology of crossbows, steel swords, horses, and firearms were overwhelmingly superior to that of his enemies, enabling Cortés to live up to the native belief that he was Quetzalcoatl, a legendary man-god.

A just fate

Cortés reached the Aztec capital of Tenochtitlán, on November 8, 1519, where the Aztec king Montezuma II welcomed him and acquiesced to his demands for gold. The inhabitants killed Montezuma for his weak leadership and, on July 1, 1520 Cortés had to fight his way to safety, losing many of his men in the process. He returned a year later to besiege the city. After capturing it he razed it to the ground.

In its place he founded Mexico City, from where he ruled as governor and captain-general of New Spain from 1522 to 1528. He sent out expeditions to Guatemala (1524–25) and led an expedition through Guatemala to Honduras

(1525–26). Cortés sailed back to Spain in 1528, and though he would return to Mexico as captain-general in 1530, exploring Baja California in 1532–36, his health failed him and he returned to Spain in 1540, dying in Seville seven years later. His remains were reinterred in Mexico City in 1629.

Francisco Pizarro, the conqueror of Peru, was born in Trujillo, central Spain. He served with Vasco Nuñez de Balboa during his explorations of Panama in 1510–19 and was present when Balboa first saw the Pacific. He sailed for Ecuador in 1526 with Diego de Almagro, when he first heard about the Inca. Both men returned five years later (1531) with an army of conquest. As archetypal conquistadors, Pizarro and Almagro lived and died by the sword. They took the Inca kingdom by treachery, capturing Atahualpa, the Inca ruler, accepting an enormous ransom for him and then killing him anyway, but Pizarro was assassinated by a follower of his erstwhile friend.

Diego de Almagro had unsuccessfully searched the Chilean desert for gold and returned to Peru to find the colony gripped by civil war. In the ensuing struggle Pizarro's brothers defeated and executed Almagro, but his followers took their revenge and the Pizarros were also killed before the colony was re-unified. Peru later became the principal source of Spanish wealth and power in the Americas.

The mean-spirited scourges of Central and South America, Hernán Cortés (**left**) and Francisco Pizarro (**above**).

Rise of the Ottoman Empire

From the obscure mountains of Anatolia in modern day Turkey, the Ottoman successors to the Seljuks arose to dispossess the thousand-year-old Byzantine empire. They captured Constantinople in 1453 and threatened the very survival of European Christendom.

Right: Mehmet II bore a striking similarity in character to the Renaissance princes he faced—educated and cultured, he nevertheless secured his throne by the murder of his infant half-brother. Illustration after a contemporary engraving.

The term "Ottoman" is a western corruption of the original Turkish name Osmanli, derived from the name of the dynasty's founder, Osman. Sultan Osman and his nomadic followers establishing an agrarian refuge in Anatolia (Asia Minor) around the 12th and 13th centuries. By the time the Seljuk Turkish state that ruled the Middle East fell into decline in the mid-14th century, the Ottomans controlled a small but resilient military state, one of a number in the region that vied for survival and supremacy. Within a few decades the Ottomans had emerged victorious, and by 1400 had extended their influence over much of Anatolia and even into Byzantine territory in eastern Europe, notably Macedonia and Bulgaria.

Their success was built on military supremacy, but also relied on the disunity and military

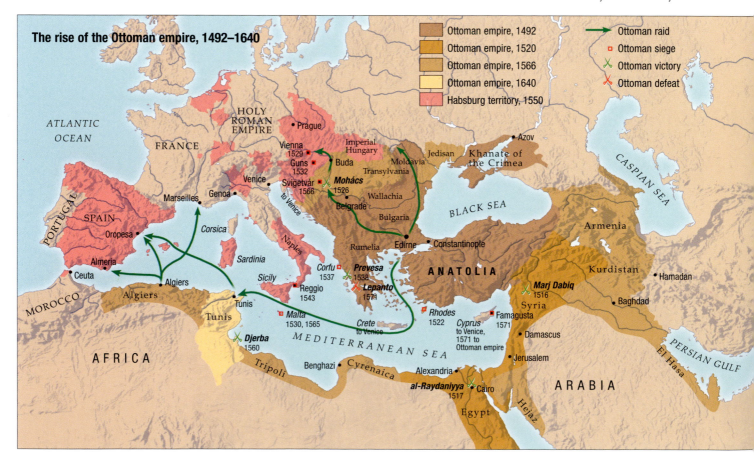

The rise of the Ottoman empire, 1492–1640

- Ottoman empire, 1492
- Ottoman empire, 1520
- Ottoman empire, 1566
- Ottoman empire, 1640
- Habsburg territory, 1550
- → Ottoman raid
- □ Ottoman siege
- ✗ Ottoman victory
- ✗ Ottoman defeat

ATLANTIC OCEAN · FRANCE · HOLY ROMAN EMPIRE · Prague · Vienna 1529 · Guns 1532 · Buda · Imperial Hungary · Azov · Jedisan · Khanate of the Crimea · CASPIAN SEA · Venice · Svigetvár 1566 · Mohács 1526 · Moldavia · Transylvania · Marseilles · Genoa · Belgrade · Wallachia · BLACK SEA · Armenia · PORTUGAL · SPAIN · Corsica · Naples · Bulgaria · Rumelia · Edirne · Constantinople · Oropesa · Sardinia · Corfu 1537 · Prevesa 1538 · ANATOLIA · Kurdistan · Hamadan · Almeria · Sicily · Lepanto 1571 · Marj Dabiq 1516 · Ceuta · Algiers · Reggio 1543 · Syria · Baghdad · MOROCCO · Algiers · Tunis · Rhodes 1522 · Famagusta 1571 · Damascus · Tunis · Malta 1530, 1565 · Crete to Venice · Cyprus to Venice, 1571 to Ottoman empire · PERSIAN GULF · El Hasa · Djerba 1560 · MEDITERRANEAN SEA · AFRICA · Jerusalem · Tripoli · Benghazi · Cyrenaica · Alexandria · al-Raydaniyya 1517 · Cairo · ARABIA · Egypt · Hejaz

1297	1394–1460	1453	1479	1492	1493	1494	1497
Venetian Marco Polo writes of his travels in China; published 180 years later they inspire explorers	Life of Prince Henry the Navigator, who sponsors Portugeuse exploration	Ottoman Turks take Constantinople and use it as a base to expand their empire and trade routes	Venice pays the Ottoman empire for trading rights in the Black Sea	While searching for a route to the Indies for the Spanish, Genoan Christopher Columbus discovers America	Founding of Hispaniola, the first Spanish settlement in the Americas	The Treaty of Tordesillas divides new territories between Spain (west) and Portugal (east)	Venetian John Cabot is the first European to make landfall in North America since the Vikings

weakness of their adversaries. A superbly efficient military organization, the well-appointed Ottoman army including the sultan's personal troops (the feared Corps of Janissaries), supported by a levy of regional militia, a powerful artillery train, and a well-trained staff.

The Ottomans defeated their enemies at Kosovo (1389) and Nikopol (1396), driving the Byzantines back toward their capital. From this point they crossed into Greece and Thrace, then advanced steadily toward central Europe, where the Balkans would become the new battleground between Christian and Muslim. In 1402, the Ottoman's capital was moved from Asia Minor to Edirne (Adrianople) in European Greece, where it posed a direct threat to Constantinople. The Byzantine empire had been crippled by fellow Christians during the Fourth Crusade. In 1204 its capital Constantinople fell to the rapacious crusaders, and had barely recovered by the time the Ottomans appeared on their eastern borders.

A magnificent achievement

Somehow the Byzantines resisted Ottoman expansion, and Constantinople became a bulwark of Christianity stemming the tide of Islam. However, the world changed in 1451, when the young Sultan Mehmet II (1430–81) succeeded his father to the Turkish throne. Fearing court intrigues, he decided to occupy his potential enemies by launching an assault on Constantinople. By March 1453 Mehmet was ready and his army laid siege. Constantinople's landward side was protected by an immense city wall, defended by a garrison of 7,000 men, while smaller walls ran along the city's waterfront. The suburb of Galata across the Golden Horn was also fortified, and a boom stretched between the two sides of the inlet. Beyond the boom Turkish galleys patrolled the Bosphorus.

For two weeks the siege guns bombarded the outer wall, then in late April the Turks hauled a squadron of galleys overland around Galata and floated them in the Golden Horn. This raised the possibility of an outflanking attack against the city's weak northern defenses, but Mehmet saved his forces for a frontal assault against the main wall. Finally in late May his gunners and engineers decided the breaches in the wall were large enough for an assault to be made, and the order was given for a full-scale attack to be launched early in the morning of May 29. The defenders were overwhelmed and Turks flooded into the city. The last Byzantine emperor died with his troops, and the victors ran riot. The following morning the sultan entered the fallen city, marking the end of an empire that had lasted for over a thousand years.

Europe was devastated by the news of Constantinople's fall, but with a divided Church and warring secular rulers, no counterattack was launched. Instead the Turks were given the opportunity to build on their success. Mehmet moved his capital to the city, which was later renamed Istanbul. From this secure base he continued his expansion into Europe

Above: A 16th-century church fresco depicts the siege of Constantinople by the Ottoman Turks in 1453.

Enemy at the Gates—the Turkish Threat

The fall of Constantinople caused European powers to realize the seriousness of the threat posed by the expansion of the Ottoman Turkish empire. From that point on, Christian and Turk would be locked in a battle for survival in eastern Europe and the Mediterranean.

Facing: A Venetian portrait by Titian of Suleiman the Magnificent, who brought Europe to its knees, but ironically helped to support the Protestant cause.

For nearly three decades Mehmet continued the remorseless expansion of his empire into Europe. Despite defeats at the hands of the Serbians (1456), Albanians (1457), and Wallachians (1462), he maintained pressure on the Balkan states to the north and east of his new European base at Istanbul. By wearing down his opponents through superior numbers and relentless campaigning, Mehmet brought Serbia under Ottoman control (1459), followed by Greece two years later. In the next two decades, Albania, Bosnia, and Herzegovina were brought into the Ottoman empire.

By 1477, smoke from burning Christian villages in Croatia could reputedly be seen from the rooftops of Venice, and by the time the sultan died in 1481 only a handful of Venetian enclaves remained in Christian hands on the eastern and northern shores of the Adriatic. Fortunately, Mehmet's successor Bayazid II (r.1481–1512) showed little desire to leave his court and Europe was granted a respite.

To a large extent, Ottoman success was a result

of Islamic fervor; the crusading zeal that had caused such suffering in the Middle East during the medieval period was being unleashed on the former zealots. However, the same fervor was also shown against fellow Muslims. When the Shah of Persia imposed Shi'ism on his subjects by force, Ottoman Sultan Selim I (r.1512–20) took up the banner of Sunni orthodoxy and invaded Persia.

Unable to make much impression on the Persians, Selim's troops turned their attention to Syria and Egypt, which were conquered in 1516–17. Ottoman expansion continued along the north African coast, the piratical city-states of Tunis and Algiers soon recognizing Turkish suzerainty. To the east expansion continued at a slower rate, but in 1534 Suleiman I the Magnificent (r.1520–66) conquered Iraq and entered Baghdad in triumph.

A grueling task

With his eastern conquest partly secured, Suleiman launched a series of attacks westward into Europe and the central Mediterranean. He captured Belgrade in 1521 and Budapest five years later, and then defeated Louis II of Hungary at the battle of Mohács in 1526, an event that had consequences for the consolidation of the Holy Roman Empire (*see page 155*). The Christian enclave of Rhodes was besieged and captured in 1521 and, with the support of the Barbary pirates of Tunis and Algiers, Ottoman warships threatened the sea lanes of Italy, France, and Spain. This maritime threat continued until the late 16th century, when Ottoman defeats at Malta (1565) and Lepanto (1571) halted further expansion.

Suleiman was a master of European politics. He supported the Protestants in their stance against the Roman Catholic Church, in an attempt to destabilize his Mediterranean rivals; it can even be argued that without Ottoman help Protestantism might never have succeeded. After the victory at Mohács, Suleiman occupied Buda (the city twinned with Pest on the Danube's eastern bank), and rather than annex Hungary, he elected to transform it into a satellite state, ruled by the Transylvanian noble John Zapolya. The kingdom was soon rocked by civil war, Zapolya's

faction losing control of most of it to Ferdinand of Habsburg, brother of Emperor Charles V. Pausing only to arrange a secret anti-Habsburg alliance with the French king Francis I (1528), Suleiman returned to Hungary, recaptured Buda, and advanced up the Danube toward Vienna. By September 1529 the Turks were at the city gates.

For three weeks Suleiman's army laid siege to Vienna, heavy guns bombarding its walls while engineers attempted to undermine the city's defenses. With the onset of winter weather in mid-October, Suleiman decided to abandon the unproductive siege and try his luck the following year. The Turks retired to Buda-Pest and the Austrians followed to besiege the city… with a similar lack of success.

Suleiman renewed his Viennese campaign in spring 1532, but Charles V barred his path with a large army. With victory unattainable, Suleiman made peace with the Holy Roman Emperor and marched back to Istanbul, which gave him the opportunity to complete his conquest of Iraq. While war with the Turks continued throughout the 16th century and the security of Austria was to be threatened again, the westward tide of Ottoman expansion had been stemmed.

Facing: On October 7, 1571 the Christian fleet of the Holy League commanded by John of Austria (d.1578) opposed the Ottoman fleet under Uluç Ali Pasha. The allied fleet of about 200 Spanish, Venetian, and papal galleys was about evenly matched with the Ottomans. But this decisive Christian victory ended the myth of Ottoman naval invincibility. It did not, however, affect Ottoman supremacy on the land. The painting of the battle, which depicts God in heaven blessing the victory, is from the Venetian school of Tintoretto.

CHAPTER 6

Window on the World—the Low Countries

Statues adorn the town hall of Bruges. The Gothic influence was to hold sway for much longer in the Low Countries than in the south of Europe, eventually melding with Italianate forms to create a uniquely northern Renaissance style.

In the 15th century, northern Europe emerged from its feudalism to embrace mercantilism and industrialism. The growth of royal authority in France and Germany gradually had an effect on the Low Countries of Holland and Flanders, regions where resistance to external (often ducal) authority had been a feature of the late medieval period. The rise of the modern state of Burgundy in the 15th century led to clashes between semi-independent cities and their ducal masters, but the collapse of the Burgundian realm following the death of Charles the Bold in 1477 changed the political landscape. From that point, real power lay with the merchants and guild members who dominated the densely populated cities.

Like the Italian states before them, the cities of northern Europe created wealth, and with prosperity came artistic patronage and the encouragement of scholarship. It was a heady time, as overseas horizons were opened by the discovery of the New World and a sea route to the Indies, while the ports of Flanders and Holland played host to shipping from as far afield as Italy, Spain, and the Baltic. By the mid-16th century the economic heart of Europe had moved from the Mediterranean ports of Venice

and Genoa to the Atlantic and North Sea ports. Within decades the Low Countries would become the most vibrant commercial centers on the continent.

Humanist study grew, creating a new spirit of inquiry that threatened to undermine confidence in the Church. This fueled theological debate, encouraged by a general spirit of anti-clericalism and a widespread disapproval of the worldliness of the Latin Church. The result was the Reformation. When this swept northern Europe in the 16th century, the stranglehold of the old Church was broken and replaced by new religious ideas and a fresh motivation for regional unity in the face of growing Catholic opposition. Increasingly, this manifested as conflict between the Habsburg empire and the newly reformed Low Country population—a religious impasse that would last a century.

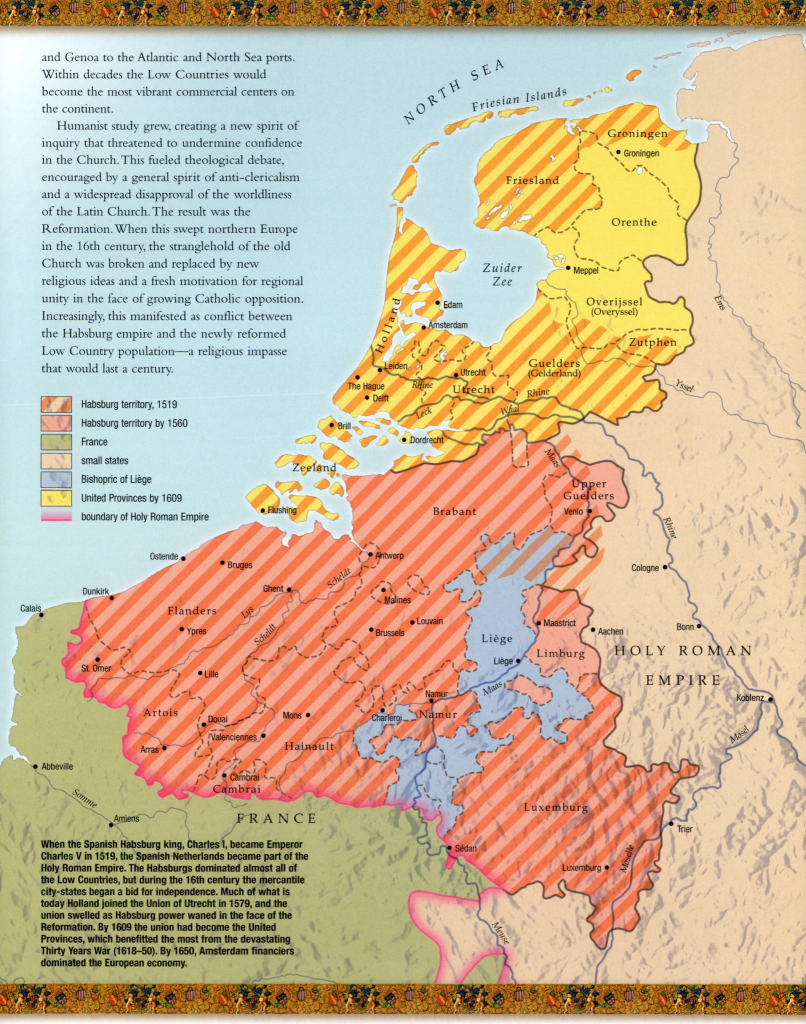

- Habsburg territory, 1519
- Habsburg territory by 1560
- France
- small states
- Bishopric of Liège
- United Provinces by 1609
- boundary of Holy Roman Empire

When the Spanish Habsburg king, Charles I, became Emperor Charles V in 1519, the Spanish Netherlands became part of the Holy Roman Empire. The Habsburgs dominated almost all of the Low Countries, but during the 16th century the mercantile city-states began a bid for independence. Much of what is today Holland joined the Union of Utrecht in 1579, and the union swelled as Habsburg power waned in the face of the Reformation. By 1609 the union had become the United Provinces, which benefitted the most from the devastating Thirty Years War (1618–50). By 1650, Amsterdam financiers dominated the European economy.

The Golden Age of Burgundy

In the late Middle Ages, the Dukes of Burgundy ruled a feudal state on the borders of France and Germany, encompassing provinces of the Low Countries and those stretching southward to Switzerland. Burgundy became a center of excellence, attracting some the finest artists and scholars of the age.

Right: Illumination from a Flemish manuscript of 1473 depicting the court of Charles the Bold.

The Burgundian dynasty was founded by Duke Philip the Bold (r.1364–1404), younger brother of Charles V of France (r.1364–80). He augmented his ducal land by marrying the daughter of the Count of Flanders (1369), which added Flanders, Artois, Nevers, and the Franche Comté to his domains. His son Duke John the Fearless (r.1404–19) continued this policy of expansion, usually at the expense of the French crown, and increasing Burgundy's political and military independence before his murder by French assassins in 1419.

Duke Philip the Good (r.1419–67) turned his back on France and allied himself with the English, who then occupied much of northern France. This gave him the freedom to extend his

domain northward to incorporate the Dutch provinces of Holland and Zealand. When English fortunes waned, Philip transferred his allegiance back to France, ensuring that Burgundy would avoid the consequences of the English defeat in the Hundred Years War.

Unfortunately, Philip was succeeded by the impetuous Charles the Bold (or Rash, r.1467–77), who possessed none of his father's military or diplomatic skills. After fighting a series of largely unsuccessful campaigns against Flemish rebels, he declared war on the Swiss Confederation and marched on Bern. He was defeated at Grandson and Morat (Murten) in 1476, then his army was destroyed at Nancy in an engagement that cost the young duke his life.

The Burgundian domain fell apart. Charles' daughter was married to Maximilian, heir to the Holy Roman Empire, who added the Low Countries to his German domains. King Louis XI of France seized the southern regions of the Franche Comté to complete the dismemberment of a once-vibrant independent state.

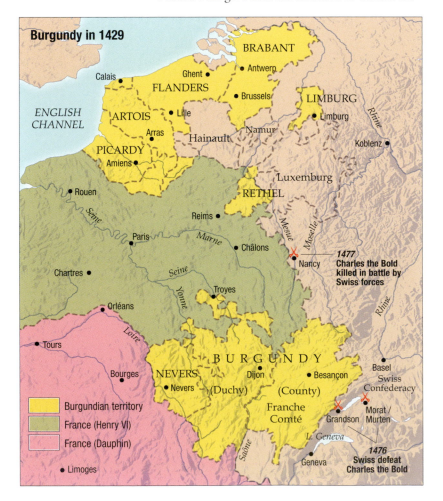

Burgundy in 1429

BRABANT
Antwerp
Calais
Ghent
FLANDERS
Brussels
LIMBURG
Limburg
ENGLISH CHANNEL
ARTOIS
Lille
Arras
Hainault
Namur
Rhine
PICARDY
Amiens
Koblenz
Luxemburg
Rouen
RETHEL
Meuse
Moselle
Seine
Reims
Paris
Marne
Châlons
1477
Nancy
Charles the Bold killed in battle by Swiss forces
Chartres
Seine
Troyes
Rhine
Orléans
Yonne
Tours
B U R G U N D Y
Basel
Bourges
NEVERS
Dijon
Besançon
Swiss Confederacy
Nevers
(Duchy)
(County)
Morat / Murten
Franche Comté
Grandson
L. Geneva
Geneva
1476
Swiss defeat Charles the Bold
Limoges

■ Burgundian territory
■ France (Henry VI)
□ France (Dauphin)

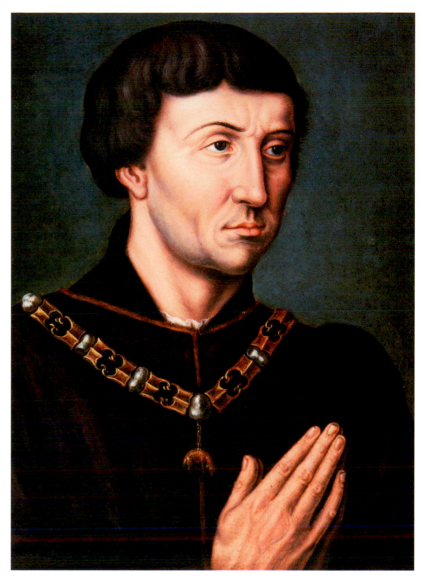

Grand decoration

During its independence, the Burgundian court attracted some of the finest artists and sculptors of the day, turning the ducal seat of Dijon into one of the most influential centers of cultural patronage in Europe, funded by profits from trade in the Low Countries. Melchior Broederlam (c.1355–c.1411) from Ypres worked in the ducal court of Philip the Bold, producing a series of carved altarpieces (including his *Presentation* and *Flight into Egypt*) that displayed an awareness of both Flemish Gothic and early Italian styles. This was particularly apparent in his triptych *The Infancy of Christ*.

The Dutch sculptor Claus Sluter was among those employed by Duke Philip to decorate the Chartreuse de Champol near Dijon (c.1350–1406), whose masterpiece was the calvary and well for the attendant church (known as The Well of Moses); he also decorated its portico and designed Philip's tomb. His work demonstrated a willingness to break with the conformities of contemporary Gothic sculpture, marking a transition from the Late Gothic to the Early Renaissance tradition of northern European religious sculpture. Unlike Italian

sculptors of a generation later, he refused to produce monochrome statues, a convention based on a misguided notion of Greek and Roman practices; like the majority of classical sculptors, Sluter embellished his figures with color, applying both paint and gilding.

The dukes of Burgundy owned several residences scattered throughout the county and the Low Countries. They were enlivened with panel paintings, Flemish tapestries, internal sculptures, elaborate furnishings, and a host of domestic items, such as gold and silver tableware, goblets, and both secular and devotional household objects. Other well-respected artists, such as Flemish painter Henri Bellechose (d.1444) and the Limbourg brothers (*see page 103*), contributed to the splendor of the ducal residences, and to the ornamentation of Burgundian places of worship. The resultant Burgundian Court Style was an amalgam of the best elements of the Late Gothic artistic movement with the first flourishing of new artistic styles from Italy.

Above: Portrait of Charles the Bold. His rash and futile attempt to seize the Swiss Confederation resulted in the loss of Burgundian power, and opened the way for the Habsburgs to take control of the Low Countries and a large part of France.

Above left: *Virgin and Child* by Claus Sluter, one of the early beneficiaries of new Renaissance patronage in Flanders.

A Gradual Revolution

Until the middle of the 15th century, the Renaissance had been limited to Italy. However, when humanism took root beyond the Alps, the scholars of the northern Renaissance went further than their Italian counterparts.

From around 1460, humanist scholarship began to influence northern Europe. To some extent this classical revival was inspired by migrant scholars, diplomats, and courtiers who ventured across the Alps from Italy, coinciding with the collapse of the Burgundian realm and the absorption of the Low Countries into the Holy Roman Empire. At the same time as the political landscape changed, so too did the way people viewed their surroundings.

The Low Countries had little need of an artistic Renaissance, since they evolved in their own unique way as the 15th century progressed, shedding their medieval roots to create an independent artistic style. The Italian Renaissance would influence northern European art later, with the migration of Italians seeking safety and patronage away from the war-weary city-states. In northern Europe, Italian influence was more directly felt in its encouragement of humanist thought. Humanist scholars studied the classics to find ethic and moral standards with which to govern contemporary society. This inevitably involved the discussion of theology, and brought into question the long-held interpretation of the Bible as expounded by the Church.

Unlike their counterparts in Italy, northern humanists began to criticize Church corruption and worldliness, and were prepared to call into question the scholasticism underpinning many existing religious ceremonies and practices, which they dubbed superstitious and illogical. This came during the closing decades of the 15th century and the first two decades of the 16th, a period marked by significant social, political, and economic changes. It was also an era when the Low Countries and their neighbors absorbed the full cultural impact of the Renaissance.

Houses of knowledge

Like the Italian city-states, the cities of Flanders and the Netherlands were highly developed trading centers, set amid an extensive network of land and sea routes. The region was prosperous, and although it lacked the rigid control that a succession of Valois kings was attempting to

impose on France, it had a hierarchy centered around land-owning aristocracy and the new breed of merchants, industrialists, and ship-owners. Court-inspired patronage was lacking after Burgundy's collapse, but secular and ecclesiastic sponsorship by wealthier members of the population was as widespread as it was in Italy; although clerical patronage was less developed without the presence of the pope.

The introduction of humanist ideas into northern Europe probably began with Italian envoys, but soon the merchants and nobles hired humanist scholars to tutor their families and form the foundation of new centers of learning. This was a period when universities appeared throughout Europe, from Aberdeen to Amsterdam, where the children of nobles and merchant families studied Latin, Greek, Hebrew, and the classics, or practiced the oratorical and written skills of Cicero and other classical authors.

While Italian artists and scholars found employment in northern courts, cities, and universities, a new breed of home-grown scholar began to appear. However, the northerners espoused classicism in a significantly different way to their Italian colleagues, who viewed their medieval past as an unhappy interlude between two great eras. To the northern humanist the Middle Ages had not been dark but rather an age during which the customs, laws, and political fabric of their society had been forged. And so access to the rediscovered classic cultures of ancient Greece and Rome led to an affirmation of their recent history, not a denial of it.

While Latin remained the *lingua franca* of scholarship, the northern humanists also realized the value of disseminating information in the vernacular, a move that would lead directly to the Protestant Reformation. It was inevitable that the spread of Renaissance humanism northward across Europe would prompt questioning of Church authority. Distance from Rome meant that unlike their counterparts in Italy, northern humanists were willing to struggle against the constraints of existing dogma, and even to break the spiritual bonds that tied them to the Church.

new printing centers

- 15th century
- 16th century
- 17th century

1499 date founded

centers of learning, university founded before:

- 1300
- 1301–1400
- 1401–1500
- 1501–1700

1290 date founded

Santiago de Compostela
1506

Coimbra
1290

Lisbon
1489 1290

Evora
1550

PORTUGAL

Sevi

The spread of learning and the growth of printing presses in Europe during the Renaissance

SCOTLAND

Aberdeen 1494
St. Andrews 1411
Glasgow 1451
Edinburgh **1507** 1582

NORTH SEA

DENMARK-NORWAY

SWEDEN

Uppsala 1477
Stockholm **1483**

BALTIC SEA

Ireland

Irish Sea

Dublin **1551** 1591

York

ENGLAND

Wales

Cambridge 1209
Oxford **1478** 1190
London **1480**

English Channel

ATLANTIC OCEAN

Caen 1432

Copenhagen **1493** 1478
Lund 1688

Kiel 1655
Rostock 1419
Greifswald 1456

Franeker 1565
Harderwijk 1648
Deventer **1477**
Groningen 1614
Emden **1554**
Hamburg **1491**

Berlin **1540**
Frankfurt 1506

Amsterdam **1523** 1631
Leiden 1574
Utrecht **1472** 1636
Osnabrück 1630
Helmstedt **1576**
Magdeburg

Louvain 1426
Brussels **1474**
Cologne **1466** 1388
Bonn **1543**
Herborn 1584
Marburg 1527
Paderborn 1614
Halle 1694
Wittenberg 1502
Leipzig **1481** 1409
Erfurt 1392

POLAND

GERMAN EMPIRE

Prague **1478** 1348

Paris **1470** c.1150
Pont-à-Mousson 1572
Metz
Trier 1473
Geissen 1607
Mainz **1448** 1476
Würzburg 1582
Bamburg **1460** 1648
Nuremberg **1470**
Olomouc 1576

Orléans 1235
Angers 1337
Nantes 1460
Poitiers 1431
Bourges 1464

Heidelberg 1386
Strasbourg **1460** 1621
Tubingen 1476
Freiburg 1457
Basel **1462** 1456
Ingolstadt 1472
Augsburg **1468**
Munich **1482**
Dillingen 1549

Tymau 1635
Vienna **1482** 1365
Linz 1669
Salzburg 1623
Graz 1585

FRANCE

Cluny **1483**
Dôle 1422
Besançon 1485
Bern **1525**
Zürich **1508**

IMPERIAL HUNGARY

Lyon **1473**

Geneva **1478** 1559
Grenoble 1339
Valence 1452

Verona 1204
Padua 1222
Milan **1470** 1559
Pavia 1361
Vercelli 1228
Treviso 1318
Venice **1469**

Bordeaux 1441
Cahors 1321
Orthez 1561
Toulouse 1229

Orange 1365
Montpelier 1289
Avignon 1303
Aix-en-Provence 1409

Turin 1405
Piacenza 1248
Parma 1502
Reggio 1188
Ferrara 1391
Bologna 1200
Arezzo 1215
Urbino 1564
Perugia 1308

Bay of Biscay

Oviedo 1604

Palencia 1208
Valladolid 1346
Salamanca 1243
Saragossa 1474
Huesca 1354
Lérida 1300
Barcelona **1475** 1430

Perpignan 1349

Ligurian Sea

Florence **1471** 1349
Pisa 1343
Siena 1246

PAPAL STATES

Adriatic Sea

Madrid **1499**
Alcala de Henares 1499
Sigüenza 1489

Corsica to Genoa

Rome **1467** 1303
Subiaco **1465**

NAPLES to Spain

SPAIN

Valencia 1500
Palma 1483
Balearic islands

Sardinia to Spain

Tyrrhenian Sea

Naples 1224
Salerno 1173

Granada 1540

Caligari 1626

MEDITERRANEAN SEA

Palermo 1637
Messina 1637
Catania 1434

Sicily

Humanists in Northern Europe

The Protestant Reformation had its roots in the humanist scholarship of northern Europe, views disseminated by the printing press and the increasing literacy of the population. However, it found expression in theological reform rather than cultural enlightenment.

Although the Reformation (*see Chapter 11*) was the most significant social and political change to affect Europe in the 16th century, it is often portrayed as an almost spontaneous event. More accurately, its roots can be traced to the spread of knowledge given extraordinary impetus by the development of the printing press (*see box below*), invented in Germany by Johannes Gutenberg (c.1397–1468).

Before mass-production printing, the road to heavenly salvation lay only in the hands of the clergy. Handwritten copies of the Bible were scarce and in Latin, a language only clerics and the most educated understood, and so the mysteries of the sacred text were preserved—a classic example of knowledge being power. As printing techniques improved, more presses appeared; in 1480 there were presses in 110 European cities, a figure that more than doubled within 20 years. As the number of books in circulation rose, more people were able to read vernacular translations of the Bible, and therefore could interpret the Scriptures for themselves instead of through the mouthpiece of a priest. It was revolutionary.

Gutenberg and the invention of printing

For centuries, books in Europe had been created by the laborious process of hand-writing every one. This task invariably fell to monks, copying from preserved Latin texts, and the language as well as the naturally tiny output the monasteries could manage ensured that books were the exclusive preserve of the Church and the elite. The world was changed with the invention of movable type and its application to a series of known practices that were integrated into a method of mass production.

The Chinese had already invented the concept of moveable type (c.1041), the individual characters formed on clay tablets, but in Europe between 1436–40 Johannes Gutenberg, a German goldsmith, conceived of using small metal blocks. Each of these bore a raised letter, and they could be arranged quickly in a wooden form before being inked by a roller to print onto paper. The inked type was printed in an adapted wine press—common along the Rhine valley. The Gutenberg press, with its metal movable type printing, brought down the price of printed materials and made books available for the masses.

Gutenberg went into business, first with Andreas Dritzehn in 1438 and then with Johannes Fust in 1450, who financed his printing experiments. On September 30, 1452, Guttenberg's Bible or the Mainz Bible (for the place where it was produced) was published, becoming the first book to be published in volume. Within three decades, printing spread across Europe and became a means of political revolution by promoting the vernacular rather than Latin as the language of literary texts.

A copy of the Gutenberg Bible. For the first time laymen could read the sacred texts in their own language and determine for themselves the mysteries contained in the Bible.

By the end of the 16th century there were an estimated 200 million books in circulation, an average of two books per head of the European population. The bulk of these works were versions of the Bible, as translated by Martin Luther and his fellow reformers (*discussed in Chapter 11*), who were prolific disseminators of information. Their thinking and speeches were eagerly set to print as pamphlets and books and widely read.

The groundwork for this revolution was laid by the simple philosophy of humanism, based on ideas began by Italian Renaissance writers such as Petrach and Giovanni Comte Pico della Mirandola. They encouraged exploration of classical sources as a means of inspiration for the modern world, and protested against the hidebound nature of the late medieval church and the way it limited human thought and action.

Erasmus, heralded and scorned

As this philosophy took shape, humanism emphasized social reform and sought to regenerate moral and spiritual life through a rebirth of the classical spirit of inquiry. Humanists championed education to encourage the quest for personal and spiritual enlightenment. In theology this involved the study of early Christianity, classical moral philosophy, and works of logical inquiry as a basis for a more progressive form of knowledge. For those of the Church hierarchy this was dangerous material, since it encouraged thinking independent of Church dogma and undermined the pulpit-thumper preaching hellfire and damnation to sinners.

In Germany humanism took on a more nationalistic flavor because students drew on the ancient Roman historian Tacitus's view of the Germans as portrayed in his book *Germania*—courageous, strong, and uncorrupted by Roman vices. This was superb material for those who questioned the authority of the Roman Church.

One of the chief propagators of this nationalist view was Ulrich von Hutten (1488–1523), a German priest and acquaintance of Martin Luther, who combined the roles of patriot and humanist. As well as several nationalist polemics against the Church, he penned the dialogue *Arminius*, a history of a barbarian German leader who defeated the Romans in AD 9. While base nationalism was confined to Germany, it helped to unify northern European opinion against the authority of the Roman Church and the Holy Roman Empire, particularly in the Low Countries.

The most significant northern humanist was Desiderius Erasmus (c.1466–1536), a Dutch ordained priest and scholar who traveled widely around Europe. At Cambridge University in England he became Professor of Divinity and Greek, and his publication of the Greek New Testament was a milestone in the dissemination of religious knowledge. His satire *Encomium Moriae* (The Praise of Folly, 1509) was widely read and much admired, but his most famous work, *Colloquia* (1522), was a masterful analysis of clerical abuses within the Church.

However, Erasmus became involved in several acrimonious debates with other intellectuals in northern Europe, which undermined his position as a founder of the reforming movement. By 1517 religious persecution had forced him to move to Flanders, and then to Switzerland, where he continued writing until his death. Despite his critics, Erasmus remained true to his goal of encouraging reform by disseminating theological knowledge. Without his efforts, Martin Luther might never have succeeded.

Above: Hans Holbein the Younger's portrait of Erasmus emphasizes the importance of printed books to the Renaissance scholar.

Toward a European Marketplace

During the Middle Ages, the Low Countries emerged as the most densely populated urban area in northern Europe, ideally placed as a trading center. During the Renaissance, urban expansion, industrialization, and the intensive development of agricultural land turned a thriving economy into a booming one.

Below: Increased mercantile trade promoted urban growth throughout northern Europe. This manuscript illumination depicts the rebuilding of Troy, but it might as well be Antwerp or Amsterdam.

The Low Countries had been embroiled in a long-running struggle with the regional feudal overlord, the Duke of Burgundy, but peace was restored when the region became part of the Holy Roman Empire in 1478. Prosperity followed soon after, despite a series of border disputes between the empire and France.

During the late 15th century the ports of Antwerp and to a lesser extent Amsterdam thrived on maritime trade (*see following page*), bringing goods from Asia, the Americas, and the Mediterranean to the Low Countries. The discovery of the New World and the flow of overseas wealth into the Habsburg empire changed the economic face of Europe and increased the sophistication of business procedures and banking. The region emerged from the relatively insular economy of the medieval age to a broader, more co-dependent international economy. This was increasingly based on international trade, tariff agreements, and the availability and demand of a wide range of hitherto unavailable goods, from spices to books, manufactured items to iron ore.

The merchants and bankers of the Low Countries created their wealth by determining where each product was in greatest demand, buying and selling products accordingly. In a more sophisticated manner, bankers traded in the future needs and products in this pan-European market. This meant that any event affecting the economy of one country could rapidly affect its neighbor and a string of trading partners on the other side of the continent. The most industrialized areas were the Spanish Netherlands (and later Holland), southwestern Germany, England, and Italy; war involving these countries, or blocking access to them, could have a serious effect on the prosperity of all the states involved in European trade.

Market value

In Renaissance Europe different areas specialized in the production of certain products, unlike the medieval economy, where each region was self-sufficient. For example, the foremost industrial areas in Europe were Flanders and the north of Italy. They boasted long-established and highly respected shipbuilding industries, metal manufacturing centers, and a skilled and guild-dominated population of artisans based in the principal cities. Both regions were known for their own form of textile production: Flanders for lace, linens, and tapestries; Italy for silks and luxury fabrics. Given their geographical positions, they were not rivals in the export of ships and metal goods, while their textiles were valued throughout Europe, so each benefited from short- and long-range exports.

Other regions were less well placed. France's silk industry was seen as inferior to Italy's. While the import of cheap Indian silks through Portugal

and the Low Countries damaged this French market, the superior Italian business remained buoyant. England exported semi-finished woolen cloth for finishing in Flanders and Brabant, but by the 16th century Spain had taken over as the principal exporter of raw wool.

From the Baltic, fur, timber, and grain were traded for French and Portuguese wines and salt. The merchants of Venice accrued much of their fabled wealth from their trade in Oriental spices and luxury goods, but once again the Portuguese challenged and eventually monopolized this trade. Slaves remained a trading commodity in the Mediterranean, and later Portuguese slavers would draw on the vast hinterland of the West African coast to begin supplying Spanish colonists in the New World with slave labor.

Across Europe, everything had a price and a potential buyer. Increasingly trade was controlled by merchant adventurers, guild masters, and bankers based in the great financial centers of Flanders, Holland, and southern Germany; the new masters of the first continent-wide trading network to emerge since the collapse of the Roman empire 11 centuries earlier.

Above: *Sale in Progress* by the studio of Quentin Metsys (c.1465–1530). Buoyant commerce led to an explosion of the middle class during the 16th century, but the pursuit of money was not always viewed with pleasure by the satirists of the Renaissance.

Left: Manuscript illumination of a tailor from J. de Cessole's *Livre des schecs moralises,* another contemporary satire on trades and commerce.

Northern Europe's Maritime Gateway

Antwerp and Amsterdam became prosperous due to a combination of geography, mercantile ability, and timing, emerging in the wake of the development of the Atlantic trading economy. During the 16th century these ports thrived, transforming the Low Countries into the fiscal powerhouses of Europe.

Below: Once the United Provinces had ejected the Spanish Habsburgs, the maritime cities began a massive expansion fueled by their growing domination of European trade. The Amsterdam of today was effectively established in the 16th and 17th centuries.

Although Antwerp was founded as a city in 1291, it only rose to prominence in the mid-15th century, when English merchants abandoned trade with the neighboring cities of Ghent and Bruges and moved their business northward. Through this trade in English cloth and other commodities, Antwerp became the most important trading port in northwestern Europe.

As its economy boomed, so did its population, while other industries benefited, such as sugar refining, printing, and diamond processing. Prosperous trade guilds built prestigious halls around the marketplace (the Grote Markt),

demonstrating where the real power lay. By the early 16th century the diamond trade had become a major industry, created by Jewish craftsmen expelled from the Iberian peninsula. Through mercantile wealth, Antwerp became a lively social and cultural center, its streets lined with so many prestigious guild houses, churches, and palaces that Italian historian and diplomat Francesco Guicciardini (1483–1540) described it as the "loveliest city in the world."

Major factors were the patronage of the Holy Roman Emperor, ruler of the Low Countries from 1515, and the banking network developed throughout Europe by Antwerp-based financial houses. As secular rulers borrowed money to finance their wars or the opulence of their courts, the interest they paid helped turn Antwerp into the financial capital of Europe.

The peak of the city's fortune came in the mid-16th century, when Antwerp's markets reaped the benefit of controlling the pricing of commodities from Italy to Sweden, gaining

interest from each transaction. This prosperity lessened after 1549, when the Portuguese withdrew their spice monopoly, so merchants ventured to Lisbon instead. It was felt that the city would recover from this setback, since her grain market profits expanded as a result of shortages, but this prosperity was short-lived.

Expelling Catholicism

The divisions caused by the Reformation led to factional fighting between rival religious groups. This reached a head in the late 16th century, when Antwerp lay on the border between two increasingly hostile states, Catholic Flanders and Protestant Holland. The city's economy never recovered from the upheavals that followed the Reformation.

To the north, the small fishing port of Amsterdam on the mouth of the Amstel was more fortunate. In 1275 it gained toll privileges from the Count of Holland, allowing its civic leaders to benefit from coastal shipping. During the 14th century it grew into a small but thriving trading port, a useful haven for Scandinavian merchants venturing south from the Baltic, or English, French, and Flemish traders who brought cloth, wool, and wine to trade for the Baltic

supplies of wood, tar, and furs. The port was the home of a growing North Sea fishing fleet, providing merchants with their own useful commodity.

Amsterdam's one great asset was its location, well away from the main theaters of war in France and Flanders, and the pirates of the English Channel. By the 15th century Amsterdam had become the largest commercial city in Holland, and during the Renaissance it grew into one of the greatest banking and commercial centers in Europe.

Like Antwerp to the south, the Reformation had a major effect on Amsterdam, but unlike its neighboring rival its location spared it from the worst excesses. As the dissemination of humanist views spread, opposition to the Church hardened across Holland, and the mercantile classes who dominated Amsterdam were eager to embrace Protestantism. The nobility of Holland were more evenly divided, but by the late 16th century their power had waned. It would be the merchants of Amsterdam who decided the fate of the province. In 1579 they rallied opposition to Spanish rule and, under the leadership of William of Orange, drove the Spanish and their Catholic supporters from Holland.

Above: A bird's eye view of Antwerp at the end of the 16th century published in Godfried Kempesen's *Civitates Orbis Terrerum* (maps of European cities). There were several such publications by other authors, which proved very popular during the 16th century.

Gothic Influence in Renaissance Art

Two distinctive art styles emerged in northern Europe, encouraged by the cultural flowering of the late medieval French and Burgundian courts. They had as profound an influence on Italian artists as the works of the Italian Renaissance had on the masters of Flanders and Holland.

Although Gothic art was established in France during the late 12th century as a style of architecture, it evolved into a label applied to contemporary visual arts. During the last decades of the 14th century a variation developed in the papal court at Avignon, a pro-French rejection of the new Italian artistic styles developed by Giotto (1266–1337) and his successors. Art historians subsequently branded this new movement International Gothic, a term derived from its spread across Europe during the following century.

From Avignon, the Gothic style became closely associated with the Valois courts of Paris, most notably those of Charles VI and Charles VII (r.1380–1422–61). It was characterized by the

bold use of color and an eye for decorative detail, transforming the elaborate linear forms of the High Gothic period into something new and powerful, imagery that suited the needs of both secular princes and the Church. The International Gothic style could be traced in painting, illumination, decorative arts, and stained glass decoration, its exuberance an influence in other countries and on other artistic traditions.

However, the most expressive form of International Gothic flourished in Flanders. The luminous quality of light in the work of Rogier van der Weyden (c.1400–64) even found popularity across the Alps in northern Italy, where he influenced artists of the Venetian and Sienese schools. In Siena its form is best characterized by the work of Stephano di Giovanni, "Sassetta" (1392–1447). Sassetta drew on the existing Sienese tradition of the vividness of color and detail, expressed most clearly in the exuberant artistry of Ambrogio Lorenzetti (c.1292–1348). While Sassetta's work remained true to the International Gothic style, it adopted the spatial awareness and perspective developed by contemporary Florentine artists such as Masaccio (*see pages 13 and 35*).

Gothic fantasy

While Sienese artists concentrated on spiritual themes, other Gothic artists undertook work for secular patrons, including the kings of France and dukes of Burgundy. At the beginning of the 15th century the medieval art of manuscript illumination was one of the most popular forms of artistic expression, and the opportunities presented in terms of color and embellishment made it a natural avenue for practitioners of the International Gothic style.

The most widely known example of this work is *Les Très Riches Heures*, an example of that 15th-century genre the book of hours, containing prayers to be recited at set hours of the day. Commissioned by the wealthy Duc de Berry, it was illuminated by the Limbourg brothers (Pol, Herman, and Jean Malouel), Dutch artists from Gelderland who worked in France and Burgundy.

Unfortunately the book remained unfinished—all three brothers died suddenly in 1416, probably victims of plague. The work remains a testimony to their artistry, landscapes combining contemporary life with fairytale fantasy, enriched by vivid color, composition, and detailing. The result is one of the most aesthetically pleasing works of the 15th century.

Other artists adapted the International Gothic movement to produce their own distinctive styles. One late practitioner was the Flemish painter Hieronymus Bosch (c.1450–1516). Although his style is so idiosyncratic and fantastical to defy easy definition, his moralistic and allegorical paintings were clearly of the International Gothic style. While some art historians claim works such as *The Garden of Earthly Delights* and *The Temptations of St. Anthony* represent a unique departure from existing conventions, the roots of his bizarre fantasy world can be seen in the semi-mythical landscapes of *Les Très Riches Heures*.

The work of Rogier van der Weyden (*Lamentation*, **facing**) and Hieronymous Bosch (*The Temptations of St. Anthony*, **above**) make an interesting comparison of the range of International Gothic. The earlier van der Weyden has much in common with his Italian contemporaries, whereas Bosch dwells in a gloomy "gothic" world of demons, in which every iconographic item symbolizes something from an often obscure canon of daily sins.

Flemish and Dutch Art

While the Renaissance was being born in Italy, contemporary artists in the Low Countries developed their own style during the 15th century, inspired as much by the skies and landscapes around them as by the development of new artistic conventions.

The Dutch or Flemish school of the early 15th century combined the level of detail shown in International Gothic treatments with a sense of perspective based on landscape, rather than the buildings preferred by Italian artists, to display their awareness of perspective and proportion. The flat topography of the Low Countries allows view to the horizon, sweeping vistas broken by linear features such as treelines, waterways, and concentrated pockets of human habitation, a landscape that lends itself to the development of perspective. The northern weather produced a range of light and conditions absent from Italy, and artists portrayed the buildings they saw, rather than attempting to reconstruct the classical structures that surrounded and inspired artists and architects of the Italian Renaissance.

By the mid–15th century, most Dutch and Flemish towns had resident craftsman painters working in private studios on behalf of secular or ecclesiastic patrons. Their ranks included Rogier van der Weyden, Petrus Christus (1410–73), Dieric Bouts the Elder (1415–75), Lucas van Leyden (1494–1533), and Hans Memling (c.1435–94), most of whom claimed inspiration from the

1364	1382	1389–1406	1416	1427	1432	c.1440	c.1450–1516
John II of France bestows Burgundy to Duke Philip the Bold, who establishes the realm's dynasty	At Roosebeke Philip the Bold defeats Flemish rebels in the name of his uncle, Count of Flanders	Flemish sculptor Claus Sluter produces his memorial to Philip the Bold at Dijon	The Dutch Limbourg brothers die before they complete their book of hours, *Les Très Riches Heures*	Start of second war between Denmark and the Hanseatic League of German, Dutch, and Flemish towns	Jan van Eyck of Limbourg paints his Ghent altarpiece, which includes the *Annunciation*	Johannes Gutenberg invents the moveable type printing press, allowing the rapid production of books	Life of Flemish painter Hieronymus Bosch, noted for his allegorical and fantastical works

pioneering artistry of Jan van Eyck (c.1385–1441).

His work set the foundations of the Flemish School of the 15th century by re-evaluating the traditional styles of Gothic painting; embracing the internationalist use of color and detail but combining them with a hitherto unimagined level of naturalistic detail. While this was partly made possible by the development of vibrant oil-based paints, Eyck's skill and eye were of great importance, as was his willingness to experiment.

Eyck's works include *The Arnolfini Marriage*, *Madonna in the Church*, and *The Annunciation*, each remarkably dissimilar to what came before, seminal studies in realism and lifelike rendition. Like their Gothic predecessors, Eyck and his successors made extensive use of symbolism and imagery, betraying the medieval roots of the Flemish society.

Evolution and influence

Later adherents of this Dutch or Flemish style were the Breugels, Pieter the Elder (1525–69), Pieter the Younger (1564–1638), Jan the Elder (1568–1625), and Jan the Younger (1601–78), all of whom combined this tradition of the dramatic use of landscape and observed detail. Both Pieters used their Flemish inheritance of intimacy and detailing and expanded it onto a bigger canvas. They also drew inspiration from Heironymus Bosch, as evidenced by their dramatic use of multiple figures filling their pictures.

Above all, the Northern Renaissance art movement was a gradual process, lacking the more decisive steps that can be traced in Italy during the same period. The beginning of one phase overlapped the end of another. Some artists employed the latest techniques to provided detailed renditions of skin and clothing, yet relied on compositions inspired by medieval traditions, while others used crude techniques to depict compelling and thoroughly modern images of exacting perspective and form.

The later Gothic and International Gothic movements died out in the closing decades of the 15th century. In northern Europe they were

replaced by the artistic conventions of the Flemish and Dutch schools who bridged the gap between the late medieval world and the Renaissance during the span of the 15th century. This Low Countries tradition then gave way to a

new generation, including Jan Gossaert ("Mabuse," 1478–c.1533), Quentin Metsys (Massys, c.1465–1530), and even German-born Hans Holbein the Younger (1497–1543), who, like many of their contemporaries, were influenced more by the painters of the Italian Renaissance than the Gothic roots of Northern European art.

Two very different Flemish artists, Pieter Breughel the Elder (**facing**) and Jan van Eyck (**left**), demonstrate the range of northern Renaissance painting. Van Eyck's fame traveled widely—the Arnolfini of his celebrated marriage picture were an Italian banking family—and in the Italian writer Bartolomeo Fazio's *Book of Famous Men* of the mid-1450s, Jan van Eyck is identified as "the leading painter of our time." The music-making angels from the right-hand panel of the *Ghent Altarpiece* triptych shows his use of luminous light and form, but van Eyck was a better exemplar of three-dimensional space than his contemporary van der Weyden. The later Pieter Breughel occupies a more parochial place, with marvellously busy scenes of everyday life, such as in *Peasant Wedding*, pictured here.

CHAPTER 7

A Sceptered Isle–Tudor England

Hampton Court was originally begun by the Lord Chancellor, Cardinal Wolsey, in 1515 as his own residence. When he fell from Henry VIII's favor, Wolsey gave the palace to the king in 1525, together with his second palace at Whitehall. Henry added greatly to Hampton Court, building the Great Hall, remodeling the chapel and constructing the King's and Queen's lodgings. It remains a masterpiece of English Renaissance architecture, a style that has since been referred to as "Tudor."

The visible effects of the Renaissance did not reach England, Wales, and Scotland in any significant way until the 16th century. The British Isles had become something of a political backwater after the disastrous Hundred Years War of the 14th century, and England's primary concerns were the continual and brutal subjugation of Scotland, Wales, and Ireland. Wales was ruled by the Lord President of the Marches from Ludlow Castle and Ireland by a Lord Deputy from Dublin Castle. In both cases their principal tasks were to put down rebellions and prevent foreign intervention using the lands as bases for an invasion of England. In all of this, there was not much use for the "new learning" of the Continent.

With its strong connections to the French court, signs of Renaissance began early in the 15th century in Scotland, but any changes were damaged when the English defeated James IV at Flodden (1513) and wiped out the Scottish nobility that had been deveoping as patrons of the arts and architecture. And so it was that a fully developed Renaissance court only came into being with the Tudors. The age of the Tudors is recognized as one of the most vivid periods of English history, thanks in particular to two astute and colorful monarchs: King Henry VIII and his daughter Queen Elizabeth I. Between them they brought their realm into the modern age.

Although entirely for his own personal and financial reasons, Henry VIII broke the stranglehold of the Catholic Church that had gathered so much wealth, lands, and power in the country since the Norman conquest. With the blood of the Houses York and Lancaster flowing through his veins Henry ruled over a united, wealthy kingdom on the verge of greatness.

Elizabeth I sat on the throne at a time when overseas exploration expanded English trade and influence, allowing business to thrive and England to change from a predominantly agricultural economy to become an important military, naval, and economic power and a real rival to other European countries. Religious differences were set aside in favor of the creation of a united nation. Elizabeth's apparently vulnerable position as an unmarried female Protestant monarch gave her the opportunity to play off one enemy country against another, all to Britain's greater gain. For the first time, these islands became an important European state.

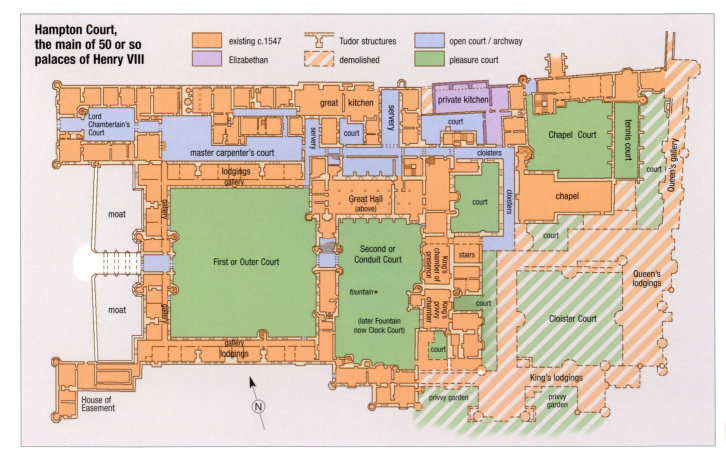

Hampton Court, the main of 50 or so palaces of Henry VIII

existing c.1547 — Tudor structures — open court / archway — Elizabethan — demolished — pleasure court

Ecclesiastical Tudor England at the time of Henry VIII

Tudor England before the Reformation was an island of numerous monasteries and smaller monastic houses. Almost all of the country's wealth lay in the hands of the Church. Between 1538–40 a revolution took place, instigated by the king, who ordered the dissolution of the monasteries; and the Church's fortune went into the royal treasury. Senior clerics who supported Henry received new Bishoprics that cut across the more important boundries.

Legend:
- Bishoprics since the medieval era
- new Bishoprics created by Henry VIII
- Council of the North
- Council of Wales
- ♰ Episcopal See
- ◉ Abbey represented in House of Lords
- • monasteries dissolved by Henry VIII, 1538–40

Some towns had more than one monastic house, indicated by the figure following in brackets.

Map labels:

Seas and waters: Firth of Forth, IRISH SEA, NORTH SEA, The Wash, ENGLISH CHANNEL, Bristol Channel, Cardigan Bay, Solway Firth, Irish Sea, Tweed, Tyne, Wear, Tees, Humber, Ribble, Dee, Severn, Thames

Regions/Dioceses: Glasgow, Galloway, Durham, Carlisle, CHESTER, York, Bangor, St. Asaph, Lichfield, Lincoln, Norwich, St. Davids, Hereford, Worcester, PETERBOROUGH, Ely, London, GLOUCESTER, OXFORD, Llandaff, Salisbury, Bath & Wells, Winchester, Chichester, Exeter, Rochester, BRISTOL

Places: Glasgow, Holyrood, St Andrews, Berwick, Lindisfarne, Jedburgh, Carlisle, to York, Durham, Shap, St. Bees, Rivaulx, Fountains, Meaux, York (10), Selby, Isle of Man, St. Asaph, Chester (5), Lincoln (7), Bardney, Anglesey, Bangor, Boston (4), The Wash, Shrewsbury (4), Lichfield, Walsingham, Holme St. Benet, Norwich (6), Lynn (5), to Bangor, Stamford (5), Crowland, Thorney, Peterborough, Ramsay, Thetford (5), Coventry (5), Cambridge (6), Bury St. Edmunds, Ely, Worcester, Pershore, Hereford, St. Davids, Gloucester (5), Colchester (3), Cirencester, Oxford (12), Ashridge, Abingdon, Waltham, to Canterbury, Malmesbury, Westminster, London (18), Rochester, Reading, Llandaff, Bristol (6), Bath, Wells, Glastonbury, Salisbury, Winchester (7), Chichester, Battle, to Canterbury, Exeter, Bodmin, Isle of Wight, Truro

The Rise of the Tudors

The Tudor age lasted for just over a century, and encompassed three generations and five monarchs. For such a dynamic family they proved surprisingly infertile, and when the line died out the Scottish Stuart dynasty inherited the thrones of England and Wales.

Below: Gilt-bronze effigies of Henry VII and Elizabeth of York, adorn the royal tomb in Westminster Abbey. The sculptures are by Pietro Torrigiano (1472–1528), who studied in Florence under the patronage of Lorenzo de' Medici.

At the start of the Tudor reign, England was not seen as any kind of a threat in Europe. Thanks to her small population of around three million and the protracted and sapping civil wars (The Wars of the Roses between the Houses of York and Lancaster) of the 1450s and 1485, England had a limited economy and was financially and economically backward. Her only perceived use was as a potential ally against another European power, or possibly a useful territory to conquer. In the late 15th century England and her satellite states of Wales and Ireland possessed no national army or navy and only a small merchant fleet.

The Tudor age began with the ascension of the chief Lancastrian claimant Henry Tudor (r.1485–1509), Earl of Richmond. Part English, Welsh, French, and Bavarian, he was the son of a wealthy nobleman. He became Henry VII in August 1485, following the defeat of the Yorkist king Richard III at the battle of Bosworth Field, all the other, more viable Lancastrian claimants having died during the wars. To unite the warring factions, Henry VII took Elizabeth of York (1465–1503), daughter of King Edward IV (r.1461–83), as his bride.

For 24 years Henry VII proved to be a shrewd

monarch who used diplomacy, justice, conciliation, and espionage to secure his kingdom. Through such careful management, he rebuilt the economic and political base of the country. His principal virtues proved to be an orderly mind and grasp of economics. He took over a bankrupt treasury but was able to leave his heir a solvent exchequer. The early 16th century was a politically turbulent age of great social instability and much of Henry's policy-making was designed to deflect the constant possibility of foreign invasion. At the beginning of the period England and Wales were predominantly agricultural economies heavily dependent on raw wool and corn exports for valuable foreign exchange. This situation changed as England started to manufacture and finish her own goods.

A Renaissance Prince

Henry used auditors to monitor the Chamber accounts and personally checked them every day. He avoided unnecessary expenditure such as warfare, but encouraged the development of manufacturing and generously rewarded people when it was deserved. He chose equally prudent advisors to work on his council, and usually presided over the meetings himself; an unusually scrupulous and controlling monarch for his age.

In November 1501 Henry VII's son Prince Arthur (1486–1502) married Catherine of Aragon (1485–1536), the youngest daughter of Ferdinand of Aragon and Isabella of Castile. Arthur died suddenly in April 1502, before the marriage was consummated. Unwilling to lose either the alliance or the handsome Spanish dowry, Henry suggested Catherine marry his second son, Henry. The Spanish monarchs agreed and the date was set for 1505, when Henry turned 14. Henry VII kept postponing the marriage for diplomatic reasons, but the union eventually took place in June 1509, only a few weeks before his death.

Thanks both to his father's prudence and his own intelligence, Henry VIII (r.1509–47) ascended the throne unchallenged and was able to establish his dynasty so firmly that he ruled without serious threat for 38 years. During this time he made his claim to be one of the great Renaissance princes of Europe, and his pursuit of

self-aggrandizement resulted in an unprecedented royal building program. As a patron, Henry VIII was interested in literature, music, and astronomy, and himself composed music and wrote works of theology. Ever out to prove his Renaissance credentials, he met the French king Francis I near Calais in 1520, where the two monarchs attempted to outdo each other in parading the splendor of their courts. Because of its extravagant spectacle the encounter came to be known as "The Field of the Cloth of Gold," and it confirmed Henry in his vision of himself as a leading light in the new Europe.

The Tudor age coincides with the mature period of the European Renaissance, but while the new thinking was influential in England, the artistic ties were not as strong once the realm had been severed from the Catholic Church (*see following page*). Accordingly the arts took a somewhat different course from mainland Europe, where painting, sculpture, and architecture were its main expression. The English Renaissance expressed itself most successfully through language, with the works of William Shakespeare, Christopher Marlowe, and Edmund Spencer.

Above: King Henry VIII by Hans Holbein the Younger. Painted in 1540, this is one of several studies made by the German painter who found his creative home in England under Tudor Renaissance patronage.

Six Wives and Henry VIII

The story of Henry VIII's marriages is as much about a drive to produce a male heir as marital felicity or a repositioning of the Church. The succession of failed alliances mirrored the great political and religious changes that helped shape Tudor England during his reign.

Below: Undated engraving from the original minature by Hans Holbein the Younger of Catherine of Aragon holding a Capuchin monkey. Henry's first wife bore him a daughter, Mary, who would become the avowed enemy of Elizabeth I, daughter of the king's second wife, Anne Boleyn, seen here, **right**, in an 18th-century engraving by Francesco Bartolozzi, after a lost portrait by Holbein.

For 16 years Henry VIII and Catherine of Aragon enjoyed a happy marriage, but from six pregnancies, Catherine bore the king only one daughter, Mary. The need for a male heir came to obsess Henry, and inevitably he blamed his wife. Henry chose to believe that God was punishing him for marrying his sister-in-law, and he tried to force Catherine to admit her previous marriage had been consummated. Meanwhile Henry's eye had been caught by Anne Boleyn (1501–36), but unlike her sister she refused to become his mistress.

Henry dispatched the Archbisop of York and Lord Chancellor, Cardinal Thomas Wolsey, to seek an annulment of his marriage from Pope Clement VII (p.1523–34). Wolsey's repeated attempts failed because Clement was beholden to the Holy Roman Emperor Charles V, who happened to be Catherine's nephew. In 1529 Henry responded by initiating a policy of estrangement from the Catholic Church. There was no religious motivation—he had already earned from the pope the title *Fidei Defensor* (Defender of the Faith) for his denunciation of Reformist Martin Luther—the reasons were purely political… and later financial.

In fury at Clement's repeated refusals, Henry took matters into his own hands, and divorced Catherine in 1533, justifying his actions by getting parliament to pass the Act in Restraint of Appeals, which stated that England was a law unto itself, no longer answerable to the papacy. In the following year the Act of Supremacy made Henry the Supreme Head of the Church of England. None of this made the king a Protestant reformer, and England remained a Catholic state until his son Edward VI came to the throne, but it meant that communication between England and Rome ended, and Church revenues benefitted the king, especially with the dissolution of the monasteries (*see page 116*).

However, Henry VIII's succession problem was not eased by ridding himself of Catherine.

He already had an illegitimate son by his mistress Anne Blount, who became Duke of Richmond (1519–36), but he was unable to name him as a successor. The duke's timely and suspicious death removed the threat to any subsequent son of Boleyn and Henry. Anne Boleyn was five months pregnant when she married Henry in secret, but she bore him a daughter, Elizabeth (1533–1603, later Elizabeth I). Increasingly frustrated, Henry wanted to get rid of Anne and was relieved to see her charged with adultery. Anne was found guilty and beheaded for high treason when Elizabeth was just two years old.

Blessed, then condemned

The king was out hunting when he heard cannon signal Anne's execution. He immediately rode to the Wiltshire home of his new love, Jane Seymour; they married 11 days later. In October 1537 Jane delivered the much-longed for son, Edward, but she died ten days after giving birth.

Given his reputation, Henry found it difficult to find another foreign bride. His advisors suggested a Protestant, to cement the split with the Church of Rome, and Henry was persuaded to marry Anne of Cleves (1515–57), a north German noblewoman. The couple married in January 1540, despite Henry being repelled by her plainness. He soon demanded a divorce and

Anne prudently acquiesced. The marriage was dissolved in June 1540 and Anne remained in England for the rest of her life, unwilling to return home a spurned bride.

Thomas Cromwell (c.1485–1540) won an earldom for arranging the marriage, and a death sentence because of Henry's disappointment. On July 28, 1540 Cromwell was beheaded, while across London Henry was married to Catherine Howard (1521–1542), the young cousin of Anne Boleyn. Although only 19, she had taken lovers from the age of 12 and stupidly continued her affairs. An initially disbelieving and indulgent Henry became enraged when he learned the truth, and in February 1542 she too was beheaded on Tower Green.

In 1543 the 52-year-old Henry married again, to twice-widowed 31-year-old Catherine Parr (1512–48). Despite growing obesity and declining health, he still hoped for more sons. Henry died in January 1547, survived by Queen Catherine. He left the crown to Edward, his only son by Jane Seymour, but if Edward produced no heirs his sister Mary would inherit the throne, with Elizabeth as the next existing heir. Henry ignored his oldest sister Margaret, who had married James IV of Scotland, but eventually the Tudors' failure to produce male heirs would allow this Scottish line to inherit the thrones of both kingdoms.

Above: An aerial view of Hampton Court, center of much drama for Henry's wives, shows its position adjacent to the River Thames. Because of the poor state of the roads, it was much faster—and much more comfortable —to take a boat along the river to the ceremonial center of Westminster. It was a sign of royal disfavor to be refused passage with the king on his boat and be condemned to taking the slow route along the muddy, rutted byways to the palace. The great moat built by Wolsey originally surrounded the palace, but has now been absorbed into the extensive gardens.

Scotland's Tragedy–The Stuarts

Scotland and England had been enemies for centuries, but as elsewhere in 15th-century Europe, the real struggle in Scotland was between the crown and the nobility. The conflict reached a climax during the Renaissance and the Reformation that followed.

Below: Originally founded as a monastery in 1128, Holyrood House became the royal residence of the Scottish monarchs. Situated at the end of the Royal Mile in Edinburgh, the building suffered much damage over the centuries, but rebuilding of the center section in the Renaissance style created a palace that served Mary, Queen of Scots in 1561–67.

Henry VIII of England and James IV of Scotland became brothers-in-law in 1504, when Margaret Tudor married the Scottish king. James was an enlightened monarch, interested in science, architecture, and military technology, but his alliance with France led to his untimely death on the battlefield of Flodden (1513) against England. Margaret became regent to her 12-year-old son, the future James V, but her marriage to the Sixth Earl of Angus lost her the support of the nobility. With fiscal and political help from Henry VIII, Margaret placed James on the throne in July 1524.

James V temporarily curbed the power of the nobility and created a centralized administration. He proved an expert in the field of European politics, giving his small country an important role through alliances with France, Spain, and the Holy Roman Empire—anyone who could help protect Scotland from the English, who remained greedy and uncertain partners, despite Henry's aid in getting him crowned. In 1538 James married Mary of Guise, forging a close alliance with France and the Catholic Church but earning the enmity of Henry VIII, who ordered an invasion of Scotland in 1542. It came to nothing, but news of a Scottish defeat at Solway Moss in November may have speeded the death of James, who was struck down by illness in his hunting palace at Falkland, Fife.

He was succeeded by his six-day-old daughter Mary Stuart, who became Queen of Scots on December 14, 1542. Henry VIII tried to arrange a marriage with his son Edward, but Mary of Guise, acting as regent, was hostile to an alliance with Protestant England. In 1548 she sent Mary to France, where she was brought up to be a staunch Catholic in the French court and betrothed to the dauphin, Francis (later Francis II).

Henry VIII responded with the "Rough Wooing," a series of brutal punitive invasions designed to force the country back into the English fold. Mary of Guise stood firm. Mary Stuart married Francis in April 1558, the same year that Mary I of England died and Elizabeth I came to the throne, re-establishing England as a Protestant country.

1485	1486	1509	1516	1534	1537	1542	1553
Wars of the Roses end with Richard III's defeat at Bosworth; Henry VII becomes king	Henry VII marries Elizabeth of York, uniting Lancaster and York, establishing the Tudor dynasty	Henry VIII marries Catherine of Aragon, widowed by Prince Arthur; he is crowned soon after	Sir Thomas More's *Utopia* tells of an ideal land, contrasting with the harsh society he lived in	Denied divorce from Catherine of Aragon by Pope Clement VII, Henry VIII establishes the Anglican Church	James V's bride Madeleine, daughter of Francis I of France, dies; he marries Mary of Guise the next year	James V dies in battle against England, succeeded by daughter Mary, Queen of Scots	Mary Tudor becomes Queen of England and reverses Catholic prejudices, burning many Protestants

Murder and intrigue

When King Henry II of France died in July 1559 Mary became Queen Consort of France, but soon her world fell apart. Her mother died in June 1560, followed by her husband six months later, leaving Mary a teenage widow. Mary's only course was to return to Scotland. In her absence the Reformation had taken hold in Scotland, encouraged by the Calvinist orator John Knox, so a Catholic queen would rule a predominantly Protestant country.

Forced to rely on often duplicitous advisors, Mary was cast adrift in a world of political and religious turmoil. In 1565 she married the handsome but vapid Henry, Lord Darnley, a great grandson of Henry VII. Darnley became implicated in the murder of Mary's secretary (and possibly lover) David Rizzio; Mary was suspected of Darnley's subsequent murder, an act probably committed by her new lover and future husband, James Hepburn, Earl of Bothwell.

Following an armed uprising, Mary was forced to abdicate in favor of her son James, who was crowned James VI of Scotland in July 1567. She sought refuge in England, whereupon Elizabeth promptly had her imprisoned. Mary remained incarcerated for almost 19 years, a rallying point for Catholics in both kingdoms, leaving Scotland split by civil war and religious strife. After her implication in a series of Catholic plots, Mary's part in the Babbington Conspiracy of 1586 led to her execution in February 1587. When he succeeded Elizabeth to the English throne in 1603, James VI ended centuries of bloody conflict, in the process founding the United Kingdom of Great Britain.

Above: Mary, Queen of Scots, was a staunch Catholic ruling over a country gripped by Protestant fever, and a queen embroiled in the plots of her advisors. Her son, James VI, seen here, **left**, in a painting by the celebrated portraitist of his day, Paul van Somer (c.1576–1621), was to become James I of the United Kingdom of Great Britain in 1603.

1558	1567	1585	1587	1588	1593	1603	1611
Mary Stuart marries Francis II of Dauphin; Mary I of England dies and Elizabeth I becomes queen	Implicated in the murder of Henry, Lord Darnley, Mary Stuart abdicates, replaced by son James VI	Elizabeth I lends English support to a Dutch rebellion against Spanish rule, triggering war	Mary Stuart is executed, becoming a martyr to Catholics in England and Scotland	England is united as it thwarts a Spanish invasion armada at the Battle of Gravelines	Richard Hooker's *The Laws of Ecclesiastical Polity* supports the monarchy and the Anglican Church	Elizabeth I dies and James VI of Scotland also becomes James I of England, uniting the British Isles	William Shakespeare completes *The Tempest*, his last major work before his death five years later

Scholars of the Tudor Era

When William Caxton started the first printing press in England, scholars finally had the means to make their ideas accessible to everyone. The result was a flowering of learning, and the standardization of the English language.

Above: Detail of Hans Holbein's magnificent portrait of Sir Thomas Moore, exemplar of the English Renaissance. Through his writing, Moore brought a European influence to humanist studies in England.

During Henry VII's reign scholars in England made an invaluable contribution to humanist writing, and traveled widely in pursuit of knowledge and new learning. Robert Flemyng (d.1483) met Guarino da Verona, who taught Greek and Latin at Ferrara, and in Rome met Pope Sixtus IV, the patron of humanist studies. William Latimer and Thomas Linacre were other notables, the latter (c.1460–1524) studying in Italy with Giovanni de' Medici, later Pope Leo X, with whom he remained friends. A third, William Grocyn (c.1446–1519), delivered the first lectures in Greek at Oxford, and taught John Colet—an outspoken critic of Church abuses—and the Reformist Erasmus.

Aristocratic patronage was also evident at this time, most notably Lady Margaret Beaufort (c.1441–1509), who founded two colleges in Cambridge: Christ's in 1505 and St. John's in 1511. In Oxford, Bishop Fox of Winchester founded Corpus Christi College, and these three institutions were centers of humanist study throughout the 16th century. However, learning was not the only benefit of the time, for without a means of disseminating the scholars' thoughts beyond the walls of elitist colleges, the English Renaissance would have faltered. The greatest boon was Gutenberg's printing press (*see page 96*), invented c.1450. In England the first press was set up in about 1474 by William Caxton (c.1422–1491). His translation of *The Recuyell of the Historyes of Troye* was the first book printed in vernacular English. Caxton printed nearly one hundred publications, about 20 of which he also translated from French and Dutch. The more notable books from his press included *The Canterbury Tales* and *Troilus and Criseyde* by the medieval English poet Geoffrey Chaucer and *Confessio Amantis* by English poet John Gower.

Sir Thomas More (1478–1535), author of *Utopia* (1516) and one-time Lord Chancellor to Henry VIII, is probably the best known of all Tudor scholars. His work described an ideal land where freedom of thought and conscience are allowed, disguising an intelligent attack on contemporary politics and social evils. *Utopia* struck a chord with the new radical times but was only read by a handful of people until it was translated from Latin into English in 1551.

More was a highly respected and learned man, with an easy command of Latin, Greek, and French, as well as theology, music, and law. He wrote pamphlets against heretics but fell out with his monarch when Henry claimed supremacy over the pope, and paid for his beliefs with his life. Charged with high treason, he was found guilty and executed along with the humanist John Fisher, Bishop of Rochester, in 1535.

In the field of mathematics, the Welshman Robert Record (c.1510–58) introduced algebra to Europe and wrote textbooks written in English that clearly explained elementary

mathematics. These included the arithmetical book *The Ground of Artes* (1543), the study of Ptolemy's astronomy *The Castle of Knowledge* (1556), and *The Whetstone of Witte* (1557), where he recorded the equals symbol (=), accompanied by the explanation "*bicause noe 2 thynges can be moare equall.*" Record's work helped to establish an important English tradition of mathematics in the exact sciences. Cuthbert Tunstall (1474–1559) was an influential mathematician, although professionally a cleric and diplomat. Tunstall was the only English author to be lauded on the Continent, thanks to his book on mathematics *De Arte Supputendi* (1522). Written in Latin and published in England, it was never translated into English, but seven later editions were published abroad and much admired.

An array of studies

The defining history book of the age was written by Raphael Holinshed (c.1535–80). Published in two volumes, *The Chronicles of England, Scotland, and Ireland* (1577) presented a history of the British Isles from the Norman Conquest to contemporary Elizabethan times. Written with a distinct Tudor bias, the work provided the historical basis for many of Shakespeare's plays.

John Leland (c.1503–52), chaplain to Henry VIII, undertook the immense task of surveying the country. After Henry's break from Rome, in 1533 he was made the king's antiquary and given orders to search secular and ecclesiastical libraries to determine the extent of the land and wealth owned by both king and Church in England. The task took him ten years, resulting in the *Commentarii de Scriptoribus Britannicis.*

The most celebrated Elizabethan antiquarian was the Londoner John Stow (1525–1605), who published a number of scientifically ordered surveys and histories. His major work on a very local and comprehensive level was a parish-by-parish history and archaeology of London spanning six centuries, published as *Survey of London and Westminster* (1598).

Richard Hooker published the *Laws of Ecclesiastical Polity* (1593), five books that outlined the laws of nature and argued that society should obey the monarch. He explained the doctrine of the Anglican Church and why it could not submit to the Roman doctrine of the Catholic Church, which did much to safeguard the Protestant Reformation in England.

Perhaps the oddest English scholar of the Tudor period was Dr. John Dee (1527–1608), Elizabeth I's mathematician and astronomer. He drew up Elizabeth's horoscope and identified auspicious dates for her. A true polymath with a great breadth of knowledge, his interests in astrology, alchemy, magic, telepathy, and the occult labeled him as a dangerous eccentric or worse, a heretic. He even claimed to have enchanted the commanders of the Spanish Armada and incited the gales that destroyed it! His proximity to the queen demonstrates the regard accorded to scientists and thinkers in England.

Left: Memorial statue to John Stow in the church of St. Andrew, London. The son of a poor London tailor, Stow became passionate about history. In about 1560 he published *The Woorkes of Geffrey Chaucer* (with *"additions that were never in printe before"*). He wrote *Annales*, a chronicle of England with a distinctly Protestant agenda to refute accusations of his popery (caused by his owning several Catholic texts) before his famous *Survey of London and Westminster*, of unique value for its account of the buildings, social conditions, and customs of London in the time of Elizabeth I.

Below: Undated engraving of alchemist, geographer, and mathematician Dr. John Dee. Dee was acquitted of charges of causing the death of Mary I by black magic.

A Protestant Realm

England and Wales became Protestant in all but name when Henry VIII severed links with the Catholic Church. The majority were unaffected, but for the nobility and clergy the move had serious repercussions, leading to decades of religiously inspired rebellion and persecution.

Henry VIII considered himself a theologian, and Pope Clement VII had once named him Defender of the Faith. But in his desire to win a divorce from Catherine of Aragon, he broke ties with Rome and created his own Church of England in 1533–4. He became head of the Church and possessor of its lands, an estimated fifth of the country. This *mortmain* (dead hand) land was released for agricultural and commercial use, and its revenues used to line the pockets of the king rather than the pope.

In 1536 Henry sent his surveyors out to investigate the monasteries. They returned with tales of worldly and licentious behavior, fiscal abuses, and general laxness. This gave Henry the excuse he needed to seize some 800 monasteries and abbeys, along with their lands. Henry gave away some land to favorites and sold the rest to the highest aristocratic bidders, thereby ensuring their fiscal loyalty to his new anti-papal cause. Henry is estimated to have gained extra revenue of £90,000 ($162,000, an astronomical sum at the time) per annum from these sales, until the last monastic estate was sold in 1540.

As part of this new initiative, in 1537 the Bible was first printed in English rather than Latin, making the Word of God accessible to all who could read. This also meant that the Scriptures were open to individual interpretation, a Protestant idea that Henry came to disapprove.

In Germany Martin Luther and his Reformers were preaching Protestantism and for Henry these new ideas provided a timely expedient. However, in his heart Henry remained a Catholic and vocally forbade any significant doctrinal changes. On his death his only surviving son, Edward VI, ascended the throne at the age of nine (r.1547–53). Under his tenure Protestantism was pursued with more enthusiasm, thanks to the influence of his protector John Dudley, the Duke of Northumberland.

Below: Undated engraving of Edward VI, son of Henry VIII and Jane Seymour. In his reign of six unhappy years, Edward's radical Protestantism was harnessed by his regency governors to move England away from his father's still-Catholic state to one of Anglicanism.

Reversals of faith

When Edward died in July 1553 the English Protestants led by Northumberland attempted to declare Lady Jane Grey (1537–54) the successor, as the great granddaughter of Henry VII. Her "reign" just lasted ten days (July 10–19) before Edward's older sister Mary (daughter of Henry VIII and Catherine of Aragon) arrived in London to secure the throne as Mary I (r.1553–58). She wanted to save Jane from charges of treason leveled by the queen's Catholic advisers, but the Grey family's involvement in Wyatt's Rebellion (January–February 1554) proved she was a dangerous Protestant figurehead. The teenaged Jane Grey was executed in the Tower of London in February 1554.

The half-Spanish Mary set about reversing all of Edward's anti-Catholic strictures. She married His Most Catholic Majesty King Philip II of Spain, and rumors abounded of a Spanish Catholic take-over of the country. The queen reacted to Protestant opposition with vigor, earning her the sobriquet Bloody Mary due to her execution of English Protestants. Houses and lands were seized, hundreds were imprisoned, many were tortured on the rack, and dozens were

burnt at the stake. Most closely watched was her Protestant half-sister Elizabeth.

The daughter of Henry VIII and Anne Boleyn, Elizabeth had a tough childhood. Her father executed her mother when she was an infant, then proclaimed his daughter illegitimate. She spent much of her childhood in exile from the court, in the care of her last stepmother Catherine Parr. She survived the intrigues surrounding the minority of her brother Edward IV and the attempted succession of cousin Lady Jane Grey. With Catholic Mary on the throne, Elizabeth lived in fear for her life, and seems to have developed a heightened skepticism about all kinds of religious belief. However, she was careful to avoid any hint of treason or conspiracy, knowing full well that her sister would have no hesitation in putting religion ahead of her family.

When Mary died Elizabeth inherited the throne. England was tired of religious persecution, and openly welcomed the new queen's more pragmatic approach to government. She followed a tough but tolerant policy, establishing Protestantism as the state religion but refusing to persecute Catholics. She avoided giving her Catholic subjects a reason to support a foreign-inspired insurrection to replace her with Mary Queen of Scots or any other Catholic claimant. Her prudence was well rewarded, for when the realm was most in danger and threatened by the Spanish Armada in 1588, Catholics and Protestants united against their common foreign enemy.

The Elizabethan Age

Elizabeth I was a pragmatist capable of uniting her country irrespective of religious belief. This same policy extended into her personal life. While Elizabeth I's advisers were dismayed at her repeated refusal to marry and produce an heir, she realized that her power rested in the ability to rule alone.

Below: The defeat of the Spanish Armada owed as much to the appalling weather as it did to English seamanship, but the removal of the Spanish threat left England free to begin its climb to naval supremacy—and free to plunder the Spanish gold galleons coming from the New World.

While still capable of child-bearing, Elizabeth attracted suitors, including Philip II of Spain, former husband of Mary I. Although Elizabeth had several lovers and favorites in court, all offers were rejected. Philip took it as an insult to himself and his country, leading to irrevocable fracture of Anglo-Spanish relations. Spain was first a diplomatic and religious opponent, then an open aggressor as the two nations came to represent the extremes of Protestant and Catholic factions in Europe.

Elizabeth and her councilors secretly encouraged the Dutch to rebel against their Spanish masters, while in return Philip funded and encouraged Catholic plots against her. In 1585 English troops sailed to the Netherlands to support the Dutch rebellion, and following the execution of Mary Queen of Scots, Catholic claimant to the English throne, a full-scale war began.

Philip ordered an armada to sail up the Channel, link up with Spanish forces in the Netherlands, then proceed to England. Once ashore, the veteran Spanish troops would have captured London and forced Elizabeth into exile. The 130-strong Spanish Armada fought a running battle up the English Channel during the summer of 1588, and although English commanders such as Howard of Effingham, Sir Francis Drake, and Sir Martin Frobisher harried them, they were unable to stop the Spaniards' progress.

When the Spanish anchored off Calais, Howard sent fireships into their anchorage and scattered the armada. A hard-fought engagement

drove the battered Spanish fleet into the North Sea, where contrary winds forced them to abandon their invasion plans. As the fleet tried to sail around the north of Scotland in an attempt to return home, a series of gales scattered the the ships towards the Irish coast. Many were wrecked along the way; barely half the original fleet limped home to Spanish ports. The conflict with Spain continued for the remainder of Elizabeth's reign but the threat of invasion had passed.

Despite uncertainties surrounding the start of her reign, Elizabeth's intelligence and political astuteness enabled her to win the support of her subjects. England and Wales prospered as never before. Their sailors and traders explored the world and the arts and literature flourished in the new air of optimism. Perhaps Elizabeth's greatest failure was her inability to provide an heir, leading to the replacement of the Tudors by the Scottish royal family, the Stuarts (Stewarts), beginning in 1603 with James I (James VI of Scotland). The Elizabethan era therefore represents the last great English hurrah, before the country became part of a greater political entity.

A literary cornucopia

The Elizabethan age was a war culture, and the queen herself was uninterested in the arts. Unlike her prodigious father, she built little and patronized painters only to the extent of buying necessary official portraits with a distinct lack of enthusiasm. However, the Elizabethan courtly circle did encourage painting—especially that peculiarly English passion, the miniature—music, and most importantly, writing. Elizabeth had enjoyed a good classical education under the humanist scholar Roger Ascham (1515–68) and spoke four languages other than her own English: Latin, Greek, French, and Italian. Ascham's most famous work is *The Schoolmaster*, published after his death in 1570, which is a manual on the teaching of children.

Elizabeth's interest in education extended to her foundation of Westminster School in 1560, a new type of institution for a new type of teaching, one that combined a humanist and

classical education with a well-rounded complement of physical activity intended to produce the courtiers and administrators for the reinvigorated England. Westminster's first headmaster was William Camden (1551–1623), a noted antiquarian. For the first time, the study of history was becoming an important part of the curriculum, and Camden's *Britannia* (1586) was a systematic history of Britain that received universal acclaim for its research and authority.

Elizabeth's reign is notable for the outpouring of remarkable literature. Inspired by Camden, the courtier Sir Walter Raleigh wrote his *History of the World* while languishing in the Tower of London; Sir Thomas North translated Roman historian Plutarch's *Lives*; and Edmund Spenser (*The Shepherd's Calendar*, 1579) and Sir Philip Sidney (*Arcadia*, 1590) published extensive works that influenced subsequent generations of poets and writers. And of course there were the plays of Marlowe, Shakespeare, and Ben Jonson. Of these, Shakespeare was to become a household name worldwide.

Above: "Good Queen Bess" presided over an England that was coming into its own in learning and Renaissance culture, even though she was uninterested in the arts. Her patronage extended to the theater and education; besides founding Westminster School in 1560, she endowed others and issued valuable charters, such as to the grammar school of Highgate village (now a part of North London) in 1564. Such charters meant that the often impoverished schools could attract sons of the aristocracy.

Shakespeare—"Not of an Age, But for all Time"

William Shakespeare was a poet, playwright, and jobbing actor who wrote popular comedies and melodramas for Elizabethan Londoners. His work has transcended time and locale to be performed in countries and languages undreamed of even in his fertile imagination.

Above: There is little certainty about Shakespeare's true appearance, beyond this engraving (which has been hand-colored later) that appeared on the frontispiece of the *First Folio* (Bodleian copy) of 1623. It appeared under the text: *Mr. William Shakespeares Comedies, Histories, & Tragedies. Publifhed according to the True Originall Copies.*

Liberally sewn with puns and contemporary political references, Shakespeare's plays told the universal stories of love and betrayal, deception and revelation, intrigue at court, and family disasters. They were eagerly received by everyone from royalty to the common rabble, demonstrating an ability to appeal to all levels. Today his works are seen as masterpieces responsible for establishing the richness and diversity of the English language. He was lauded even in his own time, as the prescient quote by Ben Johnson in the headline above proves.

Given his literary importance, frustratingly little is known about William Shakespeare. He was born in Stratford-upon-Avon in the county of Warwickshire, England in April 1564, the third of eight children of John Shakespeare, a glove-maker and wool dealer. William probably attended the King's New School in Stratford, where he would have received a good liberal education, including tuition in Latin and Greek. He is presumed to have worked as a teacher before being drawn to the theater.

In 1582 he married Anne Hathaway, a farmer's daughter from nearby Shottery. Anne was eight years older than her husband and five months pregnant with their first daughter, Susanna, born the following year. In 1585 Anne delivered twins: Hamnet and Judith. It seems that they all left Stratford for London, for reasons unknown; he probably found the lure of a touring actors' company irresistible.

By 1592 Shakespeare was working as a professional actor in London. His first known patron was Lord Southampton, for whom he would have worked at The Theatre or The Curtain. By then he was probably writing plays, and his poems *Venus and Adonis* and *The Rape of Lucrece* appeared at about that time, while his sonnets, composed in the late 1590s, were published in 1609.

There is much disagreement about the order in which most of his great plays were written— or even how many he actually wrote. Despite his prolific output, none of Shakespeare's original manuscripts has survived—his only known extant handwriting is six signatures. Similarly, there is no known attributable contemporary portrait of him. His earliest work is generally thought to be *Henry VI* (1590–91), and the first Roman tragedy, *Titus Andronicus*, was performed in 1594, the same year as his first comedy, *Two Gentlemen of Verona*. His major influences are clear: North's contemporary traslation of Plutarch's *Lives* provided much Roman history, while *The Chronicles of England, Scotland, and Ireland* (1577) by Raphael Holinshed (d.1580) was the principal source for Shakespeare's historical plays.

Grand patronage

One of Shakespeare's first London lodgings was in St. Helen's, Bishopsgate, where he probably stayed with his family. Tragedy struck when his son Hamnet died there, aged 11. His family returned to Stratford, where Shakespeare bought New Place, the best house in the town, while he remained in London. Within two years Shakespeare was working as a full member of The Lord

Chamberlain's Men, a company of actors who performed at the Globe and Blackfriars theaters.

London theaters were closed in times of trouble, as happened during the plague of 1592–94. During these periods Shakespeare wrote poetry, including his sonnets. At his peak between 1594 and 1598 Shakespeare wrote five historical plays, six comedies, and one tragedy. In 1598 he helped to establish the New Globe Theatre on Bankside, in the heart of London's entertainment center, near the brothels and gaming houses. Elizabethan theaters were rowdy, looked down on as places of licentiousness, drunken behavior, and general mayhem. The New Globe opened to a packed house with a performance of *Henry V* the following year.

Today, Shakespeare's language seems complex, but he was writing in the popular idiom and his audience easily picked up his bawdy references, *double-entendres*, and political swipes. The common folk had to stand in the "pit" to watch, where they would laugh, cry, shout, and get thoroughly and noisily involved in the performance.

With Shakespeare as their chief dramatist, The Lord Chamberlain's Men performed regularly at court for Elizabeth. When James VI succeeded to the English throne as James I, he became their royal patron and the troupe became The King's Men. James granted them a patent and doubled their pay.

By 1611 Shakespeare was living mostly in Stratford but still making frequent visits to London. His last major completed work was *The Tempest* (1611). Shakespeare died a wealthy man aged 52 about April 23, 1616—the undisputed greatest literary figure of the English Renaissance—and was buried in Holy Trinity Church, Stratford-upon-Avon.

Below: Theatergoers in London can enjoy performances of Elizabethan plays in the faithful reconstruction of the original New Globe Theatre where Shakespeare appeared. The modern version was founded by Sam Wanamaker, and has enjoyed considerable success since its opening in 1996—despite the vagaries of the English weather (it was reputedly much drier and warmer in Renaissance England).

CHAPTER 8

A World Apart— Spain and Her Empire

Spain's dramatic rise to greatness was impossible to foretell before the late 15th century. Large portions of the Iberian peninsula were in the hands of the Moors; the Spanish kingdoms were fragmented and disunited, their lands poor and infertile. But by the middle of the 16th century Spain was a major part of the Habsburg empire, a Renaissance superpower with

Spain's conquest of the Philippines, 1564–71

The first island to be pacified was Cebu, quickly followed by Leyte, Bohol, Negros, Masbate, and Panay. By 1571 Luzon was largely in Spanish hands, and Manila was established as the provincial capital.

Luzon

San Lazaro
(Philippine Islands)

Manila

Philippine Sea

Mindoro

Samar

to Acapulco.
New Spain

South China Sea

Masbate

Panay

Leyte

Cebu

Negros

Cebu

Bohol

Palawan

Zamboanga

Mindanao
southern part
to Sultanate
of Macassar

Borneo

PACIFIC OCEAN

Sulu Archipelago

Celebes Sea

When Magellan made landfall in the Philippines on March 16, 1521, he named the islands the Archipelago San Lazaro, since it was sighted on a Saturday, the day of Lazarus. The islands were later renamed the Philippines after King Philip II. Four subsequent expeditions to subdue the Filipino natives met with failure, until the fifth, led by Miguel López de Legazpi, captured Cebu. Between 1565 and 1570, his conquistadors engaged in an organized plan of annexation until the Filipinos signed a peace treaty, effectively giving Spain control of another valuable gold-producing country. Since this wealth could not be transported in a westward direction (in theory, this region belonged to Portugal, but their sailors had not reached the Philippines), the Spanish set up the "Manila Galleon" route, east to Acapulco and Mexico, and then on to Spain from there.

Newfoundland

Nova Scotia

Spain and the Habsburg's overseas empire in the Americas, 1492–1750

For the European Habsburg empire at this time, see the map on pages 58–59

Havana-Cadiz
direct route

NORTH ATLANTIC OCEAN

St. Lawrence

Georgian Bay

Lake Ontario

Lake Huron

Lake Erie

Santo Domingo
1496

Lake Superior

Lake Michigan

Hispani

Bahamas

Mississippi

St. Augustine
1565

Florida

Cuba

Matanzas
1693

Jamaica

Pensacola
1698

Havana
1515

Mississippi

Arkansas

New Orleans

Armada Española
route, to 1748

Porto Bello
1597

Gulf of Mexico

San Antonio
1718

Flota a Nueva
España route,
1580–1790

YUCATÁN

Colorado

Santa Fe
1609

Rio Grande

El Paso
1659

Zacatecas

Antigua
1542

Veracruz
1519

NORTH PACIFIC OCEAN

San Francisco

Mexico City
(Tenochtitlán)
1546

Acapulco

Culiacán
1540

Galleon route between Manila (Philippines) and Acapulco

possessions stretching from the North Sea to the southern shores of Mediterranean, and which spanned the Atlantic Ocean from the New World to the Old.

The catalyst for Spain's great success was the joining of its two principal kingdoms with the marriage of Ferdinand of Aragon and Isabella of Castile. This guaranteed the reconquest of Granada, the final expulsion of the Moors from the Iberian peninsula, and the unification of Spain as a Christian country. The same year that Granada fell, Isabella financed Columbus's first voyage of discovery. Soon a treasure fleet bore the first of what would become regular shipments of silver and gold from the New World. When Habsburg Charles became Spain's king in 1516 the country was tied to a great empire, further expanded when he became Holy Roman Emperor three years later.

As the champion of the Roman Catholic Church, Spain's exploration and subsequent conquest of much of the New World had produced the first transatlantic economy, funding a European empire that reached its apogee under that quintessential Habsburg monarch Philip II of Spain. Philip's empire dominated the Old and New Worlds, the envy of all lesser powers, while its European possessions included some of the richest states in the continent. Spain's highly successful army and extensive resources made it the arbiter of peace or war in Europe following their victory against the French in the Italian Wars. Even France was unable to rival Spanish political might, money, and political influence.

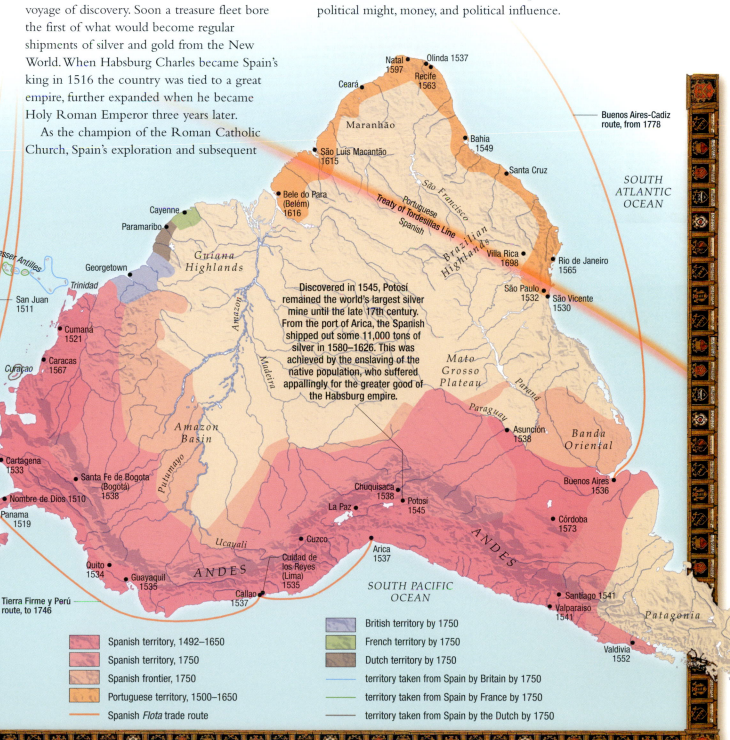

Discovered in 1545, Potosí remained the world's largest silver mine until the late 17th century. From the port of Arica, the Spanish shipped out some 11,000 tons of silver in 1580–1626. This was achieved by the enslaving of the native population, who suffered appallingly for the greater good of the Habsburg empire.

Spanish territory, 1492–1650
Spanish territory, 1750
Spanish frontier, 1750
Portuguese territory, 1500–1650
Spanish *Flota* trade route

British territory by 1750
French territory by 1750
Dutch territory by 1750
territory taken from Spain by Britain by 1750
territory taken from Spain by France by 1750
territory taken from Spain by the Dutch by 1750

The Unification of Spain

At first the unification of Spain involved the union of the thrones of Castile and Aragon, pious monarchs determined to complete the Reconquista started in the 11th century. Finally it involved the political will to weld the disparate regions of Spain into a cohesive whole.

For over six centuries, the reconquest of territory captured following the Muslim invasion of the eighth century—the Reconquista—was dominant in Spain. Castile (the "land of castles") was created as a buffer between the Moors to the south and the Christian kingdom of León to the north. By the 11th century it had become a kingdom, its growing influence during the next two centuries

Genoa. It extended to Sicily when Peter III of Aragon (1276–85) was elected ruler of the island; later Naples joined the federation. This rapid political growth was followed by almost two centuries of economic stagnation and military inertia, and by the mid-15th century the Reconquista had been all but abandoned.

Spanish fortunes improved with the marriage of Ferdinand of Aragon and Isabella of Castile in 1469. Ferdinand V (1452–1516), son of John II of Aragon, would become king in 1479; he was also Ferdinand II of Sicily (r.1468–1516) and Ferdinand III of Naples (r.1504–16). Their motto was *Tanto monta, monta tanto: Isabel como Fernando* (The one is worth as much as the other: Isabella as Ferdinand).

Right: The Catholic Majesties, Ferdinand of Aragon and Isabella of Castile, by the Granadan sculptor Alonso de Mena (1587–1646).

ensuring its dominance when the crowns of León and Castile were joined in 1230 by Ferdinand III of Castile (d.1252).

Other Christian buffer states had been formed on the Iberian side of the Pyrenees, the Kingdom of Aragon and County of Catalonia, federated through marriage in 1137. When Valencia and its hinterland was captured from the Moors in 1283 it was incorporated into the Aragonese state. The union of these three territories produced a nation with extensive maritime trading links and commercial interests rivaling those of Venice and

Ferdinand's cousin Isabella I (1451–1504) was daughter of John II of Castile and León. On the death of her brother Henry IV in 1474, Ferdinand and Isabella jointly succeeded to the throne of Castile and León. The succession was aggressively disputed by Alfonso V of Portugal, who supported the claim of Henry IV's second daughter, Juana—called La Beltraneja, because it was believed that her real father was royal favorite Beltran de la Cueva. The Treaty of Alcaçovas ended the conflict in September 1479 and La Beltraneja retired to a convent.

The Catholic Majesties

The next vital step in the unification of Spain was the resumption of the Reconquista in 1482. Fought with skilled Castilian troops and the monarchy's determination to continue the campaign whatever the human or fiscal cost, it ended on January 2, 1492, with the capture of Granada, the last independent Moorish kingdom in the Iberian peninsula. Spain was unified under the Christian banner, which earned Ferdinand and Isabella the appellation "The Catholic Majesties" from Borgia Pope Alexander VI in recognition of their service to the Church. The Spanish monarchy would remain steadfastly loyal to the Catholic Church throughout the Reformation.

War was one tool of extending royal authority, the other was domination of the nobility. In 1478 a bull issued by Pope Sixtus IV allowed Ferdinand and Isabella to appoint three inquisitors to deal with heretics and other offenders, a move designed to combat any resurgence of Muslim influence. The Spanish Inquisition (*see second spread following*) was soon used by the monarchy to threaten the nobility with relative impunity. In Castile nobles were stripped of their privileges and most of their power, replaced by royal supporters. The process was less successful in Catalonia and Valencia, where the nobility was necessary to control mercantile communities.

Ferdinand continued to consolidate royal power after Isabella's death in 1504, and embarked on a series of military campaigns that led to Spanish involvement in Italy (ostensibly on behalf of the semi-autonomous Kingdom of Naples) and conquests in North Africa (1509). On his death, Ferdinand left a kingdom unified in all but name, and a financial and military machine that would make Spain the greatest power in Europe.

The final stages of the Reconquista, campaigns of Ferdinand and Isabella

- conquered by Spain, 1481–85
- conquered by Spain, 1486–89
- Granadan territory, 1489–92
- Spanish victory, with date
- Spanish defeat, with date

Cordoba
Guadalquivir
Seville
Ecija
Ubeda
Baena
Jaen
Guadalquivir
Lucena
Alacal La Real
1485
Moclin
1483
1483
Lora
Jerez
Arcos
1483
Loja
1482
1492
Lorca
Sangonera
Cadiz
Setenil
Archidona
Granada
Guadix
Medina Sidonia
Ronda
Alhama
1483
Purchena
ATLANTIC OCEAN
Marbella
Fuengriola
Málaga
Velez Málaga
Mojacar
Algeciras
Gibraltar
Adra
Almería
to Portugal
MEDITERRANEAN SEA
Tangier
Ceuta
to Islamic Sharifs

Charles V–A Colossus on the European Stage

Charles V was born in Flanders, unable to speak Spanish, and spent most of his life in Germany. However, his empire was sustained by Spanish troops, who ensured his ultimate victory over France in a war that dominated Europe during the later Renaissance.

When Habsburg Prince Charles inherited the Spanish throne on the death of his grandfather in 1516, becoming King Charles I of Spain, he was already used to power, having inherited vast estates in Germany. This influence was strengthened in 1519, when he acquired the elective title of Holy Roman Emperor from his other grandfather, becoming Charles V.

Along with Spain's New World possessions, he inherited her interests in Italy and a war that had been raging for almost a quarter of a century.

Charles was born in the Flemish town of Ghent in February 1500, the offspring of a demented Spanish mother and a handsome but vain German father. A true Habsburg, his lower jaw protruded far enough to interfere with his speech, which left him reluctant to say more than necessary. Charles arrived in Spain to take up his inheritance in late 1517, surrounded by Flemish advisers eager to take advantage of all that Spain had to offer. Throughout his reign, he used Spanish silver; initially money raised from the taxation of Castile, later from the great Peruvian

Right: *The Emperor Charles V at the Battle of Mühlberg* (*see also page 161*). In 1548, the year following his victory over the Lutherans at Mühlberg, Charles V sat for the great Venetian painter Titian. The result, shown here, is widely considered to be one the greatest equestrian portraits ever painted. Titian made his sitter into a grave, taciturn, yet heroic figure. But there is no sense of flattery— Charles' famous jutting jaw is clearly visible, and he appears to be somberly contemplating the victory the picture celebrates instead of ostentatiously relishing his triumph.

silver mines at Potosi. By the end of his reign this influx of New World silver was in full flow.

Charles left Spain for Germany in 1520, a move that may have incited the large-scale tax rebellion in the kingdom but was necessary to strengthen his less robust tenure over his Imperial lands. He defeated Francis I of France and secured his election to the Holy Roman Empire through extensive bribes (using Spanish money gleaned from the Philippines and the Americas), the presence of his own Swabian League army (funded by the Spanish treasury), and the intimidation of rival pro-French factional leaders driven into exile by heavy-handed tactics from Charles' agents.

Vacating the seats of power

Becoming Holy Roman Emperor gave Charles power and the opportunity to tax the wealthy German states, but also brought major political, religious and military problems. Controlling the government of the German empire and safeguarding his eastern possessions was made substantially more difficult by the defeat of brother-in-law King Louis II of Hungary at Mohács (1526) at the hands of Ottoman Turks. However, he overcame military challenges, defeating Francis I at Pavia (1525, *see pages 72–3*) to secure Imperial victory in the Italian Wars, then driving the Turks from Vienna (1529) before taking the offensive against the Muslim threat by capturing Tunis (1535).

The real threat was internal social and religious unrest. The small-scale heresy of Martin Luther quickly developed into a larger Reformation movement through its appeal to the religiously disaffected laity of northern Germany. A theological clash between reformers and ecclesiastic supporters of the emperor became open warfare. Charles defeated his Lutheran opponents at the battle of Mühlberg (1547), which inspired a celebrated equestrian portrait by Titian, but the Protestant rebels were not silenced.

During his final years, Charles seemed to realize the importance of Habsburg Spain; he came to rely on Spanish advisers and military commanders, his son Philip was raised as a Castilian, and he was well aware that his strength came from Spanish troops and New World wealth. Unable to continue active rule due to severe gout, he progressively abdicated his crowns (1555–58). Philip (the heir from his marriage to Isabella of Portugal) inherited Spain, the (Spanish) Netherlands, and the Habsburg possessions in Italy. His brother Ferdinand inherited Habsburg domains in Germany, a realm which would become the Austro-Hungarian empire. Charles retired to a Spanish monastery in Estremadura, where he died in 1558, leaving behind an empire divided into two mutually supportive branches of the Habsburg dynasty that would uphold the Catholic cause in an increasingly divided Europe.

Above: *Cardinal Farnese and Charles V Leading the Army against the Lutherans*, by Federico Zuccari (1542–1609). To the Catholic artists of the later 16th century, the Holy Roman Empire's defeat of Protestantism at Mühlberg was an inspiration.

Religious Intolerance and the Inquisition

Ferdinand and Isabella were awarded the title of "the Catholic Majesties" for evicting the Muslims from Spain in 1492, but this was just one step in a process of religious and racial cleansing that came to dominate Spanish life in the decades that followed.

In November 1478 Pope Sixtus VI authorized Ferdinand and Isabella to establish a state-controlled tribunal to enforce uniformity of religious practice. It was originally charged with investigating the sincerity of those who had renounced Judaism (the Marranos) or Mohammedanism (Moriscos) for Christianity, but who were suspected of secretly practicing their original faith. Moors had been in Spain for over five centuries, and intermarried with Christians and Jews. As happens so often throughout history, religion became a factor in determining social acceptance, hence the Spanish Inquisition grew fat on intolerance.

The Spanish Church had always been opposed to heresy, and the increasingly orthodox line taken in the Middle Ages was intended to discourage dissent. By the 12th century, the Church had gained such a strong hold that heretics were regarded as enemies of the whole of Christian society. In 1231 Pope Gregory IX set up the first papal Inquisition, a word derived from the Latin verb *inquiro* (to inquire into), but which was designed to prevent the spread of heresy.

The penalties for the medieval heretic were stringent; life imprisonment for those who repented, and death for those who refused to recant. The inquisitors, usually Franciscan or Dominican monks, were expected to uncover heresy, but by the mid-13th century this process usually involved the torture of suspects. Executions were carried out by secular authorities, allowing clerics to avoid charges of un-Christian action and enforcing the link between the Church and secular government in Spain. It also permitted the Inquisition to be manipulated by unscrupulous secular powers.

Torquemada

The Spanish Inquisition of the Renaissance was distinguished from its medieval roots through its close association with the crown. Under Ferdinand and Isabella, the Inquisition formed part of the royal administration, and crown-appointed clerics supervised trials, interrogations, and executions in the name of both Church and State. It was thus as useful for rooting out political or dynastic opposition as it was for the eradication of heretics or unbelievers.

The inquisitors could question anyone or accept accusations from any informer. The accused had no right to cross-examine their accusers, and often the identity of the denouncers was kept from all but the inquisitors themselves. Once accused—fairly or not—the "heretics" had few options before them, none pleasant. They were given the opportunity to recant, admit their sins and pray for forgiveness—but this was rarely believed unless the recantation was uttered under torture. They were also required to identify other heretics on pain of further torture, creating what amounted to a self-perpetuating cycle of accusation and confession.

While confessions sometimes led to shorter prison sentences or even acquittal, those who refused to admit guilt were burned alive or chained in solitary confinement and left to die. Today, the penalties meted out for seemingly minor transgressions seem unreasonable, but the Inquisition was widely supported by a Spanish population who remained firmly opposed to reformation, heresy, or alternative faith.

The name most readily associated with the Inquisition is Tomás de Torquemada (1420–98), a Dominican monk who from 1474 was confessor to both Isabella and Ferdinand, becoming Spain's first inquisitor-general in 1478. Under his hands and those of his successors, the Inquisition grew in influence until by the late 1530s there were 19 courts across Spain and Spanish territory, including Flanders. Three more were later created in the New World. Torquemada became a major

Left: In a work of extraordinary psychological perception, El Greco (*see page 131*) captures the power of the Spanish Inquisition in his portrait of the Cardinal Inquisitor-General Don Fernando Niño de Guevera (1541–1609), painted c.1600, shortly before the cardinal became Archbishop of Seville. A sense of unease is created by the slightly three-quarter-view pose, emphasis on the glasses, and the compulsive gesture of his left hand.

Facing: *Questioning at a Trial*, from the Altarpiece of Santa Cruz, by Martin Bernat (1454–97). Also called the Alfajarin Master because his most significant work was undertaken in the parish church in Alfajarin, near Saragossa, Spain, this painter of the Early Renaissance had a linear style that reinforced the anguish of the characters he depicted.

force behind the expulsion of Jews from Spain in 1492, and during his 15-year tenure ordered the burning of some 2,000 "confessed" heretics, and the torture or incarceration of thousands more. It would take centuries for the Inquisition to disappear from Spain, in fact it lingered until the early 19th century, a symbol of religious intolerance and Spanish piety.

Art and Piety

As a pious country Spain embraced the Renaissance as a tool for devotional thinking. Life was dominated by the authorities of Church and Crown, consequently Spanish culture found expression in religious art, designed to reinforce rather than question existing values.

Right: *Portrait of Elizabeth of Valois*, the third wife of Philip II, by Alonso Sánchez Coello.

Below: *Christ Bearing the Cross* by Luís de Morales. His usually small pictures are mostly devotional, and his distinctive style was formed away from the courtly centers.

Most Spanish artistic work was commissioned by and for the Catholic Church. Court portraits of royalty and the nobility were the only other outlet for patronage. Many Spanish artists traveled to cultural centers in Italy, returning to Spain enthused with the techniques, use of color, and technical dynamism of the Italian Renaissance. Raphael and Michelangelo were much lauded by the Roman clergy, and consequently became examples for Spanish artists seeking ecclesiastical patronage. Italian Renaissance sculpture, particularly the works of Michelangelo and Benvenuto Cellini, provided essential guidelines for Spanish devotional sculptors.

Spanish art differed from contemporary non-Iberian works in its rejection of nudity, and lack of mythological and allegorical scenes. Instead Spanish artists chose tamer subjects, avoiding classical depictions in favor of works exploring the mysticism and asceticism associated with Christian spirituality, along with its attendant suffering and exultation. In the early 16th century many foreign Catholic painters found patrons in the cities of central and southern Spain, bringing with them not only Italian influences but also the new ideas emerging in northern Europe, especially those developed by the Flemish masters. Despite their more liberal upbringing, most quickly adhered to Spanish sensibilities. One of the most significant non-Spanish artists was Alejo Fernández (c.1470–1543), who was probably German but who adopted the name of his Spanish wife, along with her culture. He worked in Cordoba before moving to Seville, where his most famous work adorns the city's cathedral.

By 1550 the influence of Raphael was felt by all artists. Two of the most significant of the new breed of Spanish artists who followed his visual precepts were Vicente Masip (c.1475–1540) and his son Juan de Juanes (c.1523–79). Work undertaken by Masip in Segovia cathedral came to epitomize Spanish piety. His son explored this religious theme in greater depth, and was much sought after as a religious artist.

Light and shade

A later follower of this peculiarly Spanish devotional style was Luís de Morales (c.1520–1586), who worked in Estremadura. His intense devotional paintings earned him the nickname Morales el Divino. He painted in exacting detail, in a style reminiscent of the Flemish masters, while his elongated figures predated those of El Greco. His work is regarded as the apotheosis of Spanish asceticism.

In the later 16th century, courtly portrait painting became increasingly popular, for which Alonso Sánchez Coello (c.1531–88) and his pupil and successor Juan Pantoja de la Cruz (1551–1609) are now best remembered. Juan Fernández de Navarrete (1526–79), a deaf mute, studied in Italy before becoming a court painter to Philip II, working in the Escorial (the royal palace and mausoleum, *see page 148*) in a distinctly Venetian style. He specialized in using the colors, light, and chiaroscuro of northern Italy. Important artists who emerged later in the century included Pablo de Céspedes in Cordoba, and Vasco de Pereira and Francisco Pacheco in Seville, the latter being teacher and father-in-law of Velázquez, the great Spanish

court painter of the 17th century.

The greatest Spanish artist of the later 16th century is indisputably Domenikos Theotocopoulos (1541–1614), better known as El Greco. Born in Crete but trained in Italy under Titian, his unique style of mannerism encompassed elements of Late Italian Renaissance art. However, his emphasis on rich colors, elongated figures, and exaggerated chiaroscuro created a uniquely Spanish post-Renaissance genre of Italian Mannerism. El Greco's work conveys the ecstasy and spiritual possession so beloved of the Spanish during this period, in a manner no other native artist achieved. Although his best known works post-dated the effective end of the Renaissance, his unique amalgam of earlier Renaissance styles created paintings of great spiritual resonance—exactly the type of propaganda the Counter-Reformation needed.

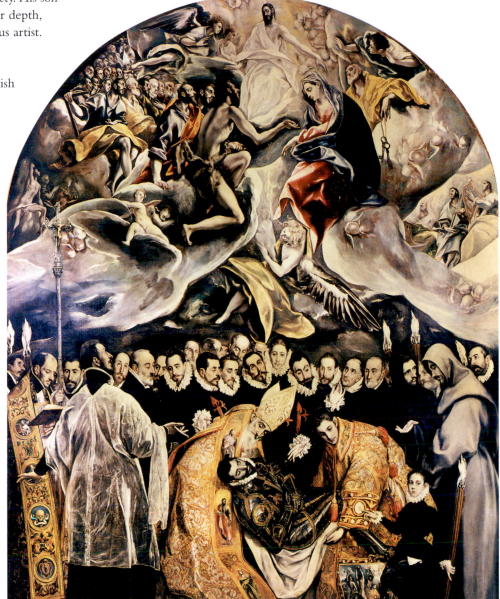

Above: El Greco's masterpiece *The Burial of Count Orgaz* (1586) is sited on a wall of Santo Tomé in Toledo, above the noble's actual burial place. As Saints Stephen and Augustine bury him, his soul rises to heaven. The work indicates El Greco's horror of unfilled space.

Left: Juan Pantoj de la Cruz' portrait of Infanta Anna and her brother, King Philip IV of Spain, (1607) illustrates the stiff formality of Spanish courtly painting.

Philip II–Master of Europe

Charles V's son Philip succeeded him as head of the Habsburg empire in Spain, and brought the country to the pinnacle of its power. His influence on the course of the Reformation and the religious division of Europe would complete the cycle begun by Ferdinand and Isabella.

Facing: Philip II Offering to Victory, part of a cycle of mythological paintings for the king that Titian began in 1553, which included *Diana and Callisto, Diana Surprised by Acteon,* and *The Rape of Europa.*

Philip II (1527–98) inherited the major portion of lands from his father; Spain (r.1556–98) and the Spanish overseas empire, the Habsburg lands in Italy, and the Netherlands. Between 1554–58 he was King of England as the husband of Mary I. Her untimely death, lack of offspring, and the unwillingness of her Protestant sister Elizabeth to marry the Catholic Philip terminated that connection and led to an attempt

Above: Alonso Sánchez Coello's portrait of Philip is quietly sedate compared to Titian's rare example in Spain of a mythological subject.

to take the country by force—his ill-fated Armada of 1588 (*see pages 118–9*).

Philip's empire was fabulously rich, thanks to New World silver and his possession of the Low Countries, the industrial heartland of 16th-century Europe. Unlike his father, he was a confirmed Spaniard, running his empire from Madrid, the capital he established in the geographical center of the Iberian peninsula. He moved his court there in 1561, then built the magnificent but austere Escorial 20 miles northwest of his city. Completed in 1584, it was used as a royal residence, mausoleum, and monastery.

Philip's empire expanded when he annexed the throne of Portugal following the death of its king, Sebastian, in battle against the Moors in 1578. Sebastian's successor Cardinal Henry died in 1580, allowing Philip to take the throne by force. A single monarch would rule the Iberian peninsula until 1640, since his son, Philip III (1578–1621), would inherit the Portuguese crown on his father's death.

Philip was a conscientious monarch, even overly so, his involvement in government often interrupting the smooth progress of State. His father had advised Philip to trust only himself. Philip took the advice literally, keeping all decision-making in his own hands. He found it difficult to establish priorities, and although he was unusually hard-working, delays in royal approvals caused the empire to grind to a halt. As an Italian subject commented, "If death came from Spain, we should live to a very great age."

Expelling the Reformation

In this era marriage was a tool of foreign policy, and Philip made full use of it, marrying four times. The first was to Maria of Portugal (1543). When she died in childbirth three years later, Philip married Mary I of England, a union that could have cemented England's return to the Roman Catholic fold. His marriage to Elizabeth of Valois sealed the Peace of Cateau-Cambrésis in 1559 and ended the wars between Spain and France. His final marriage was to the Habsburg Anne of Austria, daughter of Philip's cousin, Emperor Maximilian II, and Philip's sister Marie. This union produced his heir, Philip III.

While a consummate strategist, politician, and diplomat, even Philip could not stem the general decline in Spanish fortunes in the late 16th century. A combination of rampant inflation, military setbacks, and a reduction in the flow of New World silver eroded Spain's power. A more lasting success was his involvement in the Counter-Reformation, and through his efforts the spread of Protestantism was checked in

MAIORA TIBI

southern Europe and the Spanish Americas.

A pious monarch, Philip consummately believed in the efficacy of the Catholic faith, and actively sought to counter the spread of Protestant heresy by every means available: diplomacy, financial coercion, military threat, and the Inquisition. However, he encountered two great setbacks; the revolt of the Dutch, who created a Protestant state, and his failure to conquer Tudor England, either through marital alliance or by invasion. In the century after his death these two rivals became leading maritime powers and helped ensure the demotion of Spain from her position as the European superpower.

Spanish Humanism

Through their involvement in Italy, the Spanish played an important part in the development of the Italian Renaissance. Spanish scholars and artists embraced humanism, while adapting the cultural phenomenon to suit their uniquely orthodox environment.

Like everything in Spain, scholarship had to be subservient to the Church. There was no room for dissent, or even for liberal questioning of existing values. University patronage was ecclesiastical rather than secular, therefore Spanish scholarship was closely associated with the Roman Catholic Church, which students were encouraged to defend against its critics.

At the end of the 15th century the government of Ferdinand and Isabella enforced religious conformity through the Inquisition, military conquest, and strict secular support for Catholic orthodoxy. Jews were forbidden to practice their faith from 1492, and those who refused to be baptized into the Church were expelled. Similarly, Moors were compelled to renounce their religion or face exile to North Africa. Even the Christian population was subject to harsh restrictions, since any questioning of theological doctrine or of the authority of Church or State could result in being branded a heretic.

To ensure the maintenance of this religious orthodoxy, Spanish clerics turned to artists and scholars to provide inspiration to the laity. Many of these had experienced the Italian Renaissance and had common contact with humanist scholarship. The Spanish even founded a college in Italy within the University of Bologna in the late 14th century, to encourage the development of cultural, intellectual, and theological links between the two countries.

Most Spanish scholars and artists visited Italy during their lives, and most embraced humanist ideas before bringing this cultural doctrine back to Spain. Humanism had an influence in Spain long before the cultural effects of the Italian Renaissance were felt in northern Europe. In Spanish universities, classical studies were revived; the works of writers such as Homer, Livy, and Plato were translated into Spanish during the 15th century. This had a profound influence on the development of Spanish literature, particularly on Diego de San Pedro, whose *Carcel de Amore* (1492), an allegory of the religion of love, became an early literary classic. A growing tradition relied on allegory, romance, and the idealistic realization of human relationships, writers providing an escape from the rigid orthodoxy of everyday Spanish life. Even this found a parallel in the Spanish emphasis on mysticism as an integral part of religious belief.

Standardizing the language

In humanist scholarship, the Spanish tended to be more conservative. One of the greatest Spanish humanist works was the Complutensian Polyglot Bible of Alcala, a monumental multilingual version of the Bible dated 1514–17, although it was not published until 1522. Work began in 1502 through the patronage of the Spanish cardinal, Francisco Ximenes de Cisneros, the confessor of Queen Isabella. He wanted to

Right: A late 15th-century manuscript Illumination depicts Antonio de Nebrija with his Castilian Language Book, which became an important tool in the colonization of the New World, and the establishment of the Spanish hegemony.

1230	1283	1469	1476	1478	1479	1482–92	1500
The kingdoms of Castile and Leon are unified by Ferdinand III of Castile	Valencia is recaptured from the Moors and added to the Aragonese and Catalonian state	Isabella of Castile marries Ferdinand of Aragon	Isabella gains the throne of Castile after the dynastic struggle that followed father Henry IV's death	Tomás de Torquemada leads the Spanish Inquisition	Ferdinand becomes King of Aragon, uniting the two kingdoms	Christian Spain conducts its reconquest of territories taken by the Islamic Moors	Birth of Charles, grandson of Emperor Maximilian I and Ferdinand and Isabella of Spain

Left: This illumination shows the interior of the pharmacy of scientist and philosopher Ibn Sina, from the *Cannon Mayor*. Despite the violent removal of the Moors in 1492, Spain retained a profound admiration for Islamic navigational, scientific, and medical knowledge. Ibn Sina (980–1037) was the legendary Muslim physician who traveled extensively and wrote numerous books.

Below: A lecturer at the University of Bologna, from a 15th-century manuscript.

of Queen Isabella. He wanted to make the biblical text available in parallel columns of Latin, Greek, Aramaic, and Hebrew.

The project involved some of the leading Spanish humanist scholars of the late 15th–early 16th century, including Antonio de Nebrija (1442–1522), who rebelled against the orthodoxy of the cardinal's editing. Nebrija's book of Latin grammar (1481) became a standard dictionary throughout Christendom. At the request of Queen Isabella he produced a Spanish language version (1486), followed by the first Spanish language dictionary. This establishment of the Spanish (Castilian) language was a vital tool in the colonization of the New World.

Other Spanish humanists were less supportive of the crown. The works of Bartolome Las Casas (1476–1566) raised European awareness of the exploitation of the indigenous population of the New World. Other critics, such as the celebrated Spanish humanist Juan Luis Vives (1492–1530), conducted his writing outside Spain for fear of the Inquisition. However, the majority of Spanish scholars and artists were dependent on the Church for their livelihood, and therefore were obliged to condone its orthodox policies.

CHAPTER 9

The Late Renaissance

SWEDEN

Bergen

Christiania (Oslo)

Stockholm

Reval

SCOTLAND

Edinburgh

Newcastle

NORTH SEA

Visby

Riga

NORWAY-DENMARK

BALTIC SEA

IRELAND

Hull

ENGLAND

Kings Lynn

Lübeck

Danzig

Königsberg

Bremen

Hamburg

Stettin

to northeastern American seaboard

Bristol

London

Bruges

Antwerp

Ghent

Brussels

Deventer

Brunswick

POLAND

Cologne

Leipzig

Breslau

Caen

Rouen

Rhine

Frankfurt

Prague

Krakow

Rennes

Paris

Troyes

HOLY ROMAN EMPIRE

Nuremberg

ATLANTIC OCEAN

Loire

FRANCE

Augsburg

Danube

Bay of Biscay

Swiss Confederation

HUNGARY

Lyon

Milan

Venice

Rhône

Toulon

Aigues-Mortes

Marseilles

Genoa

Pisa

Bologna

Florence

OTTOMAN EMPIRE

Lisbon

PORTUGAL

SPAIN

Barcelona

Corsica

PAPAL STATES

Ancona

Rome

to India and Southeast Asia

Seville

Valencia

Balearic Islands

Palma

Naples

Cadiz

Malaga

Almeria

Sardinia

Crotone

to Caribbean and New Spain

Melilla

Oran

Algiers

Palermo

Messina

Syracuse

Modon

Tunis

Malta

MEDITERRANEAN SEA

Crete

Djerba

Tripoli

Ottoman sea power effectively blockaded the eastern Mediterranean from European trade. Genoa's trading routes to the Black Sea were cut, although Venice made deals that gave her merchants access to the markets of Constantinople, but not the Levant. As a result, Italy's dominance of European trading declined, while that of the Atlantic seaboard countries—Portugal, Spain, France, and the Low Countries— prospered with the new trans-Atlantic routes and those around Africa to India and Southeast Asia.

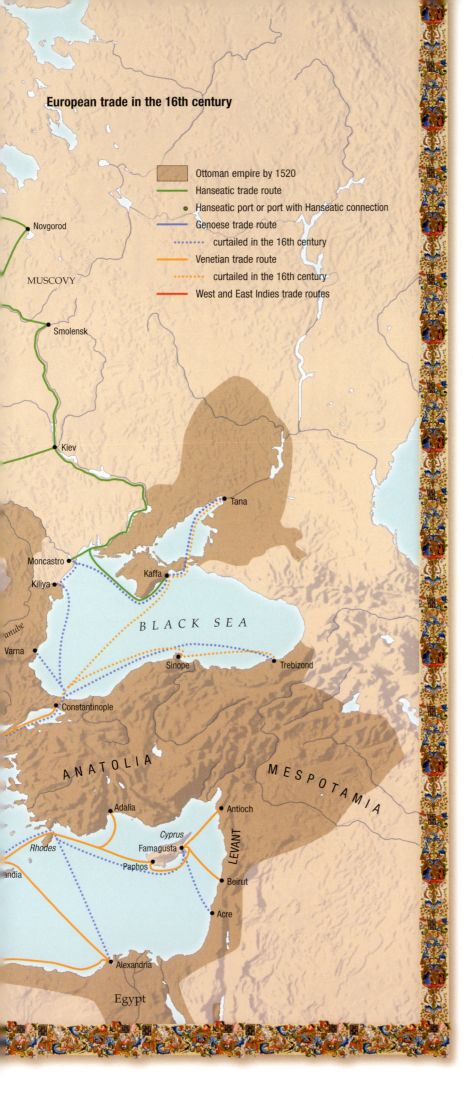

European trade in the 16th century

Ottoman empire by 1520
Hanseatic trade route
Hanseatic port or port with Hanseatic connection
Genoese trade route
curtailed in the 16th century
Venetian trade route
curtailed in the 16th century
West and East Indies trade routes

Novgorod

MUSCOVY

Smolensk

Kiev

Moncastro

Kiliya

Kaffa

Tana

Danube

Varna

BLACK SEA

Sinope

Trebizond

Constantinople

ANATOLIA

MESPOTAMIA

Adalia

Antioch

Cyprus

Rhodes

Famagusta

Paphos

LEVANT

Beirut

andia

Acre

Alexandria

Egypt

While the 15th century had been a glorious time for Italy, the century ended with invasion by a French army, and the city-states' subsequent embroilment in a dynastic struggle between two foreign powers—the Valois French and the Habsburgs. While previously, Italian merchants, bankers, and manufacturers largely dominated trade in the Mediterranean and across the Alps, this economic fortune came to an end. By the start of the 16th century the Italian city-states were in economic and political decline, their lands ravaged by marauding armies and their overseas markets cut off by the waxing and waning fortunes of war.

The one economic power in Italy to survive the war was the Republic of Venice, despite the loss of much of her overseas trading ports and territories to the Ottoman Turks, who expanded through Greece and the Balkans. Ever pragmatic, the Venetian government made a pact with the Turks that gained them mercantile privileges in the eastern Mediterranean and in Constantinople, but the other Italian maritime powers were excluded from this vital eastern trade. When the Portuguese forged a trading route around Africa, into the Indian Ocean and to the East at the start of the 16th century, Italy became an economic backwater, since the maritime powers of the Atlantic coast were better placed to take advantage of the new trading opportunities—both east and west to the New World.

The Italian Wars not only had a devastating effect on the political and economic well-being of the city-states, they also marked the end of the Italian Renaissance. Although some of the greatest cultural achievements of the age occurred during the High Renaissance of the early 16th century, the near-constant warfare that ravaged Italy sapped the self-confidence of the great patrons and idealism of its creators. As a result, many Italian painters, sculptors, and architects migrated across the Alps in greater numbers, finding better employment in Spain and France, as well as England and occasionally in Germany. Italy's disillusionment reached a climax in 1527 when Imperialist troops sacked Rome. Although artists and artisans would return to Rome and a new phase of Late Renaissance art and architecture would develop, it was clear that the great cultural movement was drawing to a close, and that the real creative impetus had moved to Spain and the countries north of the Alps.

A Slump in Mediterranean Trade

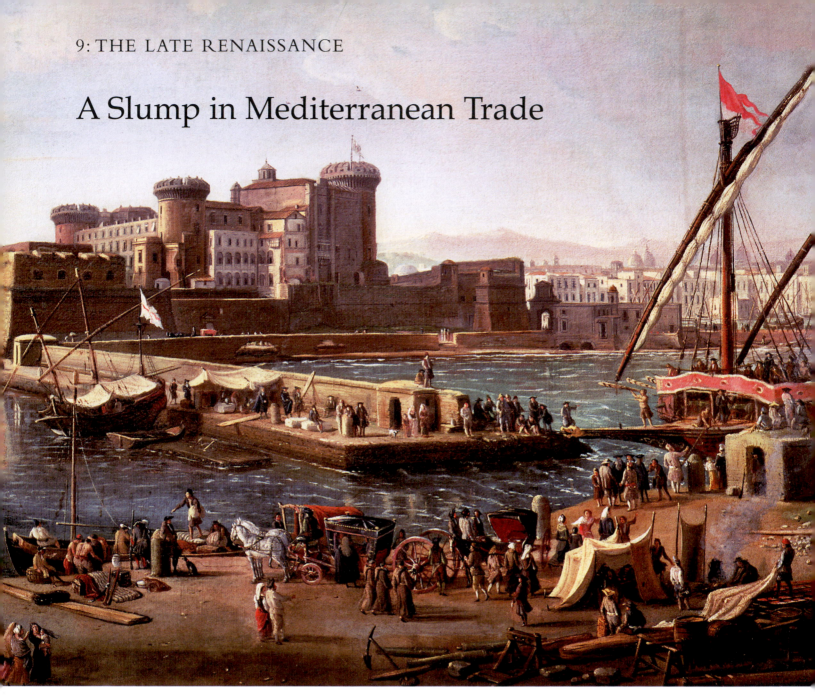

The fall of Constantinople closed access to goods shipped along the overseas trading route from the Orient. While Venice negotiated treaties with the Turks, other mercantile powers of the Mediterranean were less fortunate and had to look elsewhere to avoid economic decline.

Above: Once scenes of bustling activity, by the end of the Renaissance period the Italian docksides had been reduced to little more than local activity. *View of the Docks of Naples* by Gaspar van Vittel.

Contact between medieval Italy and the Byzantine empire had been close, both in terms of trade and culture. Venetian merchants regularly traded with the Byzantines, and from the early 13th century Venetians took over much of the declining empire's marketplaces. A thriving colony developed in Constantinople, while Venetian trading ports dotted the coast of Greece and the Aegean.

Constantinople was the conduit for trade in spices from the Orient, but this came under threat when the Ottoman Turks began to expand in Asia Minor, closing trade routes through the Anatolian and Black Sea ports to Byzantine and Venetian ships, and blocking Genoese access to their trading posts in Ionia and the Black Sea that the Seljuk Turks, predecessors of the Ottomans, had used (and encouraged Mediterranean trade). By 1356, when the Turks gained control of the Dardanelles, trade was at a virtual standstill.

There seemed little alternative but to make a pact with the enemy. While Genoese maritime trade declined steadily during the later 14th century, Venice prospered, largely due to a series of lucrative secret trading agreements arranged in the Ottoman court. Soon the only Genoese trading center in the region was the Aegean island of Chios, which had served as a Genoese port for centuries.

After the fall of Constantinople and the last remnants of the Byzantine empire, the Venetian trading agreements were reratified, becoming almost a mutual pact of non-aggression. The only restriction was that Venetian merchants were denied access to the Black Sea—if they wanted to import goods shipped along the Silk Road, they had to deal with the Turkish merchants of Istanbul or Antioch.

While other European powers were willing to fight the Turks, Venetians tended to support their fellow Christians more in spirit than military might. The long-term threat posed by Ottoman expansion seriously alarmed the Venetians, but their agreement allowed them to weather the growing economic storm, and to gain enough time to diversify. They reduced their reliance on imports and increased their small-scale manufacturing industry, principally in glass, ceramics, and jewelry.

Surrounded by competitors

The merchant traders of the remaining Italian city-states sought alternative trading opportunities. The Christian capture of Granada, Spain in 1492 meant that trade between the Atlantic and the Mediterranean was safer, although merchants were still subject to attack from pirates of the North African coast. Merchant adventurers from Pisa and Genoa tried to explore down the west coast of Africa, but the Portuguese made this route their own, protecting the main watering places of the African Atlantic coast with fortifications. The Portuguese developed the lucrative trade route to India and the slave trade between Africa and the Americas.

In the late 15th century the principal exports of the Italian city-states were textiles, predominantly silks and wools from Florence. Florentine merchants faced increasingly strong opposition from French, Flemish, and Dutch textile producers, who rivaled the Italians' output in both quality and cost. Worse, production

declined while Italy was ravaged by Habsburg-Valois rivalry as artisans and industrial workers were forced into military service, or witnessed their livelihood destroyed by rampaging soldiers. These intermittent conflicts also blocked trading routes and, with their closure, the Italians were poorly placed to revitalize their export trade.

The Mediterranean became the marketplace for northern European traders, who transported their products in large quantities by sailing ship, avoiding overland tariffs and outclassing the small and less highly developed merchant marine of the Italian city-states. Eventually competition from Portugal, Holland, and England overwhelmed the mercantile trade of the Italians, until even Venice was outclassed. Combined with steadily growing inflation and a growth in foreign tariffs, this sounded the death knell for the traditional trading powers of the Mediterranean.

Above: *The Battle of Khalenberg at the Second Siege of Vienna*, Franz Geffels. While Venice negotiated trade agreements with the Ottoman Turks, the Habsburgs faced their greatest threat as Muslim forces attempted to capture Vienna.

Below: Navigational chart of the Mediterranean on vellum, made in 1678.

Decline of the Italian City-States

In the first decades of the 16th century the Italian Wars drained the city-states of resources and manpower. Eventually, the Imperialist victory in Italy meant that the once fiercely independent city-states had become dependent on Spanish troops and a German emperor.

The city-states were pawns in the greater political game of the Italian Wars. Parts of Italy suffered considerable destruction and social dislocation. The foreign armies arrived on a grand scale, equipped with ever more destructive cannons, and cities were bomarded regardless of civilian suffering. The wars led to the sacking of cities, Prato and Brescia in 1512 and Rome in 1527 being the worst examples. Pisa had been besieged on and off throughout the 1490s, and Florence in 1529–30.

Economic recession was only one of the by-products of the conflict. Plague raged throughout the 1520s, and again in 1575–77. Typhus struck in 1505 and again in 1528, and syphilis was widespread, vectored by the navies, armies, and camp followers. With the countryside devastated, industry ruined, and the population greatly reduced by war and pestilence there came an erosion of Renaissance optimism. The decline of the economic strength that had supported cultural patronage resulted in the migration of the few scholars and artists who remained.

The sack of Rome in May 1527 by unpaid, rebellious German mercenaries, followed by the siege and fall of Florence three years later, marked the political end of the Renaissance, brutal acts characterizing the helplessness of the Italian city-states in the face of foreign interference. Florence's last flirtation with republicanism ended when Imperialists captured the city after a ten-month siege (1529–30), restoring the exiled Medici family to power as oligarchic puppets of their imperial masters.

The economic decline that had begun in the mid-15th century was accelerated by the Italian Wars. And because their financial base lay in

1444–1514	1453	1497–99	1516–18	c.1520	1526	1526	1530
Life of High Renaissance artist and architect Donato Bramante, who designed St. Peter's	Ottoman Turks take Constantinople and use it as a base to expand their empire and trade routes	Vasco da Gama rounds the Cape of Good Hope and finds a sea route to India for Portugal	Titian of Venice's first public commission, *The Assumption of the Virgin* for Santa Maria church	Italian trade and culture in decline; Spain and Portugal are booming	Ottomans under Suleiman the Magnificent conquer Hungary and make it a satellite state	Francisco de Miranda founds an Italianate school of literature in Portugal	After a short return to republicanism, Florence is besieged and captured by the Holy Roman Empire

landholdings—and war had adversely affected agricultural production—the power of the Italian nobility declined. The rise of the merchant classes during the 14th and 15th centuries had already made inroads into patrician power; now the noble houses struggled to maintain authority in cities whose economy became increasingly linked to mercantile activity. Social divisions became blurred as wealthy merchants married into the poorer noble houses, and some patricians diversified their interests by embracing mercantilism.

The economic stagnation that came in the wake of the Italian Wars gave the aristocracy an opportunity to claw back some influence. However, this was largely achieved through their active support of either the French or Imperial parties, their fortunes increasingly linked to the houses of Valois or Habsburg.

The end of a world

The pessimism felt by most Italians was captured by the artists of the late Renaissance, whose styles came to reflect the troubled times. For example, after 1494 Sandro Botticelli (1445–1510) appeared to lose the self-confidence and optimism he had expressed in earlier works, such as *Primavera* (1478) or *Birth of Venus* (1485). He summed up these feelings in an inscription he added to his *Mystical Nativity* (1500), quoting the passage in St. John's Gospel describing the loosing of the devil on the world and the coming of the second Apocalypse.

During his last years he became attracted to the preaching of the radical theologian Girolamo Savonarola (1452–98, *see pages 20–1*), as if the artist was searching for a spiritual response to the turbulence of Italy. Like other artists, the troubles affecting the city-states made it increasingly difficult for Botticelli to find patrons.

In all of Italy only Venice avoided the worst effects of the wars, and it became the artistic beneficiary of Rome's sack, as the dispersed artists and patrons who did not cross the Alps in search of a new life settled there. This was also due to the conscious policy of Doge Andrea Gritti (r.1523–38), who wanted to make his city a second Rome. Rome itself recovered in time, and contributed greatly to the later High Renaissance period, but with is infux of newcomers and a vibrant artistic school of its own, it was Venice that came to define the late Renaissance.

The name of the painter of *La Città Ideale* (The Ideal City) remains uncertain. Because of its style, several art historians have attributed it to Piero della Francesca (c.1416–92), but the majority continue to favor Luciano Laurana (d.1479), Duke Federico da Montefeltro's court architect and chief designer of the ducal palace at Urbino. In every respect, this vision represents the height of Renaissance architecture and town planning. Some of the architectural ideas set out in the painting are unprecedented, including the rows of pediments that crown several of the palaces.

Titian's Venice

By the early 16th century, Venice was the one surviving center of Renaissance culture in Italy. The work of the masters of the Venetian School, such as Titian, Giorgione, Tintoretto, and their peers, were a last great resurgence of Renaissance artistic genius.

In the 15th century Venice had been one of the great political, mercantile, and maritime powers of Europe, ruling over an extensive overseas empire that stretched down the Adriatic coast and into the eastern Mediterranean, including the islands of Crete and Cyprus. The city had become a magnet for artists and scholars, attracted by the sustained wealth of its great

merchant-families. Byzantine refugees fleeing the Turks brought their own cultural identity, which helped to shape Venice's unique amalgam of Greek and Italian culture.

Although economic decline during the 16th century meant it was less prosperous, Venice remained a center of secular and ecclesiastical patronage throughout the century, and supported numerous artists. This encouraged the development of what art historians refer to as the Venetian School, a distinctive style of art whose proponents included Giorgione (c.1476–1510), Giovanni Bellini (c.1430–1516), Titian (1490–1576), and later Paolo Veronese (c.1528–88) and Tintoretto (1518–94). Of these,

Right: Giorgione's *The Tempest* (c.1508) poses a puzzle. Is it the story of the Virgin and Christ child (possibly with Joesph during the flight to Egypt), or is she a mythical-classical figure? Giorgione's revolutionary paintings were the first in Italy to completely integrate landscape with figures, and, as this work shows, he was often more interested in the landscape, and in this case the weird light of a thunderstorm.

Tiziano Vecelli—Titian—came to symbolize both the artistic school and the city.

Titian was born in the Veneto (the Republic's mainland territories), but his family moved to Venice in 1499, where he became Bellini's apprentice, then went on to assist Giorgione, whose work profoundly influenced the young artist. After a brief foray to Padua (1511) Titian returned to Venice, where his portraiture demonstrated that his talents had developed beyond those of his tutors. Early works included *The Three Ages of Man*, *Flora*, *Sacred and Profane Love*, and *Vanity*.

Apart from his tutors, Titian was influenced by other contemporary artists, including Vivarini and Carpaccio, whose landscapes inspired later Venetian artists such as Tintoretto. The work of these members of the Venetian School was characterized by the use of warm, rich color, and the detail afforded to all aspects of their painting, including backgrounds and landscapes.

An esteemed publisher

Titian embarked on two ambitious works with classical mythological themes, *The Worship of Venus* and *Bacchus and Ariadne*, both of which broke with existing High Renaissance conventions, setting the groundwork for a new and uniquely Venetian artistic movement. Titian also received his first public commission, *The Assumption of the Virgin* for the city's church of Santa Maria (1516–18), followed by two other altarpieces. By 1516 he had become the Republic's official painter, but he continued to undertake private commissions, including some of his most memorable portraits, those of Duke Alfonso d' Este of Mantua (1516) and Venetian Doge Andrea Gritti among them.

During his later career Titian became court painter to Charles V, painting several full-length and equestrian portraits of the Holy Roman Emperor, including the acclaimed version that celebrated his victory at Mühlberg (*see page 126*). He continued the role for Charles' son, Philip II of Spain, working on a series of religiously inspired and allegorical works during his final years (*see page 133*).

While Titian and his contemporaries were developing their own artistic movement, Venice played host to humanist scholars who drew on knowledge from the eastern Mediterranean to broaden the scope of their study, promoting the growth of several academies. Of these the Neakademia of Aldus Manutius (1449–1515) became renowned for its promulgation of Greek studies and, with its associated Aldus Press,

became one of the most important scholastic publishers of the Renaissance. However, while it was sympathetic to humanist and even reformist thinking—its subscribers included major clerical reformers such as Erasmus and Thomas Linacre—like the Venetian artistic community, the Neakademia later retrenched and became a supporter of the ecclesiastical establishment; by the mid-16th century Venice was as a bastion of Catholicism rather than reform.

Above: Titian's first public commission was *The Assumption of the Virgin* for Santa Maria.

Mannerism in the Late Renaissance

The sack of Rome in 1527 was a major watershed in the development of art. The temporary end of papal artistic patronage forced artists to move to cultural centers such as Venice, Paris, and Madrid, while a new style of painting encapsulated the mood of the last great Renaissance artists.

Right: *Portrait of a Halberdier* (1528) by Jacopo da Pontormo—archetypical mannerist elongation of the body.

Below right: *Cupid Shaping his Bow* (1533) by Il Parmigianino.

Below: Narcissus (1548) by Benvenuto Cellini.

During the decade before the sack of Rome, there had been a pronounced drift away from classicism. A new breed of painters was emphasizing elegance and sophistication, and either rejecting classical influences or, more commonly, exaggerating the standard features of earlier Renaissance painting such as technical or perspective exercises, and the use of classical themes or motifs. The term "mannerism" was derived from the Italian word *maniera* (manner) and the new artistic movement remained in vogue throughout the 16th century.

At its best Mannerism was not simply a

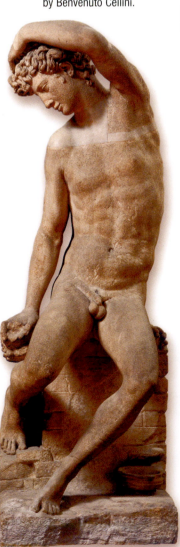

rebellion against existing artistic convention. It embraced a search for an elegance and beauty that could be expressed outside the existing boundaries of Renaissance art. It encompassed all aspects of artistry, including sculpture, architecture, and the decorative arts, and came to typify emotion in art, as well as technical or aesthetic perfection. At its worst—and there were plenty of excesses—it seemed to reflect a thinking that suggested the great Renaissance masters, da Vinci, Raphael, and Michelangelo, had done it all and could not be bettered, so why try to equal them?

Ironically, the first exponent of Mannerism was Michelangelo himself (1475–1564). Such tendencies were already evident in his *David* sculpture and his design for St. Peter's dome. His peers working in Rome and Florence before 1527 included Il Parmigianino (1503–40), Jacopo da Pontormo (1494–1557), and Rosso Fiorentino (1495–1540), all of whom contributed to the development of the mannerist style. Michelangelo and others developed the ideas first explored by Raphael, executing works distinguished from earlier Renaissance art by the use of vivid color (a trait shared by the contemporary Venetian school) and distortions of scale.

Although briefly scattered by the sack of Rome and the siege of Florence, these artists resumed their work after the Italian Wars, when many were enticed back to the Vatican by the promise of further patronage. The tendency toward exaggeration and even a move away from conventional aesthetic forms became more evident. Mannerism reached its most distinctive expression in the work of Florentine painter Giorgio Vasari (1511–74) and Flemish-born sculptor Giambologna (Giovanni [da] Bologna, 1529–1608).

Spanning the media

Vasari combined his painting with architectural work, having produced both the decoration for the Ufizzi in Florence and a posthumous portrait of Lorenzo de' Medici. However, it was Giambologna who came to epitomize the mannerist movement of the Late Renaissance, after settling in Florence in 1558. There he enjoyed Medici patronage and the friendship of Vasari, with whom he shared an affinity for the new mannerist quest for elegance. Giambologna also drew on the legacy of Michelangelo to produce sculptures depicting two or more subjects, and by 1560 had become the most acclaimed sculptor in Europe, working in both marble and bronze to produce works of sensuous beauty and dynamic energy.

Vasari gained recognition as the first art historian. Author of *Lives of the most excellent painters, sculptors, and architects* (1550), he coined the notion of a rebirth (renaissance) in painting, and traced this through three stages corresponding to a 13th- and 14th-century childhood, a 15th-century youth, and a maturity that matched the lifespan of Michelangelo.

While Mannerism was not confined to Florence and Rome, their schools came to exemplify Italian art of the late Renaissance period. Later proponents included Venetians such as Tintoretto, whose allegorical bronze of *Venus*, *Cupid*, *Folly*, *and Time* is thought by many art historians to be the perfect mannerist work. Beyond Italy, Mannerism provided an influence for the work of Cellini and the paintings of Breughel the Elder, and—in its most extreme form—El Greco.

Benvenuto Cellini (1500–71) was in and out of Rome throughout his career. While decidedly mannerist in style, the breadth of his accomplishments made him the epitome of the "Renaissance Man." He became a gold- and silversmith, even though his father wanted him to become a musician. To popes and princes he provided jewelry, basins, rings, crucifixes, and androgynously sensuous small sculpted figures in bronze and precious metals. In his autobiographical *Life* (1558–66), he is revealed as a complex character—bisexual, and violent in defense of his friends' and his own reputation.

Mannerism continued to be a stylistic force

throughout the 16th century, eventually merging into the more flamboyant Baroque style of the early 17th century. In the compilation of art histories in the early and mid-20th century it was general to regard Mannerism as a period of artistic decadence following the High Renaissance. Now it is more commonly seen to be an important movement in its own right, representing the culmination of artistic exploration that characterized the Italian Renaissance.

Above: *The Dream of Alessandro Farnese* (1566–68) by Tintoretto.

Below: *Perseus Rescuing Andromeda* (c.1570) by Giorgio Vasari.

Architecture of the Late Renaissance

If Italian architecture of the Early Renaissance is characterized by the adoption of classical motifs in building design, projects of the later Renaissance represent the development of a unique Italianate style, exported throughout Europe in the 16th century.

During the late 15th and early 16th centuries, a succession of popes embarked on a series of building projects aimed at turning the Vatican and its surroundings into a modern city worthy of the Supreme Pontiff. The most ambitious was initiated by Pope Julius II (p.1503–13), who commissioned the rebuilding of St. Peter's Basilica, large sections of the Vatican Palace, and even the surrounding neighborhoods; the largest example of urban renewal of its day. Rome came to be regarded as the cultural and architectural epicenter of the High Renaissance movement.

Like Julius himself, most of the artists and architects who participated in this revival were not Romans, but were eager to participate in the High Renaissance transformation of the Papal See. The terms High Renaissance or Late Renaissance are essentially artistic. In architecture a far smoother transition can be traced from the earlier Renaissance designs of Brunelleschi to the later Italianate structures of Julio Romano, who incorporated mannerist notions of elongation and exaggeration.

Donato Bramante (c.1444–1514) is generally regarded as the founder of High Renaissance architecture, since he received Julius's commission to rebuild St. Peter's, basing his floor plan on a giant Greek cross, with smaller similar crosses at its angles. Only the central crossing of this complex but potentially elegant design was built, since both Julius and Bramante died before its

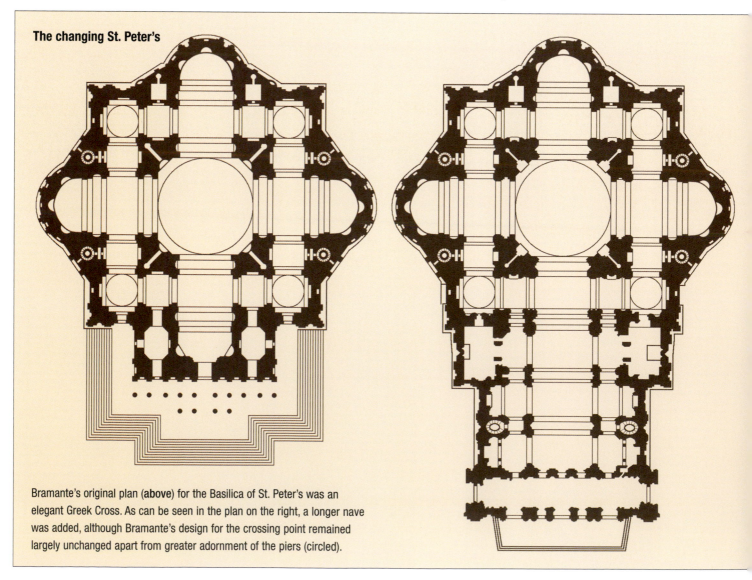

The changing St. Peter's

Bramante's original plan (**above**) for the Basilica of St. Peter's was an elegant Greek Cross. As can be seen in the plan on the right, a longer nave was added, although Bramante's design for the crossing point remained largely unchanged apart from greater adornment of the piers (circled).

real inception. The design was modified by a succession of artists and architects (including Raphael and Michelangelo), but the basic proportions of Bramante's original design were preserved, as was the addition of a massive cupola, redesigned in the mannerist style by Michelangelo then finally completed by Giacomo della Porta (c.1540–1602) and Pope Sixtus V's architect-engineer, Domenico Fontana (1543–1607).

Like other High Renaissance buildings in Rome, the design of St. Peter's was inspired by the classical remains that surrounded it, but this new breed of architects took existing designs a stage further. They abandoned the austere lines of the Early Renaissance and introduced a more ornate reinterpretation of classical designs. Della Porta's façade for St. Peter's became an authoritative model for many buildings in the Baroque style. The façade, fairly simple in design, is embellished by half-pillars, pilasters, panels and niches. As such it is hardly ecclesiastical in character and more resembles the style of a palace. [continued on 148]

Left: Michelangelo's dome for St. Peter's was completed by Giacomo della Porta, whose apparently simple façade hides a complexity of elements that make it more suited to a palazzo than a church. Bramante's original dome was more spherical than Michelangelo's and much plainer, lacking the ornate ribbing and mannerist upper drum and topping steeple.

Renaissance urban planning

Palmanova is one of the finest examples of Renaissance urban planning. Founded by the Republic of Venice in 1593, it is a fortified town in the shape of a nine-point star. It stands on the plains of Friuli, 90 miles northeast of Venice, and was designed to defend the republic's eastern borders from both the Habsburg empire and from the Ottoman Turks, who had formerly invaded Friuli and almost reached Treviso. The Siennese painter Francesco di Giorgio Martini (1493–1502) outlined many imaginary ideal town plans in his *Tratto di Architettura* (*Treatise on Architecture*, c.1470), but in Palmanova the Venetians realized them. The town was built according to Giulio Savorgnan's designs, which reflect not only an urban center capable of defending itself, but one which is also an ideal environment for living. The circular street plan provides for easy communication while providing the maximum building space, while the radial streets naturally lead to the splendid central piazza, linking all the gates and the defensive wall road. The plan below is from *Civitates Orbis Terrarum*, published about the time Palmanova was christened; right, an aerial view today.

Severe and gloomy, Philip's Escorial

The choice of granite as the building material adds to the Escorial's severity. The palace commemorated Philip's victory over the French on August 10, 1557, which was San Lorenzo's Day, hence the name: San Lorenzo de El Escorial. The rectilinear complex is modeled on the gridiron on which San Lorenzo was roasted to death. The enormous stretch of plain walls is broken only by three entrances, with the main portal topped by an Italianate pediment.

King Philip II of Spain took a keen interest in every aspect of the Escorial's construction, which took 21 years (1563–84). The initial design—based on the biblical description of Solomon's temple—was undertaken by Juan Batista de Toledo, a pupil of Michelangelo, but passed to the severe Juan de Herrera. Conceived as a monastery, the Escorial is also a complex comprising a mausoleum, church, library, and a palace. Its gloomy halls became Philip's preferred residence, and his extreme religiosity precluded any of the more frivolous elements of Late Renaissance Italianate style. The absence of decoration marked a break with the ornateness of earlier Spanish architecture.

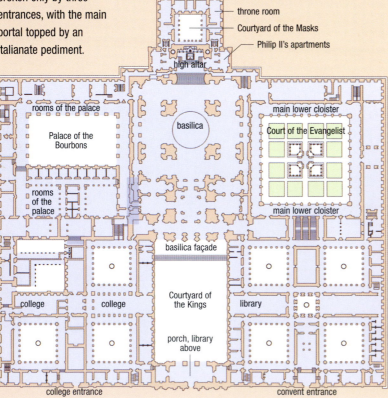

gallery of the Royal Chambers
throne room
Courtyard of the Masks
Philip II's apartments
high altar
rooms of the palace
basilica
main lower cloister
Palace of the Bourbons
Court of the Evangelist
rooms of the palace
main lower cloister
basilica façade
Courtyard of the Kings
college
college
library
porch, library above
college entrance
convent entrance

Italianate flavors

The sack of Rome in 1527 halted building work and architects were hired by patrons elsewhere in Italy, or beyond the Alps. In France, Germany, and the Netherlands they came into contact with the existing architectural heritage based on Gothic ecclesiastical design, which in turn inspired the architecture of civic buildings and even fortresses. Here the High Renaissance style became "Italianate," a term widely misused through its readoption in the 17th century by later advocates of mannerist architecture such as England's Inigo Jones (1573–1652).

To the princes of Europe, Italianate involved the addition of *gravitas* and enrichment to existing designs, since it was deemed that a slavish adoption of pure Italian architecture was inappropriate. Therefore the châteaux commissioned by Francis I in France or the royal palaces of Henry VIII in England were designed around vernacular lines, but embellished by

Italian architects to incorporate the latest style.

The exception was Dutch architect Cornelis Floris (c.1515–75), whose design for Antwerp's town hall (1561–66, pictured above) represented a northern European adaptation of Italian mannerist design. Spain was the only country outside Italy to adopt true Italian High Renaissance architecture, as evidenced by Philip II's Escorial (*see box, left*) outside Madrid, although its austere appearance is at odds with the more decorative traditions encouraged by the mannerist movement in Italy.

The true legacy of Donato Bramante can be found in the later work of Giulio Romano (c.1492–1546) in Rome and Mantua, and Giorgio Vasari and Bartolomeo Ammanati (1511–92) in Florence, whose mannerist decorations and sculptures inspired later advocates of Italianate. Like the artistic style to which it was linked, this form of architecture survived into the 17th century, when it was amalgamated into the Baroque style of the southern German states and Mediterranean Europe.

Left: The dome of the Villa La Rotunda near Vicenza was inspired by the Pantheon.

Palladio and the Neo-Classical Movement

Few Renaissance men had such an impact on the subsequent course of European architecture as Andrea Palladio (1508–80). Unlike many of his contemporaries, who were moving away from a purely Classical style, Palladio studied the ancient Roman remains and adhered to the results of the numerous drawings he made. These included minute details of column and capital decoration, as well as their proportions. He started a simple stonemason, but the patronage of Giangiorgio Trission, a patrician of Vicenza, launched him on a prolific career, mostly in the region around Venice (although he designed few buildings in the city itself, apart from churches). Palladio's work included palaces, churches, and civic buildings, but his is best known for country villas. While some of these were leisure retreats for the wealthy, many were also working farms, and they combine spaces for family living, farm storage, and administration, as well as rooms for lavish entertainment.

In 1570 Palladio published *I Quattro Libri dell' Architettura* (*Four Books of Architecture*), in which he elaborated every conceivable kind of structure from bridges to palaces, and also commented on the work of the ancient Roman architect, Vitruvius. These books, as much as the visible evidence of his creative genius, inspired an entire generation of European architects, most notably in England, men such as Inigo Jones, Robert Adam, and Lord Burlington.

Above: Palladio's plan and elevation for a symmetrical villa, similar to the Villa La Rotunda, but with a higher raised dome.

Left: When he visited Italy in his early 20s, Inigo Jones (1573–1652) became enamored of Palladio's buildings, and brought the Classical stye to England, where his first commission was the Queen's House at Greenwich. The innovation of this palace earned him the name of "architect."

Above: A later Palladian was Scotsman Robert Adam (1728–1792), who built many great country houses. Here, the domed hall of Kedleston Hall, Derbyshire, is a fine example of his elegant interior design, combining all the Classical elements to create serene harmony.

Literature and Music of the Renaissance

While the cultural achievements of the Renaissance are dominated by the development of scholarship and art, a similar transformation took place in the fields of popular literature, poetry, and music.

Below: Jan van Eyck's group of angels represent the ideal Renaissance *a capella* choir of eight to ten liturgical singers.

Late medieval literature and poetry were traditionally divided into two types. Works aimed at the well-read nobility usually drew on a medieval tradition of romance, chivalry, and legend, but less structured prose was produced for a more populist market. In the 15th century humanism transformed literature, and the rapid growth of printing allowed works to reach far wider audiences. The rediscovery of the epic poems of antiquity made a profound impression on 15th-century writers, who almost immediately switched from chivalric deeds to classical themes, with the exception of the courtly circles of France and Burgundy. Elsewhere, Roman and Greek mythology became interwoven with earlier medieval legends and works of fantasy to produce a new and widely popular literary subject.

The development of the novella or prose tale was one of the most successful literary accomplishments of the Renaissance. Although prose tales had been written earlier, they were considered vulgar and populist, but the introduction of classical themes helped to elevate their status. The earliest practitioners were Giovanni Boccaccio (1313–75) and Franco Sacchetti (c.1333–1400), who adopted a colloquial style of writing that made their works accessible to a wider audience. During the 15th century Poggio Bracciolini (1380–1459) and Masuccio Salernitano (c.1415–80) developed this a stage further, incorporating rich characterization and parody in their writing. By the 16th century the development of printing led to the proliferation of novellas.

Madrigal history

Unlike scholars and artists, musicians had no surviving classical legacy to refer to, so they sought inspiration from contemporary artistic

developments. In this they were so successful that a critic writing in 1477 stated that music written four decades before was not worth listening to, since it was unworthy of the new age.

The only musical influence to survive from antiquity was the Platonic dictum that music should be subservient to the written word, and this influenced the way music was perceived and written. Although some composers tried to categorize music as a science (*see Harmony of the spheres, page 38*), they were unable to elevate the perception of music onto the same cultural level as other forms of artistic expression.

Music, too, was divided—between that in service to God, and the secular courtly madrigal at the top end and populist, bawdy street theater. Most Renaissance church music was *a capella* (lit. "for the chapel"), the best known composers being Josquin Desprez (c.1440–1521), Giovanni Pierluigi da Palestrina (c.1525–94), and Orlande de Lassus (1532–94). Their works encompassed hymns, motets, psalms, and Masses. As printing popularized books, so it did music, in the form of scores, much as we know them today. Parisian Pierre Attaingnant was the first to use the technique of printing notes, text, and staves in a single impression, one of his first being a Mass by Jean Mouton, published in 1532.

During the Renaissance most of the influential composers came from France and the Low Countries; the singers and composers of the papal choir were recruited from northern Europe, until the 16th century, after which they chiefly came from Spain and Italy. Northern Europe's musical domination provided a foundation for the development of the madrigal, which had come to epitomize Renaissance musical expression by the 16th century, when Venice had become a musical capital. Venetian composers and publishers were hugely influential in the transformation of the madrigal into a predominantly Italianate form of expression.

Composers and musicians also found employment in the courts of Europe, therefore the tastes of patrons influenced composition through their commissions. Germany, Spain, and England had a strong tradition of ecclesistical medieval music, and this influenced religious music in the rest of Europe. The Church embraced new styles of music to demonstrate that it was not resistant to cultural change. Later in the 16th century Protestant reformers also turned to religious music as a tool to propagate their spiritual message.

CHAPTER 10

A Flickenteppich–
Renaissance Germany

Given the geographical proximity of southern Germany and Switzerland to the seat of the Italian Renaissance, it is surprising that it took almost a century for the rebirth of classical culture to make an impact beyond the Alps. To the sophisticated rulers of Renaissance Italy, the Holy Roman Empire was a dirty, uncivilized land, still locked in backward, medieval ways. This prejudicial view was hardly accurate. The urban centers of Switzerland and southern Germany were thriving, while along the Baltic coast the trading ports of the Hanseatic League might have entered a period of decline but still remained populous and busy marketplaces, linking the interior of Europe with the natural resources of Scandinavia and Russia. While political control of this sprawling German empire was nominally in the hands of the Holy Roman Emperor, his power was limited to his own feudal demesne; elsewhere Germany was a patchwork of small ducal realms, minor principalities, and independent city-states.

Even before the first effects of the Renaissance were experienced in Germany, the region had undergone its own cultural transformation. Long traditions of scholarship and learning made the region receptive to the new ideas coming from the Italian Renaissance, but a greater concern with textual criticism than was evident in Italy meant that the Northern Renaissance was more occupied with matters of personal morality. Italian classicists glorified the diginity of man, while their German counterparts concentrated on man's worthlessness in the face of God.

Encouraged by the art movements of the neighboring Low Countries, German painters, sculptors, and architects began to experiment, pushing the boundaries of the Late Gothic style that was omnipresent in 15th-century Germany. Eventually German artists created their own style, blending the Renaissance with the Gothic to create a cultural movement uniquely Germanic in style, exemplified by the work of Cranach, Grünewald, and Dürer.

The Renaissance spirit of inquiry struck a chord with the German population and its rulers, many of whom had become disillusioned with the Church. This discord and the invention of the printing press would lay the groundwork for the Protestant Reformation that would bring the cultural achievement of the Renaissance to a close.

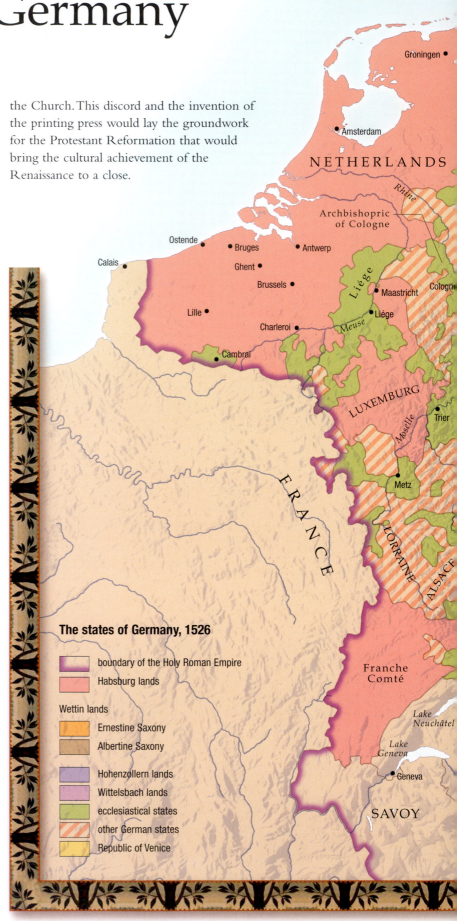

The states of Germany, 1526

- boundary of the Holy Roman Empire
- Habsburg lands

Wettin lands

- Ernestine Saxony
- Albertine Saxony

- Hohenzollern lands
- Wittelsbach lands
- ecclesiastical states
- other German states
- Republic of Venice

HOLSTEIN

• Lübeck

MECKLEMBURG

POMERANIA

• Hamburg

Stettin •

Archbishopric
of Brmen

• Bremen

Brunswick-
Lüneburg

BRANDENBURG

POLAND

Oder

Brunswick-Wolfenbüttel

• Berlin

• Münster

Magdeburg •

Wittenberg •

SILESIA

Halberstadt •

HESSE

Eisleben •

Mühlberg •

Oder

Eisenach

Gotha • Erfurt •

SAXONY

Dresden •

Archbishopric
of Trier

• Marburg

Zwickau •

Elbe

Fulda •

Annaberg •

Archbishopric
of Mainz

Prague •

Frankfurt •

Rhine

Würzburg •

• Bamberg

BOHEMIA

• Mainz

KINGDOM ØF BOHEMIA
before 1526

MORAVIA

Palatinate
of the
Rhine

• Worms

• Nuremberg

• Heidelberg

Upper
Palatinate

Rattisbon
(Regensurg) •

• Strasbourg

WÜRTTEMBERG

Danube

Ingolstadt •

BAVARIA

Passau •

Danube

Vienna •

• Augsburg

Inn

AUSTRIA

Munich •

Rhine

Lake
Constance

Salzburg •

Enns

HABSBURG
HUNGARY
after 1526

• Basel

Zurich •

Salzburg

rn

SWISS
CONFEDERATION

TYROL

Styria

Carinthia

Trent •

REPUBLIC
OF
VENICE

TURKISH
HUNGARY
after 1526

DUCHY
OF MILAN

Lake
Garda

• Milan

Venice •

ADRIATIC
SEA

Istria

The Holy Roman Empire

The Holy Roman Empire was a vast area of territories, bishoprics, and cities, stretching from the Netherlands in the west to Bohemia and Hungary in the south, and from the Baltic Sea to the Alps. It became both the breeding ground of the Reformation and a bastion of Catholicism.

The Holy Roman Empire (*Heiliges Römisches Reich*) developed from the Treaty of Verdun (843). It emerged as a successor state from the eastern portion of Charlemagne's Frankish kingdom, and survived until its dissolution by Napoleon in 1806. By the 16th century it consisted of the lands of the nine Electors plus numerous small states and cities. These varied in size and importance as family lines merged or

Below: Regalia of the Holy Roman Empire.

disappeared. Each of the hundreds of small territories was controlled by their individual rulers, but in theory remained under the overall control of the Holy Roman Emperor.

Since the Middle Ages the emperor had been elected to his position by the Electors, who varied between six and ten, principally: the King of Bohemia, the archbishops of Mainz, Trier, and Cologne, the Duke of Saxony, the Markgraf of Brandenburg, and the Count Palatine of the Rhine. The Archbishop of Mainz took precedence over all other electors. Within a month of the death of an emperor, the Archbishop of Mainz or the Archbishop of Trier would summon the other electors to Frankfurt to choose the next incumbent.

When an election was convened many important people would gather (ambassadors, noblemen, princes) and debate the candidates, then all but the electors were ordered out of the city. The electors convened in the cathedral chapel, where they swore to abide by majority decision and choose the worthiest candidate. Whoever received over half the votes was elected. In due course his successor, known as King of the Romans, would be elected in the same way.

The theory behind this remarkably democratic process was fine, but in practice it frequently failed. Although the title of Holy Roman Emperor was elective, it was often bought through bribery and corruption. And although non-hereditary, the title was often passed from father to son, since they had the influence and funds to buy the position. The structure was also convenient for the numerous principalities and free city-states, for they were collectively hard to govern and were left with a free hand in their own territories.

A Habsburg empire

When the Habsburg Archduke Maximilian of Austria and ruler of the Low Countries was elected King of the Romans in 1486 and emperor in 1493, he made sweeping social and administrative reforms. At his first election his position was precarious. He was a refugee from Hungarian-held Austria, but his victory over the Turks at Villach in 1492 bolstered his claim to the

| **962**
Otto the Great becomes the first Holy Roman Emperor, establishing the empire | **1372**
Swabian League of southern German cities is defeated in a civil war with the emperor | **1419**
Supporters of reformer Jan Huss rebel against German rule in Bohemia, beginning the Hussite Wars | **1444**
Realist artist Konrad Witz paints *The Miraculous Draught of Fishes* | **1488–1534**
The Swabian League defends southern German cities from Switzerland and Bavaria | **1489**
Sculptor Viet Stoss carves the altar of St. Mary's church, Kraków, Poland | **1515**
Painter Matthias Grunewald completes his altarpiece at the Isenheim hospital chapel | **1516**
Grandchildren of Maximilian marry son and daughter of king of Hungary, assuring Habsburg authority |

Left: Portrait of Emperor Maximilian I by Albrecht Dürer, the Austrian ruler who brought the Holy Roman Empire into Habsbug hands.

empire, and his reforms were designed to strengthen the Habsburg hold over Germany. In doing so Maximilian I sought to give the German princes what they wanted, but without diminishing his own position. In 1495 he established the *Reichsammergericht* (Imperial Court of Justice) and a new structure for the Imperial Diet (parliament), in 1500 the *Reichsregiment* (a permanent Council of Regency), and in 1512 the *Reichsschlüsse* or "Mandates" of the Imperial Diet.

With the creation in 1495 of three Colleges of the Diet—*Kurfürstenrat* (Electors), *Fürstenrat* (Princes, which included secular and ecclesiastic princes), and *Collegium der Reichsstädte* (Imperial Cities)—Maximilan effectively surrendered all direct rule of the empire. But in so doing he also made the House of Habsburg indispensable to the German princes, since they only received these rights through his holy office. Voting rights were jealously guarded and associated with great prestige.

Ultimately the *Reichsregiment* proved unsatisfactory to Maximilian's successor Charles V, who worked to reduce its authority; it was dissolved in 1531.

The three emperors of the Renaissance period were all Habsburgs. Maximilian's son Philip the Handsome married Joanna the Mad of Spain (*see picture, page 60*) and his daughter Margaret wed Philibert of Savoy (her second marriage). Philip and Joanna's sons Charles and Ferdinand in turn inherited the Holy Roman Empire. In 1519 Charles V succeeded his grandfather by beating Francis I of France in the election. And then in 1526 the last king of Hungary, Louis II, was killed at the battle of Mohács by the Ottoman Turks, and Bohemia and what was left of Hungary went to Charles, who now held sway over a sprawling Habsburg empire that dominated Europe for over a century. Charles abdicated in favor of his brother Ferdinand I in 1556, dying in 1558. Ferdinand ruled until his death in 1564.

1523	1524–25	1525	1530	1531	1536	1547	1806
Albrecht Dürer expresses his Protestantism through the *Last Supper* woodcut	German peasants revolt against taxation, Imperial rule, and local lords	At the Battle of Frankenhausen lords defeat the peasantry, ending their rebellion	Lutherans form the Schmalkaldic League in response to Charles V's anti-Lutheran stance	Charles V dissolves the Reichsregiment, a ruling council that reduced the emperor's influence	Bavarian portrait painter Hans Holbein the Younger becomes court artist to Henry VIII of England	Schmalkaldic Protestants are defeated by the Holy Roman Empire at the battle of Mühlberg	Napoleon dissolves Holy Roman Empire and creates the Confederation of the Rhine

Germany's Renaissance

Encouraged by the patronage of German princes, humanist scholars eventually ventured north to the universities of central Europe, and in their wake came the cultural movement that had swept Italy and would adapt itself to the German psyche.

Facing below: The *Mariacki Altarpiece* in the Church of Our Lady, Krakow, Poland by Viet Stoss is an example of crowded Gothic tradition melded with a Renaissance sense of proportion.

Below: *Holy Blood*, sculpture in wood by Tilman Riemenschneider, a combination of northern Gothic with Italian Renaissance sensibility.

To put the lie to the Italian prejudice that Germany was a country of poverty and ignorance, several universities had been founded across central Europe during the 14th century, including those of Prague (1348), Vienna (1365), Heidelberg (1386), and Leipzig (1409). By the mid-15th century many of the lecturers in these seats of learning had studied in Italian universities such as Bologna, Pavia, and Padua. They returned to Germany enthused by the newfound humanist emphasis on the classics, and by the late 15th century many German universities had become recognized for their humanist scholarship.

Although the Holy Roman Emperor had little direct political power, he could influence the spread of patronage and culture within the imperial borders. Both Frederick III (r.1452–93) and his successor Maximilian I encouraged the migration of humanist thinkers to Germany.

On their arrival the immigrant scholars found a different form of patronage from that of ecclesiastical Italy. During this period, Germany developed a reputation for high-quality metalwork, and in southern cities such as Nuremberg and Augsburg artisans produced arms and armor, watches, and scientific instruments of the finest quality. Like the city-states of Italy, these cities were largely independent, and their inhabitants displayed a self-confidence and a zeal for commerce that made them important hubs of trade and sources of wealth. They also enjoyed recycling some of their wealth into educational and artistic patronage.

The emperor and German princes seemed to be fixated by a chivalric notion of culture based on the existing Gothic tradition, although this changed during the final years of the 15th century. Maximilian took the lead as a patron of Italian art and learning. He had a personal interest in art and letters and made his Viennese court a lively center of humanist culture. His nobles followed suit, and so it was wealthy patrons from the cities and universities who were more willing to embrace the art and culture that was beginning to reach Germany,

although there was some ecclesiastical patronage too. However, the Renaissance in Germany did not become a slavish copy of the High Renaissance movement of Italy, but combined the new influences with the existing High Gothic tradition, creating a uniquely German perspective.

Artists rejected

German artists of the early 16th century used Italian notions of light and shade, perspective, and color, combined with the Gothic tradition of exquisite attention to surface detail, what might today be called photo-realism, and vivid imagery. For example, the wood and stone sculptor Tilman Riemenschneider (c.1460–1531) from Würzburg produced limewood carvings that seamlessly combined the two artistic traditions. Viet Stoss (c.1450–1533) relied more on the High Gothic traditions of northern and eastern Germany, but he too adapted Italianate notions of composition and human proportion to create his carvings.

Since German artists and scholars lacked the extensive network of ecclesiastic patronage available to their counterparts in southern Europe, they were forced to rely on the support of the civic community. Increasingly, princes, nobles, and civic grandees sought humanist scholars to educate their children or to teach in their regional universities, or they decorated their palaces, castles, and homes with examples of art inspired by visits to Italy, or brought north via the highly developed trade routes that crossed Germany from the Alps to the Baltic.

It is a unique German phenomenon that while scholars and theologians were widely respected and encouraged to participate in the cultural enrichment of the court, artists and sculptors were never afforded the same social status. As Dürer

remarked on a visit to Venice, "Here I am a gentleman, but at home I am a parasite." This emphasis on one aspect of culture at the expense of another continued well into the 16th century, but at least the status afforded to academics and theologians meant that humanist ideas permeated German courts. And that—combined with the political muscle afforded by the new printing presses—made Renaissance Germany the principal catalyst for religious reform.

Above: Leipzig was only one of several German cities to have founded a university by the start of the 15th century. This view from a *Civitates Orbis Terrarum* dates from the start of the 16th century.

The Growth of Social Unrest

When humanist thinking began to work its effects on German cities, the Renaissance met a wall of resistance in the sprawling conglomeration of states. The Holy Roman Empire was a chaotically organized confederation of conflicting interests that sponsored unrest at every level.

Facing: Detail from *The Martyrdom of Ten Thousand Christians Under King Sapor* (1508), painted by Dürer for Prince Friedrich the Wise, Elector of Saxony. The painting refers to an incident that allegedly took place in Turkey after the Roman emperor Constantine's conversion to Christianity. The Persian king, Shapur (Sapor), began a systematic persecution of Christians living in his domains on the grounds that, having come under the protection of Rome, they were now his enemies. However, as with almost all of Dürer's allegorical work, this painting is more of a contemporary comment on the social and religious unrest sweeping through Germany than it is a historical image.

The Black Death culled over half of the Holy Roman Empire's population in the mid-14th century, and it was only by the mid-15th century that Germany's cities recovered to the levels they had attained before the Black Death, and in the following century the increase continued. Urban regeneration led to fresh demand for production, and a resurgent mercantile class appeared to satisfy it. However, although the physical and economic scars of the Black Death had healed, its psychological impact lingered. The old views of life, death, God, and the role of mankind had been shaken, and many laymen began to question the religious certainties that had appeared immutable during the Middle Ages. This coincided with the spread of humanist ideas and its attendant encouragement of inquiry.

The scattered, loose confederation of small states that made up the Holy Roman Empire created a provincial regionalism that hindered the Habsburg emperor's ability to counter the spread of religious dissent and social unrest. Since the universities were mostly funded by local rulers they were not the ecclesiastic colleges of southern Europe. Therefore, religious reform was not the restricted preserve of theologians, as in Italy or Spain, but became the responsibility of the princes and leaders of urban communities.

During the 15th century German dukes and princes were frequently engaged in warfare, with each other, with their emperor, against rebels within their own territories, and against the free cities whose wealth they coveted (*see following page*). Germany was gripped by bouts of dynastic warfare, interspersed with waves of pestilence or famine. The princes were clearly found wanting as moral and spiritual role models. And the mid-15th-century regeneration of German cities meant that the agrarian economy that sustained the nobility was being eroded, as wealth became concentrated in the blossoming mercantile centers. While the feudal lords were able to tax some of the cities, others retained their independence and even formed military and political alliances to defend themselves from feudal neighbors.

Discontent grows

The most effective urban alliance was the Swabian League (1488–1534). Supported by the emperor, it comprised more than 26 south German cities and many nobles, knights, and prelates, and safeguarded their interests against attack by the Swiss Confederation or the feudal ruler of Bavaria, Duke Ulrich of Württemberg. The league had a court, a powerful army, and a formal constitution. In 1519 it backed the election of Charles V in opposition to Duke Ulrich, who supported the candidacy of the French king Francis I. Charles then relied on the league's military power to expel Ulrich from Württemberg after he had occupied the free Imperial city of Reutlingen. The league also played a leading role in defeating the peasants in the peasants' revolt of 1525. Its dissolution in 1534 resulted from the opposition of interests between its feudal members and its cities, and from the divisive religious arguments caused by the Reformation. Many Protestant members joined the Schmalkaldic League in 1530 (*see page 161*). Later attempts by Charles V to restore the Swabian League as a bolster to Catholicism failed.

The division between the feudal nobles of the Swabian League were typical of other smaller political leagues in Germany. The increasing employment of mercenary troops such as the *landsknechts* benefited the emperor and the cities, because they could pay the troops' wages more readily than the increasingly impoverished German nobles.

While, as we have seen, the Habsburg emperors maintained a firm hand over their administrative bodies, they were unable to control the Church within Germany. Unlike the ecclesiastical hierarchies of France or England, German Church lands were directly controlled from Rome. This also meant that the emperor was unable to prevent the visible excesses of what was still a late medieval Church in Germany, or to control the agitation of humanist reformers who sought to combat these deficiencies.

Unrest was becoming widespread. As humanist Ulrich von Hutten (1488–1523) put it, why should Germans pay for Roman churches when Italy was wealthier than Germany? As religious, social, and political tensions grew, the opportunities presented to humanist reformers were amplified, ensuring that the seeds of the Reformation fell on fertile ground.

German Free Cities

The patchwork of free cities within the Holy Roman Empire was a rich, vibrant hotbed of political, commercial, and religious activity. Autonomous and flourishing, they provided the perfect breeding ground for the German Renaissance, and later the theological revolution that led to the Reformation.

Within the Holy Roman Empire, a number of cities emerged during the Middle Ages, either free (*freie Stadt*, or the plural *Städte*), governed by a city council or dominated by an independent bishop, or Imperial (*Reichsstädte*). The numbers of both varied according to the political climate and at times reached as many as several hundred. Although important, they were often small in area, comprising only a few square miles each. This led to them being referred to as a *Flickenteppich*, or patchwork carpet.

The "free" status gave cities an enviable degree of autonomy. Imperial cities were answerable only to the emperor; the free cities to their internal civic organizations. Cities within the empire without this protective status were located within feudal territory and governed by a noble landowner.

The organization of the Holy Roman Empire was dominated by the nobility, but the importance of the *Reichsstädte* meant that they wanted to be involved in government, particularly to have a

voice in debates about taxation. The *Reichsstädte* were only officially allowed representation in the *Reichstag* during the 15th century and, initially, their voice counted for less than that of the nobles. The nobles in whose territories the free cities flourished resented their independence, freedom from local taxation, and ability to vote at Imperial Diets.

At the Nuremberg Diet of 1522–23, nobles attempted to destroy the power of the cities by imposing Imperial customs duty on them. The *Reichsstädte* indignantly protested to the emperor. Charles V needed the financial support of the wealthy merchants and the banking house of Fugger, who operated from the *Reichsstadt* of Augsburg. Jacob Fugger (Jacob the Rich) had lent substantial funds to the Habsburgs, which helped secure Charles' election as Holy Roman Emperor, and he was reluctant to increase the power of the German nobility. He duly reversed the Diet's decision.

Allied against the empire

Most of the free cities were located in southwest Germany, where the diverse political landscape allowed important cities such as Augsburg, Frankfurt, and Nuremberg to flourish as free political entities. Elsewhere, in Bavaria and the north, the nobility was mostly too powerful to lose significant control over its cities, the

Both: Views of Augsburg (below) and Cologne at the end of the 15th century, from woodcuts for *Liber Chronicarum* of c.1493 by Hartmann Schedel. The Latin words reflect the derivation of the modern names for the cities: Augusta Vindelicorum became simply Augusta, then Augsberg; Colonia Agrippinensis became simply Colonia, then Köln (Cologne).

· COLONIA ·

exception being members of the medieval Hanseatic League.

This league (from the word *Hansa*, a company of merchants) grew along the northern coastline of Europe in the 12th century to foster trade and protect its alliance. The principal Hanseatic ports were Lübeck, Bremen, and Hamburg, but at various times over a hundred towns from Holland to Poland were members. The league was not strongly organized and by the 16th century competition between its members, German princes, and foreign mercantile states had reduced its importance.

It was possible to be a Hanseatic town as well as an Imperial free city. Emperor Frederick II made Lübeck (one of the founding members of the Hanseatic League) a *freie Stadt* in 1226, but some important Hanseatic cities achieved the status much later, such as Bremen in 1646. The free cities and *Reichsstädte* played a significant part in the Reformation. At the Diet of Speyer (1526), a coalition of Protestant and Catholic cities convinced Charles V to proclaim a religious truce across the empire, although his conciliatory attitude was more dictated by Imperial foreign policy with regard to Pope Clement VII, France, and the aggression of the advancing Turks.

The political climate had changed by the time of the second Diet of Speyer (1529), when Charles V returned to his anti-Lutheran position. Protestant cities found common cause with Protestant nobles and united against the emperor. The truce between the Catholic and Protestant cities was shattered when Lutherans formed the Schmalkaldic League in 1530. Under the league's protection the Reformation spread rapidly through the empire, and although it was defeated by an Imperial army at the battle of Mühlberg (1547), Protestant survival in northern Germany was assured.

The Peasants' Revolt

One of the most striking images to emerge from Germany during the late 15th century was Albrecht Dürer's engraving *Four Horsemen of the Apocalypse*, symbolizing the social and religious unrest that was sweeping the country, as well as the ever-present specters of famine, plague, war, and death.

Facing: Dürer was influenced by a variety of events and currents of thought including humanism, the growing frequency of peasant revolts, political division between German leaders and the papacy, and the Renaissance. These perturbations were never more expressively rendered than in the *Four Horsemen of the Apocalypse* woodcuts.

Above: The pastor of Wert, near Nuremberg, preaches about the freedom of mankind at the spring carnival. Itinerant "hedge priests" and local pastors were at the forefront of German peasant unrest in the early 16th century.

Although towns and cities were vital to the economic and cultural development of Germany, the majority of the population eked out a living in a landscape dominated by great forests, vulnerable to the changes of climate, fertility of the land, and the dictats of feudal superiors. Many peasants were no longer serfs, since the breakdown of the feudal system, although pockets of serfdom remained until the 19th century. The feudal yoke was replaced by often crippling taxes to the local lord, Church, and emperor. Those who lived in towns and cities, in particular those without citizenship, also held grievances, since they were ineligible to serve in municipal assemblies or to hold public office.

In England, where the feudal system had disintegrated in the late Middle Ages, the peasants had revolted in 1381, a tense situation only defused by the many empty promises of reform given by the young king, Richard II. In Germany, any similar unrest was thwarted by the patchwork carpet of states, which made large enough gatherings of malcontents impracticable.

However, at the beginning of the 16th century, social unrest spurred by rising taxation and a succession of bad harvests led to peasant revolts in several European countries. The most significant were the Doza revolt in Hungary (1514), the uprising of Slovenian serfs (1515), and the great peasants' revolt in Germany (1524–25).

A contemporary account of peasant grievances is detailed in the *Twelve Articles of the Swabian Peasants*, a petition drawn up at the start of the rising. They demanded basic rights, principally to choose their own pastors, and to cut wood and hunt. They wanted a say in the introduction of laws that affected them and resented tithes and taxes, in particular the *Todfall* (death tax). They denounced serfdom and "oppression" by their lords.

Equally importantly, the *Twelve Articles* mentioned the Gospel: "The gospel is not the cause of revolt and disorder, since it is the message of Christ… the peasants demand that this gospel be taught them as a guide in life." Luther's impassioned protests against the Catholic Church (*see pages 178–9*), the dissemination of the German Bible, and the feeling of heightened religiosity provided extra impetus to social unrest.

Luther's rejection

In early 1525 Lutheran follower Thomas Münzer (1489–1525) helped incite rebellion in Thuringia and Saxony, which swept across southern Germany. Monasteries and churches were looted, partly as revenge for centuries of religiously inspired taxation. Over 250,000 peasants took part, who expected Luther's blessing in what they saw as a religious as well as a secular revolution.

Luther's response was critical to the development of the Reformation. In April 1525 he showed his support for the main tenets of the rebellion in his *Friendly Admonition to Peace concerning the Twelve Articles of the Swabian Peasants*. However, while Luther might criticize corrupt nobles and their oppressive taxation of peasants, he was no advocate of anarchy or social revolution, particularly if by association it would lose him noble allies. Luther was leading a crusade on the excesses of Rome and he did not want political division with the temporal powers of emperor or nobility to get in the way of theological reform.

His reaction was polemic: "In my earlier pamphlet I had no occasion to condemn the peasants, because they promised to yield to law… But they rob and pillage and act like mad dogs… They have loaded themselves with horrible sins against God and men, for which they deserve a manifold death of body and soul." It was a calculated reversal of position, and saved the Reformation.

At the battle of Frankenhausen in May 1525, the forces of the *status quo* defeated the peasantry. During the savage reprisals that followed, as many as 100,000 peasants were executed, Münzer among them. It became clear that the success of the Reformation depended on the support of the secular German princes rather than the masses, consequently Luther and his supporters did not foster support of the peasantry.

German Art of the Renaissance

During most of the 15th century, German art was dominated by the International Gothic style, but gradually artistic influences from both Italy and the Low Countries helped to shape a new blend of Gothic and the Italianate influences.

Right: *Crucifixion* by Matthias Grünewald. Two versions were painted, this—the *"Small Crucifixion"* of 1510 appears to be a preparatory work for the larger Isenheim altarpiece of 1515. The agonized pose of Christ is identical in both, but the foreground characters are considerably altered.

German painter and sculptor Hans Multscher (1400–67) from Ulm was one of the first artists to emerge from the confines of High Gothic tradition. His altarpieces displayed a sound understanding of these older conventions, but he augmented his work with acutely developed observance of humanity and human action that gave refreshing individuality to his characterizations.

In Basel, German-born painter Konrad Witz (c.1400–45) developed a realism that mirrored that of Flemish contemporary Jan van Eyck (*see page 105*), clearly an influence. Witz had traveled in the Low Countries, since his father was an artist who enjoyed Burgundian patronage. He set *The Miraculous Draught of Fishes* (1444) in Lake Geneva, one of the earliest examples of a recognizable landscape.

A Low Country influence was detected in the work of Martin Schongauer (c.1430–91), who remained true to the International Gothic style and was influenced by the detailed art of the mid-15th century Flemish master Rogier van der Weyden (*see page 103*). Schongauer was a leading engraver, and his work influenced many later German artists including Albrecht Dürer (*see following spread*).

Dürer's contemporary Matthias Grünewald (c.1475–1528) of Aschaffenburg combined the roles of painter and architect, having trained in Alsace, probably in the study of Schongauer, although his medium was

Above: *Holy Family* by Martin Schongauer of c.1490.

oil paint. He assimilated the best of the Flemish and Italian works he came across, combining them in his most important work, the altarpiece of Isenheim, in Alsace (1515). His use of agonized human forms harked back to a darker, somewhat fantastical medieval Gothic tradition, but his use of color to express emotion was a new departure in German art. Working during the era of Martin Luther, Grünewald and Dürer's art expressed the personal, spiritual, and moral struggles endured by many of their contemporaries.

Victims of the Reformation

Witz may have been a source of inspiration for a new breed of south German painters who became known as the Danube School through their development of landscapes. Bavarian-born painter and etcher Lucas Cranach the Elder (1472–1553; *see pictures, pages 176 and 179*) was based in Wittenberg, where he produced religious works for the Elector of Saxony. He became a friend of Martin Luther, and, following his switch to Protestantism, Cranach concentrated more on portraiture rather than religious subjects, since this was where the patron's tastes lay.

Contemporary Albrecht Altdorfer (1480–1538) was a town architect, but developed an interest in painting and printmaking. Patronized by Emperor Maximilian I, this Bavarian artist specialized in landscapes and epic battle scenes. Further down

Left: Albrecht Altdorfer's *The Departure of Saint Florian* (1520) shows the painter's interest in combining human events with a natural background. With the notable exeption of the Venetian Giorgione, this fascination with nature is a typically northern trait, but with some of Altdorfer's pictures, nature becomes the very subject. This is exemplified in his *St. George and the Dragon* (1525), in which the two protagonists are almost lost at the base of a painting bursting with exuberant forest foliage.

the Danube, Wolf Huber (1490–1553) operated in Passau and Ratisbon. All three shared an ability to produce extraordinary detail in miniature in a modernized International Gothic style in tune with the works of the Italian High Renaissance.

Despite his Flemish training, the religious works of Bavarian Hans Holbein the Elder (c.1465–1524) betrayed a strong Italian influence. He is probably best remembered as the father of the gifted Hans Holbein the Younger (c.1497–1543), who became court painter for Henry VIII of England. The younger Holbein displayed a skill for portraiture that owed much to both the Italian and Flemish schools.

The upheaval of the Reformation made it difficult for German artists to obtain patronage.

In the absence of ecclesiastic patronage and with secular patrons reluctant to commission religious themes, many moved abroad (like Holbein the Younger) or abandoned their craft (like Grünewald). While Cranach the Elder and others attempted to create an iconographic Protestant style, the reformers were opposed to anything that retained links with the Catholic Church. For a similar reason, the sensuality of the Italian Mannerists was avoided in favor of more pedestrian portraiture. In this climate, German Renaissance painting withered and all but died.

Architecture—always more of a necessity than painting—did better, but the great days of German and Bavarian building belong to the 17th-century Baroque than to the Renaissance.

Albrecht Dürer

Most art historians agree that the great artist of the Renaissance outside Italy was Albrecht Dürer. As a painter and engraver he knew no equal, combining the Gothic German traditions of his childhood with the new and vibrant style of the Italian Renaissance.

Born in Nuremberg in 1471, the young Dürer was apprenticed to local artist Michael Wolgemut during the late 1480s, but in 1492–94 he worked in Basel, Switzerland, were he began to experiment with the art of woodcut engraving by providing images for a Swiss publisher. In 1494 he married teenage bride Agnes Fey, and the young couple traveled to Italy, visiting Venice in 1496.

They returned to Nuremberg, where he soon established a reputation as a printmaker, a famous example of this early work being his *Four Horsemen of the Apocalypse* (1498, a series of woodcuts), which also indicated his sense of spiritual and intellectual unease. From 1500 he was increasingly sought after by secular patrons, who commissioned his painting of the *Adoration of the Magi* (1504). Dürer was in Italy 1505–07, during which time he visited Giovanni Bellini and Giorgione in Venice. On his return to Nuremberg he painted his panels of *Adam and Eve*, which brought him to the attention of Maximilian I, who brought Dürer to his court in 1512.

In this respect, Dürer was very different from his contemporaries who, as we have seen, were not as highly regarded as were scholars and writers. He was proud of his social as well as artistic achievements, and painted several self-portraits, which show him as a handsome, sophisticated gentleman, rather than a lowly craftsman. The self-portraits, on which he lavished care and attention, were also useful advertisements of his skills to his noble patrons.

Dürer produced some of his best engraving work in his capacity as Habsburg court artist, his output included a series of 192 woodcuts (*The Triumphal Arch*, 1515) and numerous other widely acclaimed individual and grouped engravings. In 1513–14 he created the greatest of his copperplate engravings: *The Knight, St. Jerome in His Study*, and *Melencolia I*, all containing rich iconographic detailing. These works were probably designed to be viewed together, an exercise in raising the intensity of his art and displaying this genius to his audience.

Overcoming the Reformation

It was during this period that he came into contact with the teachings of Martin Luther and, despite his adoption of Protestantism, the patronage of the Holy Roman Emperor continued, Charles V retaining Dürer in his Flemish court. Returning to Nuremberg in 1521, Dürer was in great demand as a portrait painter of leading reformers, producing engravings of humanist acquaintances Erasmus, Philip

We must conclude that Dürer was proud of his appearance, because he painted several self-portraits during his life. This one, painted when he was 26, portrays the artist as a Renaissance prince, man of the world, and well-traveled sophisticate. The serenity of the painting is in direct contrast to his violent, Gothic engravings, such as the *Apocalypse* series, an example of which is shown on page 163. Dürer was equally at home in the medium of water color, and his *Hare* (**facing**) and *Great Piece of Turf* (both about 1503) are remarkable for their precision and detail.

Melanchthon, and Willibald Pirckheimer, as well as a *Four [Protestant] Apostles* panel commissioned by Nuremberg Town Council.

Durer's fascination with the world, curiosity about the workings of nature, and keen powers of observation were the keys to his success. He had the ability to express the beauty and even the ugliness of nature in its most natural form, features he shared with Italian artists such as Bellini. His early woodcuts, such as the *Apocalypse* series (1498), have a more Gothic flavor, so his second Italian journey clearly had a profound influence on him.

Through his letters we can detect a somewhat obsessive nature, demonstrated by his constant striving for the essence of a subject and restless quest for knowledge and enlightenment.

His portraits attempt to delve into the heart of a person. Dürer was extremely learned and fully understood the Italian emphasis on the dialog between scientific theory and art, producing his own treatise on geometric proportion shortly before he died.

By the time of his death in 1528, Dürer was one of the most widely recognized artists in northern Europe, his engravings sold or reproduced far beyond the confines of his native Germany. The 16th-century art critic Giorgio Vasari described Dürer as that "most marvelous painter." It has been argued that Dürer was so great and popular an artist, so searching and rounded a thinker, that he was almost a Renaissance in his own right.

CHAPTER 11

A House Divided–
The Reformation

In the early 16th century an initial expression of religious discontent encouraged by the failings of the Church and the spread of humanist scholarship found a willing audience among the laity of Europe. For centuries the Church had abused its position of trust as a spiritual and moral guiding force. The rise of humanism during the Renaissance created an educated elite that was prepared to question long-accepted values, and the Church came under growing criticism due to its corrupt political structure, rigid interpretation of theology, and immoral worldliness. This criticism struck a chord among the increasingly urbanized population, many of whom formed their own opinions as a result of access to mass-printed pamphlets and books published in their own vernacular languages, rather than the elitist Latin of the clergy.

This was followed by an altogether more radical phase, when theological reformers led by Martin Luther took the Church to task. When the papacy refused to reform, the radicals took matters into their own hands. They created their own ecclesiastical structure, operated according to the new humanist interpretation of theology, and formed their own views on the importance of the sacraments, salvation, and the priesthood of all believers—a conception that permitted entire communities to participate in this spiritual revolution.

After the initial Reformation came other, even more extreme reforms. The most significant was Calvinism, named after radical theologian John Calvin, a hard-line Protestant who developed Luther's ideas a to a further stage. Combined with the evolution of extremist sects such as the Anabaptists, this prompted a Catholic backlash that became known as the Counter-Reformation. This sought to reimpose the old doctrines on an often unwilling European population. Christendom was split into Catholic and Protestant camps, which inevitably led to a spiral of religious wars, massacres, and repression, the effects of which can still be felt today.

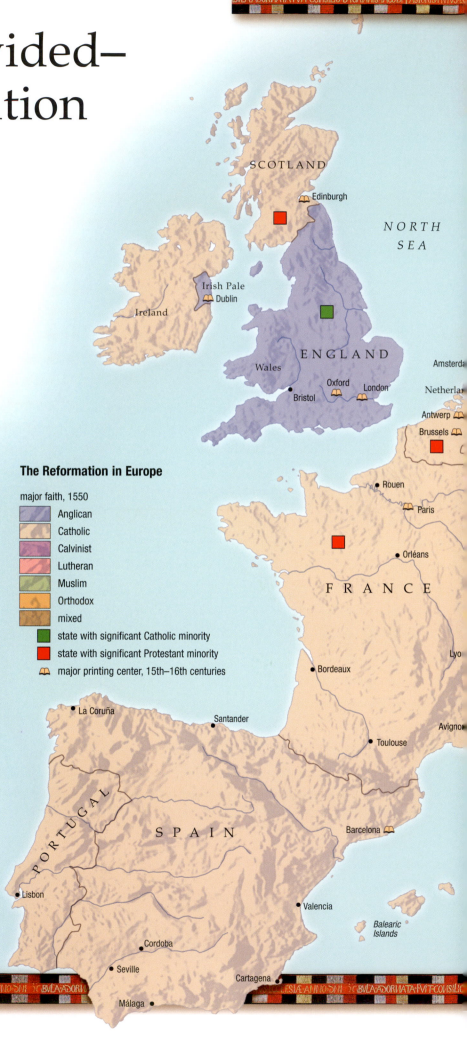

The Reformation in Europe

major faith, 1550

- Anglican
- Catholic
- Calvinist
- Lutheran
- Muslim
- Orthodox
- mixed
- ■ state with significant Catholic minority
- ■ state with significant Protestant minority
- 📖 major printing center, 15th–16th centuries

ESTONIA

LIVONIA

Riga

COURLAND

RUSSIA

Polotsk • • Smolensk

Christiania
(Oslo)

Stockholm

SWEDEN

BALTIC SEA

Vilna • • Minsk

NORWAY-DENMARK

Copenhagen

Königsberg

Prussia

LITHUANIA

Kiev

Danzig

Lübeck

Stettin

Emden • Hamburg

Bremen

Brandenburg

Berlin

Emperor Charles V
defeats a Lutheran
army in the name of
Catholicism

Warsaw

POLAND

UKRAINE

HOLY
ROMAN
EMPIRE

Wittenberg

Leipzig

Mühlberg
1547

Saxony

Dresden

Deventer

recht

Cologne

Bonn

uxemburg

Frankfurt

Mainz

Worms

Prague

Area of Hussite revolt,
1419–37; many continued to
adhere to the teachings of
Jan Huss into the 16th century

Lemberg

Krakow

Silesia

BOHEMIA
To Habsburgs
after 1526

Bamberg

Nuremberg

Peasants War
1525

Bavaria

Strasbourg

Augsburg

Moravia

MOLDAVIA

Jedisan

Vienna

Buda

TRANSYLVANIA
to Ottoman empire by 1541

Jassy

Munich

Basel

Zurich

Swiss Confederation

Bern

Tyrol

Austria

Salzburg

IMPERIAL HUNGARY

HUNGARY
to Ottoman empire by 1541

Geneva

Trent

Mohács
1526

WALLACHIA

Bucharest

Milan

Savoy

Venice

Belgrade

BLACK
SEA

Parma

Ottoman Turks
defeat last king of
Hungary, Louis II

BULGARIA

Genoa

Modena

PAPAL

Nish

Saluzzo
to France, 1559

Florence

Urbino

Montenegro

Sofia

Siena

STATES

Ragusa

Edirne
(Adrianople)

Constantinople

Corsica

Rome

Subiaco

Thessalonica

O T T O M A N   E M P I R E

NAPLES

Rumelia

Naples

Izmir

T Y R R H E N I A N
S E A

Sardinia

Morea

Athens

Caligari

Sicily

Messina

Reggio

Rhodes

Palermo

Syracuse

Candia

Crete

169

The Pre-Reformation Church

The roots of the Reformation lay in a growing secular dissatisfaction with the late medieval Church. Although the conciliar movement attempted to force change on reluctant popes, little real effort was made to end the clerical abuse and shortcomings of the 15th-century Church.

Contemporary engravings of John Wycliffe (**right**) and Jan Huss (**below**)—both men were dedicated to undermining the power of the papacy.

During the 14th century the Great Schism brought the papacy into disrepute, and this, combined with other examples of misgovernment within the Church, led to the spread of heresy. In the medieval sense, "heresy" may be interpreted as meaning any religious convictions that the Roman Catholic Church regarded as contrary to its teachings, or liable to undermine its pre-eminent position. In a

narrower sense, it also meant any attitude that might reflect the papacy—and that includes the cardinals and leading ecclesiactical princes—in a poor light. During the 12th century the heretical Waldensians in the Alps and the Albigensians in the south of France were crushed by crusaders sanctioned by the pope. During this same period the notion of individual piety gained ground, as did a spread of mysticism; both developments that aroused deep suspicion among the clergy.

English cleric John Wycliffe (1320–84) even declared that an unworthy pope need not be obeyed. Since, his rejection of the rituals and doctrines of the established Church were mixed with elements that suggested social reform, his doctrine was anathema to both papacy and the monarchy. In Bohemia, Jan Huss (c.1369–1415) developed Wycliffe's theories, but concentrated on the growing worldliness of the Church, and he called for a return to a simpler interpretation of religion. While denouncing the pope as the Antichrist, Huss encouraged the view that the faithful laity could reform the Christian religion, encouraging a "grass roots" rebellion against the structure of the Church.

1415	**1512–17**	**1516**	**1517**	**1519**	**1520**	**1521**	**1521**
Bohemian Jan Huss is executed for preaching the reformist views of John Wycliffe	The Fifth Lateran Council discusses the ending of clerical abuses such as sales of indulgences	Humanist Desiderius Erasmus questions the Church's interpretation of Scripture in his Greek New Testament	Martin Luther posts his 95 Theses in Wittenberg, stating his objection to the sale of indulgences	Luther breaks from the Roman Church and establishes his own doctrine the following year	*The Freedom of a Christian Man* sets out Luther's belief in salvation through faith	Interpretation of the Scriptures, *De legis litera sive carne et spiritu*, is published by Andreas von Karlstadt	Refusing to retract his views, Martin Luther is banned from preaching at the Diet of Worms

Critics of the Church attacked the widespread financial and moral abuses of the 15th century—claiming that the papacy was little more than a bank to administer the pope's temporal affairs. For many, the greatest form of financial abuse was the sale of indulgences. During the Middle Ages many monasteries had beome bloated with wealth earned from selling God's forgiveness for sins committed in body or spirit. Prelates all over Europe had cashed in on the cash-for-remission business, the theory being that a penitent could receive a reduction of the time their soul would spend in Purgatory if they received an indulgence from an ordained priest—and nothing was for free.

Money absolves sin

The practice of selling indulgences began as a means of raising revenue, but increasingly the distinction between reducing the period of atonement for sins and the attainment of salvation and therefore entry to heaven became entwined. As one contemporary couplet ran, "The moment the money tinkles in the collecting box, a soul flies out of purgatory." The implication was that money could buy eternal celestial happiness. Erasmus summed up the criticism of this system when he said that the Church "measured Purgatory by the hourglass… as if it were a mathematical table." He added, "Suppose some merchant, soldier, or judge, parts with some small piece of ill-gotten money. He at once conceived… [that] his whole life [is] quite cleansed."

Another much-criticized practice was the sale of Church offices. The pope could appoint cardinals as he saw fit, and in 1487 alone Innocent VIII (belying his name) sold no fewer that 24 senior clerical posts. This allowed wealthy laymen to accumulate substantial wealth from sees they never visited; offices could even be passed down like a secular inheritance.

Among the lower ranks of the Church, priests were often resented for the fees they charged for almost everything: conducting weddings and funerals, hearing confession, or giving the last rites. Worse, their worldliness often extended to the keeping of mistresses, an abuse of their priestly vows of celibacy that extended through the ranks of the clerics as far up as the pope. In the country, monasteries grew rich from their extensive landholdings (some taken in lieu of

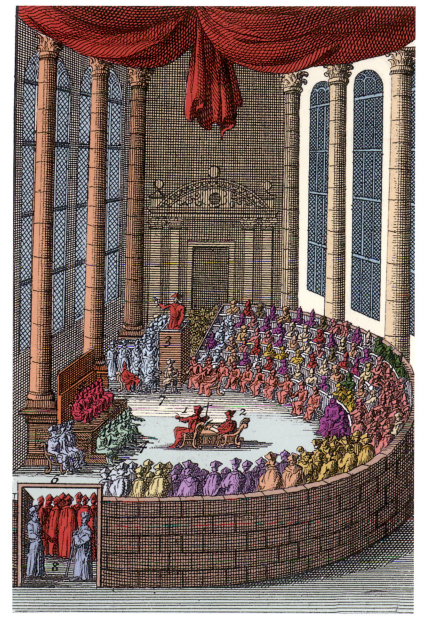

indulgence payments), while in the cities sees became as much business centers as they were the spiritual House of God on earth.

Although the conciliarists attempted to reform the Church in the late 15th century, a succession of popes managed to avoid major changes to the system. During the decades that followed, attempts to force reform were repeated, this time supported by secular princes who feared a widespread reformist revolt. It was too little, too late. By the time the Fifth Lateran Council sat to discuss the ending of clerical abuses (1512–17), Luther was already drawing up the *Ninety-Five Theses* that would bring about the Protestant Reformation.

Above: At the Council of Trent (1545–63) the main objective was the definitive determination of the doctrines of the Church, in answer to the heresies of the Protestants, and a thorough reform of the inner life of the Church by removing the numerous abuses. It was insufficient to satisfy the Lutheran Protestants.

The Influence of Humanist Theology

The general tenor of disapproval leveled by the lay community against the late medieval Church was only a partial cause of the Reformation. If it were not for the rise of humanism, it is unlikely that the critics of the Church could have gained such widespread support.

Below: Contemporary illustration of a teacher encouraging discussion among his scholars at a university of the 15th century.

While humanism involved renewed interest in the classical writings of antiquity, usually Latin and Greek texts, this intellectual movement was not necessarily religious in nature. Rather, classical study encouraged individuals to employ the classical tools of logic and philosophy, with the concomittant demand toward inquiry. This also meant that humanists focused on human ability, rather than divine power or religious mysticism.

By the mid-15th century humanist scholars began to apply their new training in Platonic logic to question the doctrines and superstitions that characterized the late medieval Church. By the time of Desiderius Erasmus (c.1466–1536) humanism had spread throughout Europe, and a form of religious scholasticism had appeared in Italy and Spain, where the Church employed humanist scholars to provide a logical support for orthodox religious doctrines.

By contrast, humanist scholars who operated beyond the confines of Church academia developed a different approach. God had given man certain intellectual gifts, therefore man could use these to discover his own spiritual identity. The ability of humanist scholars to study biblical texts in their original language, combined with the development of printing, encouraged the idea that through the examination of Scripture, man could gain a better understanding of his faith. The Church rejected this, arguing that since the pope was God's representative on earth, only the pontiff and his clerics could interpret God's word through the Scriptures. Erasmus set about discrediting the scholastic theology that supported the Church's position and used logic to bring into question the mysticism and superstition that underlay much of late medieval Christian worship.

The Bible reinterpreted

The humanist movement encouraged a revival of philosophy. The medieval universities had been dominated by Aristotle, but humanists insisted on the importance of other forms of philosophy: Stoic, Epicurean, Skeptic, and Platonic. The revival of Christian Platonism became the dominant philosophical and theological movement of the late 15th century.

Erasmus aimed to create a more practical form of Christianity, one which was suitable for all Christians, not just those who supported the rigid confines of established orthodoxy. His *Greek New Testament* (1516) pointed out the significant errors in the standard Vulgate used by the Church, proving that the established interpretation of the Scriptures was fallible. Erasmus challenged orthodox biblical interpretation that rested on corrupt texts or anachronistic assumptions. Later, reformers such as Luther and Calvin would argue that the original "evangelical" interpretation of the Bible had been lost through medieval corruptions of translation and papal censorship, and only the Protestant reformers, working from original sources, could present a clear and original interpretation of God's word.

By encouraging fellow humanist scholars to read the Bible in its original language, Erasmus encouraged others to question the standard interpretation imposed by the Church. At the time, most Catholic scholastics believed that theology was a science, to be learned and taught by qualified clerics. Erasmus challenged this, arguing that "the philosophy of Christ" (the message of Christianity) could be learned by any pious educated person who studied the Bible.

When this notion was developed a stage further and humanists encouraged laymen to read the Bible translated into the vernacular, the Church was unable to contain the move away from its strict—and often self-serving— interpretation of God's word. It proved impossible to reconcile humanist inquiry and Catholic orthodoxy, forcing theologians to consider ways of breaking the bonds that bound them to the Church, creating an unbridgeable divide between reformers and Catholics in the process.

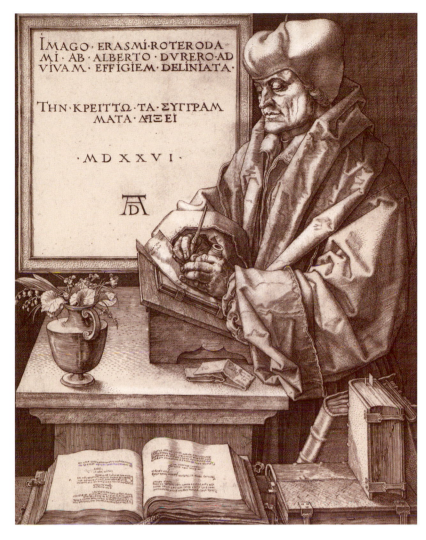

Above: Engraving by Albrecht Dürer of Erasmus at work on his manuscripts.

Left: Low respect for the office of the pope by Germans is indicated in this engraving depicting German mercenaries mocking Pope Clement VII during the sack of Rome in 1527.

Salvation and the Sacraments

In the early 16th century, the notions of salvation, the importance of the sacraments, and the interpretation of Scripture were crucial, since any theological error was widely regarded as leading to eternal damnation. In a spiritual age, man had to redefine his own beliefs.

Facing: The power of the medieval Church over every aspect of people's lives is excellently conveyed in this painting by Rogier van der Weyden. Called the *Altarpiece of the Seven Sacraments* of c. 1445, this is a detail of the open center panel: *Baptism, Confirmation, and Confession.*

As theologians re-examined the original biblical texts, the greatest divergence from the Catholic Church lay in the theology of salvation and its related issues of justification, predestination, grace, and the sacraments. Salvation was closely linked to the example set by Jesus. His ultimate sacrifice and resurrection were considered to be a guarantee from God of the existence of a saving grace; finding the favor of God. The theological question was how was this to be achieved.

The most widely-held interpretation was that by imitating His life one could achieve grace, which gave rise to the conceptions of charitable works, celibacy, piety, and so on. Another interpretation centered on redemption. Through His life, death, and resurrection, Christ demonstrated the ability to renew himself; allowing a rebirth of faith (an interpretation characterized by the theology of Baptist Christians).

The central issue here was sin. Some theologians argued that since Adam, man had diverged from the sinless path God had intended. This left no room for personal redemption, and all the good works in the world could not save a naturally sinful soul from damnation. Christ's life showed a way out of this predicament with the intercession of God himself, a divine saving grace that could save the elect and give the "fallen man" a chance of eternal bliss. Human works, however individually worthless, were witnessed by God, and counted toward a final reckoning.

The notion of Purgatory was introduced because nobody knew how much grace was needed to gain entrance to Heaven. By the Middle Ages, the notion was that when a body died, the soul would spend a period in Purgatory, depending on its worldly guilt. For those unsure of salvation, the thought of spending aeons in limbo was far from comforting. The Catholic solution was simple: purchase an indulgence and reduce time in Purgatory. Other methods involved pilgrimage, crusade, or patronage of ecclesiastical projects.

The rites preserved

The sacraments, most still observed today, are rites that involve the benevolent conveyance of God's grace to a recipient through the intervention of a cleric. Through the observance of long-established ceremonies, clerics could perform the miracle of consecration, bringing the spirit of God into a ritual to serve as His vehicle in the distribution of divine grace. The seven sacraments include baptism, confirmation (the ratification of baptism on a sentient being), matrimony, and the last rites—stages through life where the granting of grace was considered important. Another sacrament is ordination, whereby a candidate bestowed with a special and irrevocable grace to become a minister, or bestowed with an apostolic succession.

Finally there are two special sacraments. The first is the Eucharist, where through consecration an offering of bread and wine was converted into the body and blood of Christ (transubstantiation), which allowed Him to die again, thereby permitting the grace of the faithful. The final sacrament is penance, where personal sins were repented according to a set pattern, involving contrition, confession, the satisfaction of an act of penance, regeneration (signifying a mending of the ways), and final absolution, the removal of the taint of sin by a priest.

The system of grace was an emotive issue in the early 16th century because it invited Church corruption. Humanist research showed how the sacraments had largely been invented by the Church in the preceding centuries, their emphasis more due to the maintenance of Church domination of religious life, since only ordained priests could dispense grace. Holding services in Latin helped to maintain the position of the priest, because most laymen were unable to follow the rites involved, which increased the mysticism of the sacraments. The priest was paid for bestowing grace, and so the richer you were, the better the afterlife became. Reformers who were able to offer an alternative path to salvation were obviously going to be the beneficiaries of a greatful populace capable for the first time— thanks to the invention of printing and the stream of cheaply produced books that resulted— of working out for themselves the shaky ground on which the medieval Church was founded.

Martin Luther

Although he was not the first theologian to challenge the practices of Roman Catholicism, Martin Luther captured the public imagination. By highlighting doubt about orthodox practices, he laid the foundation for the Protestant faith.

Left: Portrait of Martin Luther by Lucas Cranach the Elder, who was a friend of the revolutionary theologian.

Son of a Saxon miner, Martin Luther (1483–1546) never broke free of his humble roots. He excelled at the local school, and in 1501 began attending courses in humanist philosophy at the University of Erfurt. Luther underwent a spiritual awakening in July 1505, when he joined the reformed Augustinian order against his father's wishes; two years later he was ordained as a priest. His superior intellect allowed Luther to progress through a series of theological studies and earn a doctorate in theology and a seat as the dean in the seminary at Wittenberg.

For years, Luther had been racked by doubt over his worthiness, the notion of "saying" (expressing wisdom or truth), and the attainment of salvation. He was influenced by the humanist William of Occam and the ancient teachings of St. Augustine, who helped him reach the conclusion that man's grace could not be purchased, but could come from faith alone, through the grace of God. Did the Bible not say that "The just shall live by faith" (*Romans I:17*)? This conclusion broke with accepted teaching, and highlighted the shamefulness of the sale of indulgences.

On October 31, 1517 Martin Luther tacked a statement of faith on the church in Wittenberg; the *Ninety-five Theses or Disputations on the Power and Efficacy of Indulgences*. The document was both a statement against the selling of indulgences and an invitation to other scholars to join the debate. He argued that God was omnipotent and omnipresent, and would decide which souls

Above: An unsigned, undated engraving gives the Catholic version of Luther, portrayed here as an instrument of the devil. The bagpipe was a well understood medieval symbol for Satan, so Luther is seen as doubly damned— playing the devil's tune and being his creature.

would receive salvation and which would be condemned to eternal damnation. Salvation was therefore a gift from God and one which humans were unable to influence, therefore the sale of indulgences was irrelevant.

Justifying his faith

Luther was unhappy to see fellow Germans being duped by sales from the pope's "treasury of merits" to provide financial gain for the Church. He added that "The true treasure of the Church is the holy gospel of the glory and the grace of God." This was not just an attack against the sale of indulgences, but an assault against the fundamental roads of the Catholic faith and the structure of the Church.

Luther arranged the distribution of his theses around Saxony. When word of Luther's actions reached Rome, Pope Leo X (p.1513–21) sent orders that Luther's Augustinian superior should demand an end to his rebellion. Luther refused to demur, since by that time he had earned the support of Frederick III "the Wise," Elector of Saxony (1486–1525). Leo tried a more conciliatory approach, sending a papal legate to meet Luther in Augsburg to discuss his concerns. Luther refused to demur, despite the risk of a heresy charge.

The impasse continued until, in June 1519, Luther stated he did not consider the pope infallible, which led to a final break with Rome. As Luther put it, "We have cared for Babylon, but she has not healed; let us then leave her." In 1517, Luther had not sought a split with the Church, only the chance to reform her. By 1520 it was clear that he had to create his own Church, based on "justification by faith alone." By his actions Luther not only refused to acknowledge the spiritual supremacy of the pope, he also denied the value of ritual as a means of salvation.

For Luther, there was no need for priests to interpret God's word. The Christian was saved by faith, his belief in God. God had granted man his free grace, so by embracing faith and being reborn, the sinner could be cleansed and renew his path to salvation. Luther called on German princes to reform the Church within their own states, remodeling it to encompass this new interpretation of God's will. Luther had opened Pandora's Box, but what followed would surprise him as much as it did the pope.

The Impact of Lutheranism

By the summer of 1520, the rift between Martin Luther and Leo X was unbridgeable. Emperor Charles V sided with the pope and Luther was outlawed, but his reforms were undertaken by the laity and theologians on his behalf, turning much of northern Germany toward Protestantism.

In June 1520 Pope Leo X excommunicated Martin Luther from the Church, accusing him of 41 heresies, "objectionable to pious ears, misleading to simple minds, and contrary to Catholic teaching." He described Luther as "the wild boar who has invaded the Lord's vineyard." Luther consigned his writ of excommunication to the flames.

By this time Luther's challenge to the papacy had also become a matter of politics. Before his election, Charles V had promised that no one within the bounds of his empire would be excommunicated without a fair hearing. This was aimed to appease Luther's supporter Frederick the Elector of Saxony, and through Frederick's

Below: An unknown 16th-century painter depicts Protestant reformers gathering. The figure in the left foreground probably represents Luther.

mediation Charles summoned Luther to appear before him and the Imperial Diet at Worms in 1521. When he arrived Luther was asked if he had written the treatises and pamphlets arrayed in front of him. Luther readily acknowledged his authorship, adding, "I am bound by the Scriptures I have quoted and my conscience is captive to the Word of God. I cannot and I will not retract anything, since it is neither safe nor right to go against my conscience."

Unimpressed, the largely conservative diet condemned him, and in May 1521 the resulting Edict of Worms, signed by the emperor, placed Luther under the ban of the empire, which prevented him from preaching and was a step toward being branded as a heretic. For his safety, the Elector of Saxony sheltered Luther in his castle at Wartburg. By banishing Luther, the emperor sided with the pope and the orthodoxy of the Catholic Church. While this stemmed Luther's preaching, it imposed a secular solution on a spiritual problem, a situation many humanists found intolerable.

A complete doctrine

Although Luther returned to his seat at Wittenberg in 1522, his fate depended on political developments within Germany. He would remain in Wittenberg for the rest of his life, working on a set of Catechisms (1529) and his German translation of the Bible, which was published in 1534 and became the mainstay of German Protestant worship.

In his middle age Luther became increasingly irascible, resisting attempts to refine his theological work and opposing further reform. For Luther, the Scriptures constituted the word of God—there was no need for their interpretation by any ecclesiastical structure. The pious would discover its true meaning for themselves. As for the sacraments, he only recognized the importance of baptism, which reminded the recipient of God's saving power, and the Eucharist, which for Luther represented the true spirit of Jesus Christ. For him it was God who turned bread and wine into the body and blood of Christ, not some mystical, miraculous transubstantiation. To the Catholic Church, this was heresy, as was his belief in justification by faith, without the mediation of clerics.

However, his idea that all were equal in the eyes of God—his priesthood of all believers—was altogether more dangerous, since it was interpreted as an attack on both ecclesiastic and

secular powers in Europe. This doctrine influenced the German peasantry to rebel against their feudal overlords (*see page 162*), but Luther quickly retracted anything that seemed to incite or support this type of rebellion.

For all his emphasis on spirituality, Luther was pragmatic enough to realize that the ultimate survival of his reformed Church was to be determined not by the peasantry, but by the princes and noblemen who governed Germany.

Through their support, Luther's followers presented a document to the Imperial Diet at Augsburg in 1530 that established the groundwork for a Protestant Church. The Augsburg Confession by Philip Melancthon (1497–1560) became the doctrine that inspired secular princes and civic leaders to adopt the reformed faith, despite the opposition of Charles V. The Protestant faith would survive and prosper.

Urban Reformers

In the wake of Luther's initial plea for reform, several urban reformers took the Protestant Reformation a stage further. Cities were ideal homes for Luther's "priesthood of all believers," since their inhabitants were used to working together for the good of their community.

At first the Reformation in Germany was mainly an urban phenomenon. Reformers found these communities ripe for the introduction of Lutheran ideas, since many already had universities or colleges of theological study as a means of improving the standards of their local clergy. Many of these clerics abandoned the Catholic Church in favor of the Lutheran faith.

German cities (particularly free cities) boasted a highly developed sense of civic pride and solidarity, their citizens working together for the good of trade and the standing of their homes. This made them microcosms of the larger country, where the technical elements of the Protestant Reformation could be tested and applied. As Erasmus put it, "What else is the city but a great monastery?"

While a German prince might order the conversion of his entire state, in cities religious reform had to come as a result of the willing participation of the whole community. This made the Reformation both a political challenge and a unique social and religious experiment. Luther's disciples hoped to make these burghers good Christians, as well as good civic citizens, where the entire city could embrace reform and safeguard its development through the maintenance of civic order, community

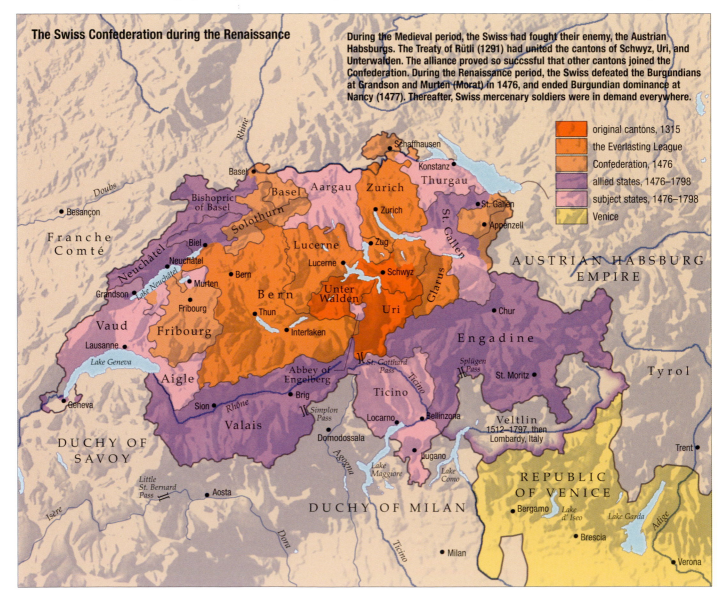

The Swiss Confederation during the Renaissance

During the Medieval period, the Swiss had fought their enemy, the Austrian Habsburgs. The Treaty of Rütli (1291) had united the cantons of Schwyz, Uri, and Unterwalden. The alliance proved so succssful that other cantons joined the Confederation. During the Renaissance period, the Swiss defeated the Burgundians at Grandson and Murten (Morat) in 1476, and ended Burgundian dominance at Nancy (1477). Thereafter, Swiss mercenary soldiers were in demand everywhere.

- original cantons, 1315
- the Everlasting League
- Confederation, 1476
- allied states, 1476–1798
- subject states, 1476–1798
- Venice

involvement, and the continuation of regular secular and spiritual life within a Protestant setting.

Three cities in particular played a crucial role in the development of the Lutheran Church, each guided by a charismatic reformer. In Switzerland at Zurich Huldreich Zwingli (1484–1531) was able to draw on the unique nature of the Swiss cities, which were even freer of feudal domination than their German counterparts. As a reformer, Zwingli was influenced by Erasmus, and while still a parish priest in Glarus he published works of humanist scholarship, developing a reputation that earned him a clerical appointment in Zurich (1518).

Incomplete reform

Zwingli's preaching and writing became increasingly antagonistic to Catholic doctrines, and although the city was nominally part of the see of the weak and unpopular Bishop of Constance, he failed to denounce Zwingli before the priest won over the townspeople to his cause. Although the anti-German Zwingli was not a Lutheran, he eventually adopted a version of Protestantism virtually identical to that espoused by Luther.

In 1522 Zurich formally became a Protestant community that Zwingli hoped would become "The Kingdom of God on Earth." He encouraged the removal of idolatrous images and crucifixes from the city's churches, since they would distract from the people's display of piety. More importantly, he devised a new form of Protestant baptism and Mass more in keeping with the reformed faith. However, his eucharistic doctrine set him at odds with Luther, causing the

first of many rifts between the Protestant reformers.

In the Swiss city of Basel, German-born reformer Johannes Oecolampadius (1482–1531) was appointed as a preacher in 1515, but after working elsewhere and undergoing a crisis of faith he returned with his reforming zeal renewed (c.1522). He introduced Protestant reform similar to that adopted by Zwingli, although Oecolampadius was more willing to follow Luther's lead. He supervised the abolition of Mass and Catholic religious festivals, emphasizing that the reformed religion needed pure faith, not mysticism.

Alsacian Martin Bucer (1491–1551), a former Dominican monk, served as the main reformist preacher in the independent German city of Strasbourg for a quarter of a century after 1524. He acted as a humanist mediator between Luther and Zwingli, and later encouraged the radicalism of John Calvin.

In none of these three cases did the urban reformer agree unequivocally with either Luther or his fellow reformers. This indicated that although the Reformation was a *fait accompli*, a unity akin to that enjoyed by the Catholic Church remained an unattainable goal.

Above left: Martin Bucer (Butzer) was one of the leaders of the German Reformation in the south. An ardent admirer of Erasmus, he withdrew from the Dominican Order after hearing Luther preach. Bucer died in Cambridge, England.

Above: The Swiss pastor Huldreich Zwingli enjoyed greater freedom of speech than his German contemporaries due to the Confederation's independence from both the Catholic Church and feudal overlords.

Toward the Second Reformation

To some radical reformers, Luther had not gone far enough. These groups included the Anabaptists and the supporters of Karlstadt, but due to political and social factors, both of these sects were bound to fail. Instead, the new standard bearer of the Reformation would be John Calvin.

While Luther remained reluctant to adopt any significant doctrinal changes to Lutheranism, urban reformers helped to found the Protestant Lutheran faith as a workable alternative to Catholicism. Others sought more radical avenues of reform. One such group were the Anabaptists, a term coined by Zwingli in reference to their re-baptism.

The founder of the sect was theologian Thomas Münzer (1489–1525), who broke with Lutheranism. Like other critics of Lutheranism, the Anabaptists based their doctrine on the scripture, believing that this represented the unequivocal Word of God and must be followed implicitly (*sola scriptura*). They also believed in *sola experientia* (spiritualism), claiming that an internal religious experience and transformation by God were needed for one to attain grace.

Other fundamentalist notions included the embrace of martyrdom, the belief in the imminent Second Coming, and a revolutionary belief in common ownership of property. After encountering increasing hostility and persecution by opponents of all faiths, Anabaptists led by Johann Matthiesen seized the city of Münster to serve as a rallying point for the Anabaptist faithful. In 1535 their martyrdom was assured when the city fell to a vengeful Imperial army.

Andreas von Karlstadt (1480–1541) was a contemporary of Luther at Wittenberg but went further, calling for the establishment of a "new Jerusalem" through radical reformation, widespread iconoclasm, and a social revolution that benefited the peasantry, elevating them to full membership of a community run according

Above: A 16th-century engraved portrait of the French theologian and reformist John Calvin.

to the Word of God, as written in Scripture.

While von Karlstadt's concept of "proto-Puritanism" pre-dated the more fundamentalist forms of Protestantism of later decades, they were based on his belief in the supremacy of Scripture, which brought him into conflict with the more liberal line adopted by Luther, as did disagreements over the Eucharist and baptism. He was marginalized through his calls for social reform, which was a contributory factor in the peasant uprisings of 1524–26.

Protestant Rome

It fell to a French theologian, John Calvin (1509–64), to suggest a viable Protestant alternative to Lutheranism. A brilliant scholar, he was educated in the humanities and law at the universities of Paris and Orléans and destined for a bright humanist career before his adoption of Luther's reforms in about 1533. To avoid persecution, he left France for Basel, where he published his *Institutes of Christian Religion* (1536), a work that established his credentials as a leading Protestant reformer.

Calvin was invited to assist the reformer Guillaume Farel (1489–1565) in Geneva, but his

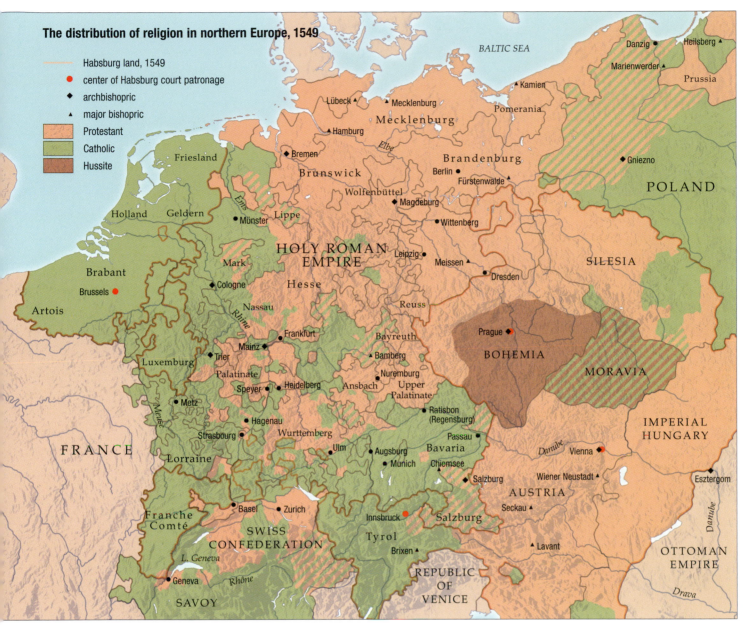

The distribution of religion in northern Europe, 1549

- Habsburg land, 1549
- ● center of Habsburg court patronage
- ◆ archbishopric
- ▲ major bishopric
- Protestant
- Catholic
- Hussite

BALTIC SEA

Danzig · Heilsberg

Marienwerder · Prussia

Kamien ▲

Lübeck ▲ · Mecklenburg

Pomerania

Hamburg ▲

Mecklenburg

Elbe

Brandenburg

Bremen ◆

Brunswick

Berlin · Fürstenwalde ▲ · Gniezno ◆

Wolfenbüttel

Magdeburg ◆

POLAND

Friesland

Holland   Geldern   Lippe

Münster ·   Mark

Wittenberg ·

Leipzig ·   Meissen ▲

HOLY ROMAN
EMPIRE

SILESIA

Brabant

Brussels ●

Artois

Cologne ◆   Hesse

Nassau

Reuss

Dresden ·

Rhine

Frankfurt ·

Mainz ◆

Trier ◆

Bayreuth

Bamberg ▲

Prague ◆

BOHEMIA

MORAVIA

Luxemburg

Palatinate

Speyer ·   Heidelberg ·   Ansbach   Upper
Palatinate

Nuremburg ·

Metz ·

Meuse

Hagenau ·

Wurttemberg

Ratisbon
(Regensburg) ◆

IMPERIAL
HUNGARY

FRANCE

Strasbourg ·

Ulm ·   Augsburg ·   Passau ▲

Munich ·   Bavaria

Danube   Vienna ●

Lorraine

Chiemsee ▲

Esztergom

Salzburg ·

Wiener Neustadt ▲

Franche
Comté

Basel ·   Zurich ·

Innsbruck ●   Salzburg

Seckau ▲

AUSTRIA

SWISS
CONFEDERATION

Tyrol

Lavant ▲

L. Geneva

Brixen ▲

OTTOMAN
EMPIRE

Geneva ·   Rhône

REPUBLIC
OF
VENICE

Danube

SAVOY

Drava

---

radical and increasingly uncompromising radicalism led to his expulsion (1538), at which point he sought refuge in Martin Bucer's Strasbourg. On his return to Geneva in 1541, Calvin imposed his will over the city council, convening an assembly of ministers and lay "elders" to assist the elected council in their work. From then on the city was run along austere, godly lines, creating what Calvin termed the "Protestant Rome."

During his later years he re-edited his *Institutes* and refined his theological views into what amounted to a new, more radical brand of Protestantism. Calvinism (or the Reformed Religion) represented a second wave of the Reformation, free of the confused doctrines of Lutheranism. It also provided a theological basis for Presbyterianism, Puritanism, and Southern Baptism.

Calvin's doctrine shared many characteristics of Lutheranism, including belief in "justification by faith alone," but he held divergent views on the importance of the Scriptures and sacraments, and on the relationship between God and mankind. In Calvin's eyes, man was insignificant to God. His doctrine of predestination meant that God had pre-determined who was to receive grace and who would be damned. It was not for man to comprehend God's purpose, only to meet His demands and purpose without question.

It was an uncompromising view, coming at a time when Protestantism was under threat from a resurgent Roman Catholicism. The advent of Calvinism and the Counter-Reformation led to extremism on both sides, and Europe would soon be plunged into a cycle of religious wars that would rage intermittently for over a century. This period of conflict also crushed what remained of the Renaissance, an era created amid a general feeling of renewal, and which ended amid the acrimony and incompatibility of a religious divide.

Left: While new techniques of mass printing had given the Reformation its impetus, and helped bring Renaissance humanist thinking to the masses, the ease of publishing pamplets led to a proliferation of conflicting arguments. The ensuing flood of literature resulted in a religious chaos that led to war and the end of the Renaissance.

Genealogical Tables of the Renaissance

Genealogical tables, or family trees, do not appeal to everyone—some find them easy to read, others not. And yet no other graphic device shows as clearly the lines of power running through a dynasty. Moreover, in a period as politically complex as the Renaissance, genealogical tables illuminate the tangle of inter-dynastic alliances through marriage, from the north of Europe to the south, west to the east, and all points in between. In the following tables 18 major dynastic alliances are indicated by differently shaped and colored devices, like the three examples shown to the left of this column. Each appears twice in either the same or different tables to show the link.

Cosimo de' Medici

The Medici of Florence

CAPITALS denote duke
Bold **CAPITALS** denote pope

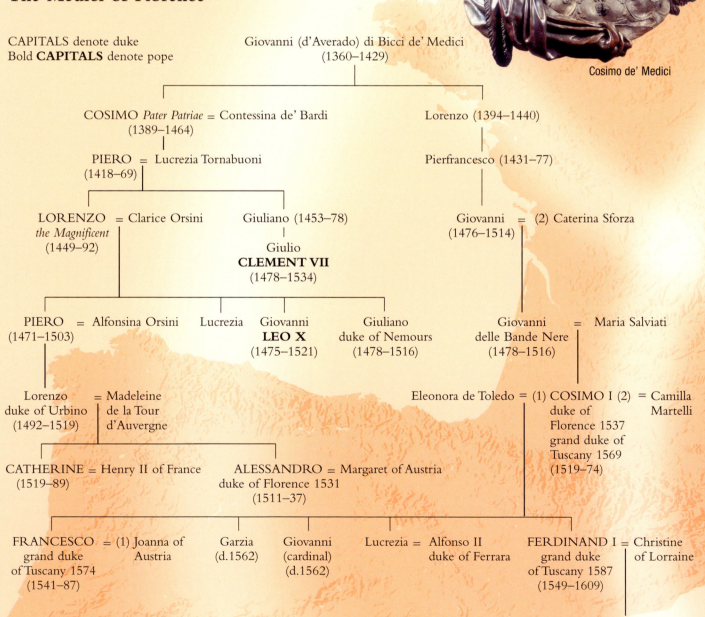

Giovanni (d'Averado) di Bicci de' Medici (1360–1429)

COSIMO *Pater Patriae* = Contessina de' Bardi (1389–1464)

Lorenzo (1394–1440)

PIERO = Lucrezia Tornabuoni (1418–69)

Pierfrancesco (1431–77)

LORENZO = Clarice Orsini
the Magnificent (1449–92)

Giuliano (1453–78)

Giovanni = (2) Caterina Sforza (1476–1514)

Giulio
CLEMENT VII (1478–1534)

PIERO = Alfonsina Orsini (1471–1503)

Lucrezia

Giovanni **LEO X** (1475–1521)

Giuliano duke of Nemours (1478–1516)

Giovanni delle Bande Nere = Maria Salviati (1478–1516)

Lorenzo duke of Urbino (1492–1519) = Madeleine de la Tour d'Auvergne

Eleonora de Toledo = (1) COSIMO I (2) = Camilla duke of Martelli Florence 1537 grand duke of Tuscany 1569 (1519–74)

CATHERINE = Henry II of France (1519–89)

ALESSANDRO = Margaret of Austria duke of Florence 1531 (1511–37)

FRANCESCO = (1) Joanna of grand duke Austria of Tuscany 1574 (1541–87)

Garzia (d.1562)

Giovanni (cardinal) (d.1562)

Lucrezia = Alfonso II duke of Ferrara

FERDINAND I = Christine grand duke of Lorraine of Tuscany 1587 (1549–1609)

COSIMO II grand duke of Tuscany (1590–1621)

Rulers of Milan—Visconti, Sforza, and Valois (of France)

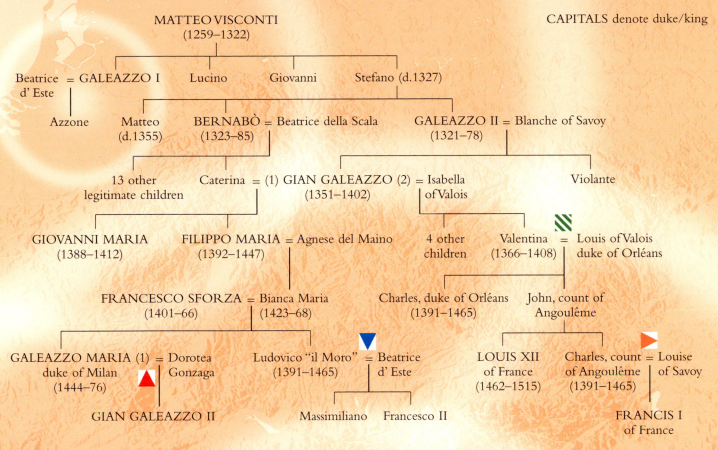

MATTEO VISCONTI
(1259–1322)

CAPITALS denote duke/king

Beatrice = **GALEAZZO I**   Lucino   Giovanni   Stefano (d.1327)
d' Este

Azzone   Matteo   **BERNABÒ** = Beatrice della Scala   **GALEAZZO II** = Blanche of Savoy
    (d.1355)   (1323–85)   (1321–78)

13 other   Caterina = (1) **GIAN GALEAZZO** (2) = Isabella   Violante
legitimate children   (1351–1402)   of Valois

GIOVANNI MARIA   **FILIPPO MARIA** = Agnese del Maino   4 other   Valentina = Louis of Valois
(1388–1412)   (1392–1447)   children   (1366–1408)   duke of Orléans

FRANCESCO SFORZA = Bianca Maria   Charles, duke of Orléans   John, count of
(1401–66)   (1423–68)   (1391–1465)   Angoulême

GALEAZZO MARIA (1) = Dorotea   Ludovico "il Moro" = Beatrice   **LOUIS XII**   Charles, count = Louise
duke of Milan   Gonzaga   (1391–1465)   d' Este   of France   of Angoulême   of Savoy
(1444–76)   (1462–1515)   (1391–1465)

GIAN GALEAZZO II   Massimiliano   Francesco II   **FRANCIS I**
of France

The Gonzaga dynasty of Mantua

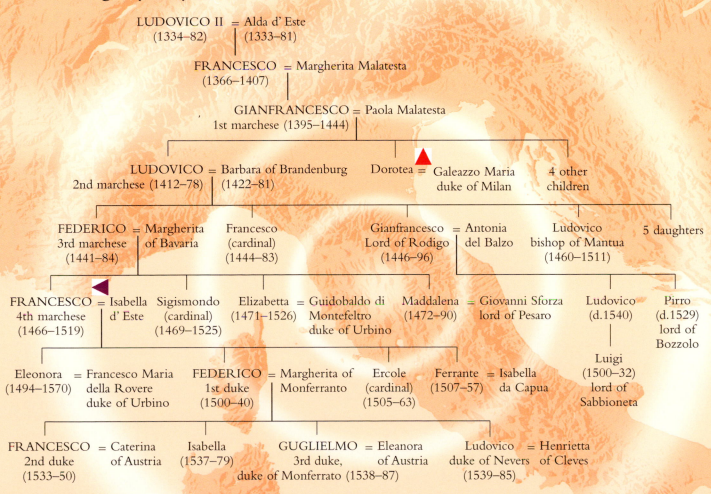

LUDOVICO II = Alda d' Este
(1334–82)   (1333–81)

FRANCESCO = Margherita Malatesta
(1366–1407)

GIANFRANCESCO = Paola Malatesta
1st marchese (1395–1444)

LUDOVICO = Barbara of Brandenburg   Dorotea = Galeazzo Maria   4 other
2nd marchese (1412–78)   (1422–81)   duke of Milan   children

FEDERICO = Margherita   Francesco   Gianfrancesco = Antonia   Ludovico   5 daughters
3rd marchese   of Bavaria   (cardinal)   Lord of Rodigo   del Balzo   bishop of Mantua
(1441–84)   (1444–83)   (1446–96)   (1460–1511)

FRANCESCO = Isabella   Sigismondo   Elizabetta = Guidobaldo di   Maddalena = Giovanni Sforza   Ludovico   Pirro
4th marchese   d' Este   (cardinal)   (1471–1526)   Montefeltro   (1472–90)   lord of Pesaro   (d.1540)   (d.1529)
(1466–1519)   (1469–1525)   duke of Urbino   lord of
                                                  Bozzolo

Eleonora = Francesco Maria   **FEDERICO** = Margherita of   Ercole   Ferrante = Isabella   Luigi
(1494–1570)   della Rovere   1st duke   Monferranto   (cardinal)   (1507–57)   da Capua   (1500–32)
        duke of Urbino   (1500–40)   (1505–63)   lord of
                                                          Sabbioneta

FRANCESCO = Caterina   Isabella   **GUGLIELMO** = Eleonora   Ludovico = Henrietta
2nd duke   of Austria   (1537–79)   3rd duke,   of Austria   duke of Nevers of Cleves
(1533–50)   duke of Monferrato (1538–87)   (1539–85)

The Este dynasty of Ferrara

CAPITALS denote duke

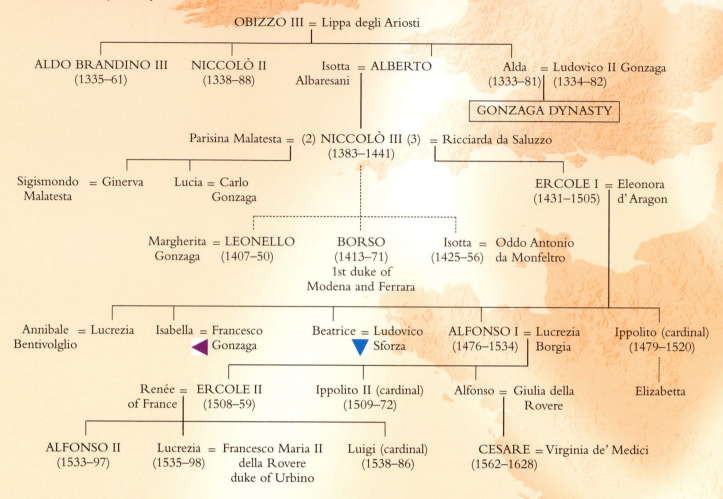

OBIZZO III = Lippa degli Ariosti

ALDO BRANDINO III (1335–61) NICCOLÒ II (1338–88) Isotta Albaresani = ALBERTO Alda (1333–81) = Ludovico II Gonzaga (1334–82)

GONZAGA DYNASTY

Parisina Malatesta = (2) NICCOLÒ III (3) (1383–1441) = Ricciarda da Saluzzo

Sigismondo Malatesta = Ginerva Lucia = Carlo Gonzaga ERCOLE I (1431–1505) = Eleonora d' Aragon

Margherita Gonzaga = LEONELLO (1407–50) BORSO (1413–71) 1st duke of Modena and Ferrara Isotta (1425–56) = Oddo Antonio da Monfeltro

Annibale Bentivolglio = Lucrezia Isabella = Francesco Gonzaga ◀ Beatrice = Ludovico Sforza ▼ ALFONSO I (1476–1534) = Lucrezia Borgia Ippolito (cardinal) (1479–1520)

Renée of France = ERCOLE II (1508–59) Ippolito II (cardinal) (1509–72) Alfonso = Giulia della Rovere Elizabetta

ALFONSO II (1533–97) Lucrezia (1535–98) = Francesco Maria II della Rovere duke of Urbino Luigi (cardinal) (1538–86) CESARE (1562–1628) = Virginia de' Medici

The Duchy of Burgundy

CAPITALS denote duke

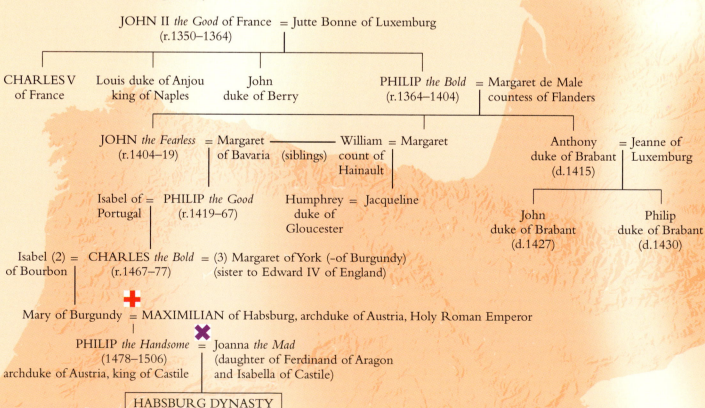

JOHN II *the Good* of France = Jutte Bonne of Luxemburg (r.1350–1364)

CHARLES V of France Louis duke of Anjou king of Naples John duke of Berry PHILIP *the Bold* (r.1364–1404) = Margaret de Male countess of Flanders

JOHN *the Fearless* (r.1404–19) = Margaret of Bavaria —— (siblings) —— William count of Hainault = Margaret Anthony duke of Brabant (d.1415) = Jeanne of Luxemburg

Isabel of Portugal = PHILIP *the Good* (r.1419–67) Humphrey duke of Gloucester = Jacqueline John duke of Brabant (d.1427) Philip duke of Brabant (d.1430)

Isabel (2) of Bourbon = CHARLES *the Bold* (r.1467–77) = (3) Margaret of York (–of Burgundy) (sister to Edward IV of England)

Mary of Burgundy ✚ = MAXIMILIAN of Habsburg, archduke of Austria, Holy Roman Emperor

PHILIP *the Handsome* (1478–1506) archduke of Austria, king of Castile ✖ = Joanna *the Mad* (daughter of Ferdinand of Aragon and Isabella of Castile)

HABSBURG DYNASTY

The Valois kings of France and the House of Bourbon

CAPITALS denote king

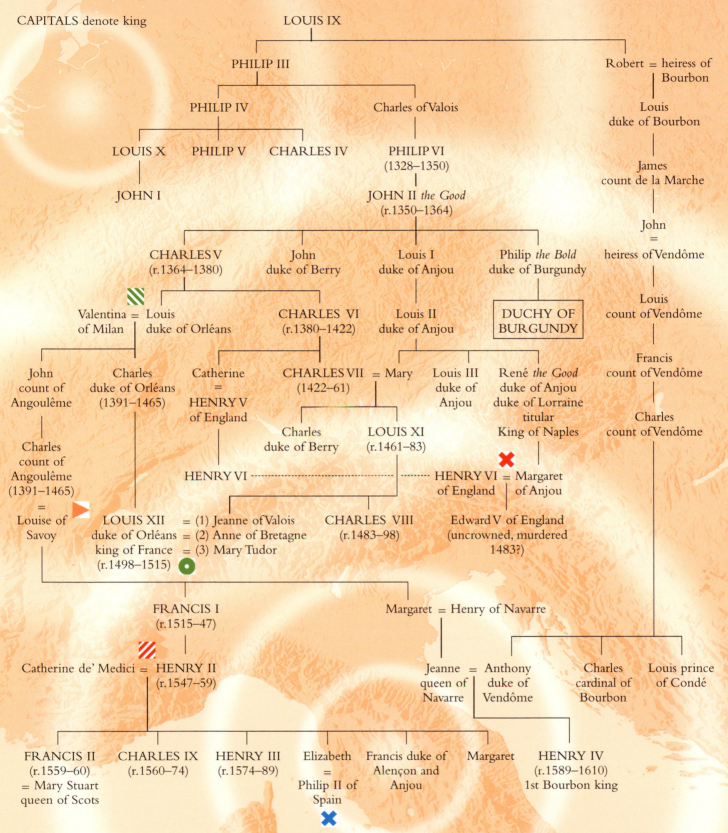

LOUIS IX

PHILIP III — Robert = heiress of Bourbon

PHILIP IV — Charles of Valois

Louis duke of Bourbon

LOUIS X — PHILIP V — CHARLES IV — PHILIP VI (1328–1350)

James count de la Marche

JOHN I

JOHN II *the Good* (r.1350–1364)

John = heiress of Vendôme

CHARLES V (r.1364–1380) — John duke of Berry — Louis I duke of Anjou — Philip *the Bold* duke of Burgundy

Louis count of Vendôme

Valentina = Louis of Milan duke of Orléans — CHARLES VI (r.1380–1422) — Louis II duke of Anjou — DUCHY OF BURGUNDY

Francis count of Vendôme

John count of Angoulême — Charles duke of Orléans (1391–1465) — Catherine = HENRY V of England — CHARLES VII (1422–61) = Mary — Louis III duke of Anjou — René *the Good* duke of Anjou duke of Lorraine titular King of Naples

Charles count of Vendôme

Charles duke of Berry — LOUIS XI (r.1461–83)

Charles count of Angoulême (1391–1465) = Louise of Savoy

HENRY VI -- HENRY VI = Margaret of England | of Anjou

LOUIS XII duke of Orléans king of France (r.1498–1515) = (1) Jeanne of Valois = (2) Anne of Bretagne = (3) Mary Tudor — CHARLES VIII (r.1483–98) — Edward V of England (uncrowned, murdered 1483?)

FRANCIS I (r.1515–47) — Margaret = Henry of Navarre

Jeanne = Anthony queen of duke of Navarre Vendôme — Charles cardinal of Bourbon — Louis prince of Condé

Catherine de' Medici = HENRY II (r.1547–59)

FRANCIS II (r.1559–60) = Mary Stuart queen of Scots — CHARLES IX (r.1560–74) — HENRY III (r.1574–89) — Elizabeth = Philip II of Spain — Francis duke of Alençon and Anjou — Margaret — HENRY IV (r.1589–1610) 1st Bourbon king

187

The Tudor dynasty of England, to the Stuarts

CAPITALS denote king/queen

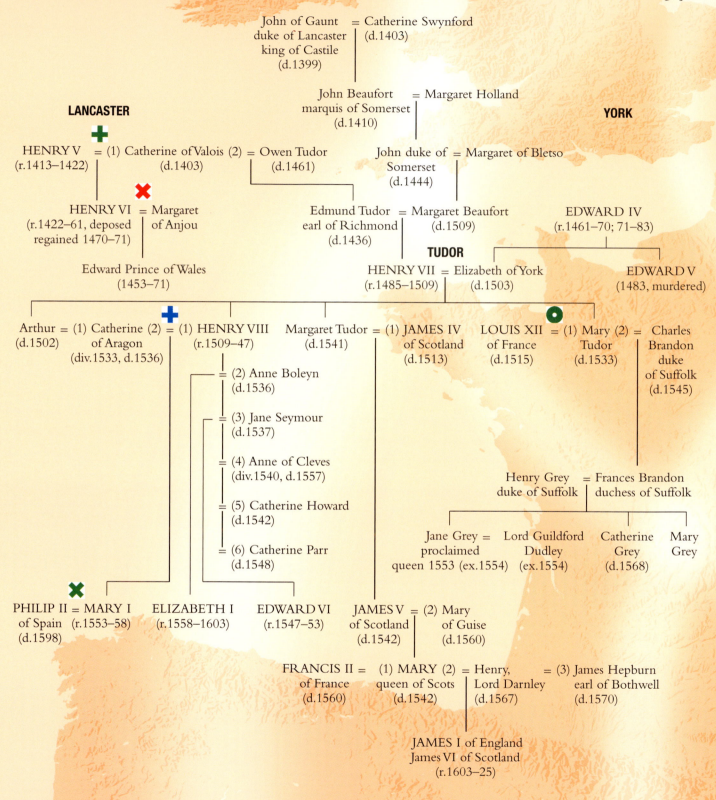

The Ottoman sultans during the Renaissance

Mehmet II 1451–81	Mehmet II 1595–1603
Bayazid II 1481–1512	Ahmed I 1603–17
Selim I 1512–20	Mustapha I 1617–18; 1622–23
Suleiman I (II) 1520–66	Osman II 1618–22
Selim II 1566–74	Murad IV 1623–40
Murad III 1574–95	Ibrahim I 1640–48

The Habsburgs

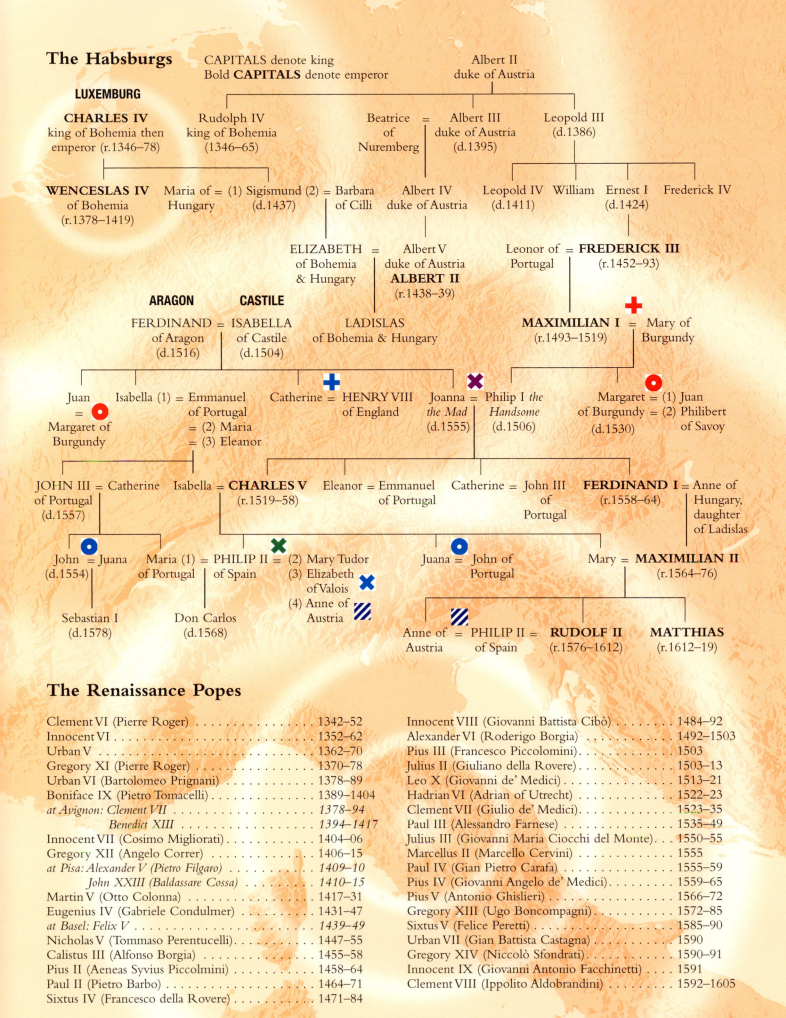

CAPITALS denote king
Bold **CAPITALS** denote emperor

Albert II duke of Austria

LUXEMBURG

CHARLES IV king of Bohemia then emperor (r.1346–78)

Rudolph IV king of Bohemia (1346–65)

Beatrice of Nuremberg = Albert III duke of Austria (d.1395)

Leopold III (d.1386)

WENCESLAS IV of Bohemia (r.1378–1419)

Maria of Hungary = (1) Sigismund (d.1437) (2) = Barbara of Cilli

Albert IV duke of Austria

Leopold IV (d.1411) — William — Ernest I (d.1424) — Frederick IV

ELIZABETH of Bohemia & Hungary = Albert V duke of Austria **ALBERT II** (r.1438–39)

Leonor of Portugal = **FREDERICK III** (r.1452–93)

ARAGON — **CASTILE**

FERDINAND of Aragon (d.1516) = ISABELLA of Castile (d.1504)

LADISLAS of Bohemia & Hungary

MAXIMILIAN I (r.1493–1519) = Mary of Burgundy

Juan = Margaret of Burgundy

Isabella (1) = Emmanuel of Portugal = (2) Maria = (3) Eleanor

Catherine = HENRY VIII of England

Joanna the Mad (d.1555) = Philip I the Handsome (d.1506)

Margaret of Burgundy (d.1530) = (1) Juan = (2) Philibert of Savoy

JOHN III of Portugal (d.1557) = Catherine

Isabella = **CHARLES V** (r.1519–58)

Eleanor = Emmanuel of Portugal

Catherine = John III of Portugal

FERDINAND I (r.1558–64) = Anne of Hungary, daughter of Ladislas

John (d.1554) = Juana

Maria of Portugal (1) = PHILIP II of Spain = (2) Mary Tudor (3) Elizabeth of Valois (4) Anne of Austria

Juana = John of Portugal

Mary = **MAXIMILIAN II** (r.1564–76)

Sebastian I (d.1578)

Don Carlos (d.1568)

Anne of Austria = PHILIP II of Spain = **RUDOLF II** (r.1576–1612) — **MATTHIAS** (r.1612–19)

The Renaissance Popes

Clement VI (Pierre Roger) 1342–52	Innocent VIII (Giovanni Battista Cibò) 1484–92
Innocent VI 1352–62	Alexander VI (Roderigo Borgia) 1492–1503
Urban V 1362–70	Pius III (Francesco Piccolomini). 1503
Gregory XI (Pierre Roger) 1370–78	Julius II (Giuliano della Rovere) 1503–13
Urban VI (Bartolomeo Prignani) 1378–89	Leo X (Giovanni de' Medici) 1513–21
Boniface IX (Pietro Tomacelli) 1389–1404	Hadrian VI (Adrian of Utrecht) 1522–23
at Avignon: Clement VII *1378–94*	Clement VII (Giulio de' Medici) 1523–35
Benedict XIII *1394–1417*	Paul III (Alessandro Farnese) 1535–49
Innocent VII (Cosimo Migliorati) 1404–06	Julius III (Giovanni Maria Ciocchi del Monte) . . . 1550–55
Gregory XII (Angelo Correr) 1406–15	Marcellus II (Marcello Cervini) 1555
at Pisa: Alexander V (Pietro Filgaro) *1409–10*	Paul IV (Gian Pietro Carafa) 1555–59
John XXIII (Baldassare Cossa) *1410–15*	Pius IV (Giovanni Angelo de' Medici) 1559–65
Martin V (Otto Colonna) 1417–31	Pius V (Antonio Ghislieri) 1566–72
Eugenius IV (Gabriele Condulmer) 1431–47	Gregory XIII (Ugo Boncompagni) 1572–85
at Basel: Felix V *1439–49*	Sixtus V (Felice Peretti) 1585–90
Nicholas V (Tommaso Perentucelli) 1447–55	Urban VII (Gian Battista Castagna) 1590
Calistus III (Alfonso Borgia) 1455–58	Gregory XIV (Niccolò Sfondrati) 1590–91
Pius II (Aeneas Syvius Piccolmini) 1458–64	Innocent IX (Giovanni Antonio Facchinetti) 1591
Paul II (Pietro Barbo) 1464–71	Clement VIII (Ippolito Aldobrandini) 1592–1605
Sixtus IV (Francesco della Rovere) 1471–84	

Index